Interpreting Nietzs

Interpreting Nietzsche
Reception and Influence

Edited by Ashley Woodward

continuum

Continuum International Publishing Group

The Tower Building	80 Maiden Lane
11 York Road	Suite 704
London SE1 7NX	New York, NY 10038

British Library Cataloguing-in-Publication Data
A catalogue record for this book is available from the British Library.

ISBN: HB: 978-1-4411-5241-1
     PB: 978-1-4411-2004-5

Library of Congress Cataloguing-in-Publication Data
Interpreting Nietzsche : reception and influence / edited by Ashley Woodward.
   p. cm.
  Includes bibliographical references and index.
  ISBN-13: 978-1-4411-5241-1
  ISBN-10: 1-4411-5241-5
  ISBN-13: 978-1-4411-2004-5 (pbk.)
  ISBN-10: 1-4411-2004-1 (pbk.)
  1. Nietzsche, Friedrich Wilhelm, 1844–1900.   I. Woodward, Ashley.

B3317.I65 2011
193–dc22
                                     2011004029

Typeset by Newgen Imaging Systems Pvt Ltd, Chennai, India
Printed and bound in Great Britain

Contents

Acknowledgements

This book owes much to the international scholars who have contributed such fine chapters. I would like to thank not only them, but also those Nietzsche scholars who were not able to contribute, but who expressed much encouraging enthusiasm for the project. Thanks are due to Joanne Faulkner, who in addition to contributing a chapter of her own, aided in finding contributors for some of the other chapters. Thanks to the editors at Continuum for their immediate interest in the idea and for seeing it to completion. This book has its origin in a seminar on Interpretations of Nietzsche held at the Melbourne School of Continental Philosophy. I would like to dedicate this book to all the students of the MSCP.

Ashley Woodward

Abbreviations

Editions of Nietzsche's collected works in German are abbreviated as follows:

KGW *Kritische Gesamtausgabe: Werke*, G. Colli and M. Montinari (eds). Berlin and New York: Walter de Gruyter, 1967–.

KSA *Sämtliche Werke. Kritische Studienausgabe*, G. Colli and M. Montinari (eds), 2nd ed. Berlin and New York: Walter de Gruyter, 1980.

Given the variety of different translations of Nietzsche's works, and preference of some of authors to employ their own translations, no consistency of referencing to translations of individual works across the chapters of this book has been attempted. However, general references to Nietzsche's works (as opposed to specific translations or editions) frequently employ the following abbreviations. Letters refer to book title, followed by the abbreviated title of the chapter or number of the section, or when required, both. For example, TI 'Socrates' 5 refers to *Twilight of the Idols*, 'The Problem of Socrates', Section 5.

A	*The Anti-Christ*
BGE	*Beyond Good and Evil*
BT	*The Birth of Tragedy*
D	*Daybreak*
EH	*Ecce Homo*
GM	*On the Genealogy of Morality*
GS	*The Gay Science*
HAH	*Human, All Too Human*
HL	'On the Uses and Disadvantages of History for Life' (*Untimely Meditations* 2)
TI	*Twilight of the Idols*
TL	'On Truth and Lying in a Non-Moral Sense'
WP	*The Will to Power*
Z	*Thus Spoke Zarathustra*

Notes on Contributors

Ciano Aydin is an Assistant Professor at the University of Twente, a full special Thomas More Professor of Philosophy at Delft University of Technology, and a Senior Researcher at the Radboud University Nijmegen. He is a member of the Nietzsche Research Group, and is working on the compilation of a Nietzsche dictionary. He has published in, among others, *The Journal of Nietzsche Studies* and *Transactions of the Charles S. Peirce Society.*

Carolyn D'Cruz is a Lecturer in Gender, Sexuality and Diversity Studies at La Trobe University. She is author of *Identity Politics in Deconstruction: Calculating with the Incalculable* (Ashgate, 2008), and has published articles that largely focus on relations between deconstruction and justice.

Joanne Faulkner is an ARC Postdoctoral Fellow with the School of History and Philosophy, University of New South Wales. She is author of *Dead Letters to Nietzsche* (Ohio University Press, 2010) and *The Importance of Being Innocent* (Cambridge University Press, 2010), and co-author of *Understanding Psychoanalysis* (Acumen, 2008). She has published a number of articles, some of which have been about Nietzsche, and others of which, about Irigaray.

Duncan Large is Professor of German at Swansea University. He is the author of *Nietzsche and Proust* (Oxford University Press, 2001) and *Nietzsches Renaissance-Gestalten* (Verlag der Bauhaus-Universität Weimar, 2009), and co-editor of *The Nietzsche Reader* (Blackwell, 2005/6). He has translated Sarah Kofman's *Nietzsche and Metaphor* (Athlone and Stanford University Press, 1993), as well as Nietzsche's *Twilight of the Idols* (Oxford University Press, 1998) and *Ecce Homo* (Oxford University Press, 2007).

J. Harvey Lomax is a Professor of Political Science at the University of Memphis. He has served two years as Visiting Research Professor in Philosophy at the University of Heidelberg where Karl Löwith earlier taught. His publications include *The Paradox of Philosophical Education: Nietzsche's New Nobility and the Eternal Recurrence in* Beyond Good and Evil (Rowman and Littlefield, 2003) and translations of Karl Löwith's *Nietzsche's Philosophy of the Eternal Recurrence of the Same* (University of California Press, 1997) and

Heinrich Meier's *Carl Schmitt and Leo Strauss: The Hidden Dialogue* (University of Chicago Press, 1995).

David Rathbone holds degrees from the University of Melbourne, Australia and from the New School for Social Research, New York. He was a founding member of the Melbourne School of Continental Philosophy, and has also taught many courses in Philosophy at the University of Melbourne. He is facilitator of the Australasian Nietzsche Society, and an avid blogger (criticalidealism.net.au).

Jon Roffe is the founding convenor of, and a lecturer at, the Melbourne School of Continental Philosophy. He is the co-editor of *Understanding Derrida* (Continuum, 2004), and *Deleuze's Philosophical Lineage* (Edinburgh University Press, 2009).

Sean Ryan has lectured and tutored French and German philosophy at the University of Melbourne for the past fifteen years. He publishes primarily on Heidegger and has recently completed a doctoral thesis on Heidegger's interpretation of Nietzsche.

Matthew Sharpe is a Lecturer in Philosophy and Psychoanalytic Studies at Deakin University. He is the author or co-author of several monographs, including *Slavoj Zizek: A Little Piece of the Real* (Ashgate, 2003), *Understanding Psychoanalysis* (Acumen, 2008), and *The Times Will Suit Them: Postmodern Conservatism in Australia* (Allen and Unwin, 2008).

Mark Tomlinson is a member of the Melbourne School of Continental Philosophy and a postgraduate student at the University of Melbourne. He has written for *Critical Horizons* and *Parrhesia: A Journal of Critical Philosophy*.

Daniel Townshend teaches philosophy at Deakin University. His research focuses on ancient, medieval, and contemporary political philosophy.

Robert T. Valgenti is Assistant Professor of Philosophy at Lebanon Valley College in Annville, PA. His research interests and publications include work on Kant, hermeneutics, twentieth-century Italian philisophy, and the connection between food and philosophy. He is an active translator and promoter of Italian philosophy in the United States.

Ashley Woodward is a member of the Melbourne School of Continental Philosophy and an editor of *Parrhesia: A Journal of Critical Philosophy*. He is author of *Nihilism in Postmodernity* (The Davies Group, 2009) and *Understanding Nietzscheanism* (Acumen, 2011), and a co-editor of *Sensorium:*

Aesthetics, Art, Life (Cambridge Scholars Publishing, 2007) and *The Continuum Companion to Existentialism* (Continuum, 2011).

Yue Zhuo is Assistant Professor of French at Yale University. Her research focuses on twentieth-century French literature and theory. She has published on Pascal Quignard and Roland Barthes and translated Walter Benjamin into Chinese. She is currently preparing a book entitled *Bataille et la préhistoire.*

Introduction

Whose Nietzsche?

Ashley Woodward

Friedrich Nietzsche has been one of the most influential of all modern philosophers, and his work continues to wield a powerful fascination. A staggering number of books on Nietzsche have been published since he first began to receive attention in the mid-1880s, and they continue to appear at a steady pace today. This book is not quite like any of the others. It is neither an introduction to Nietzsche's philosophy, nor a scholarly study of that philosophy. Rather, it is a guide to understanding some of the main books on Nietzsche which have already appeared. It is an introduction to *interpretations* of Nietzsche; a guide to interpreting Nietzsche through his reception in and influence on the works of other philosophers.

Nietzsche's writings are often as ambiguous as they are fascinating, and have given rise to many radically different interpretations. Many of the most influential interpretations have come from philosophers who are both significant and challenging in their own right, philosophers such as Martin Heidegger, Gilles Deleuze, and Luce Irigaray, to name only a few. This book provides an introductory survey of landmark readings of Nietzsche throughout the twentieth century, giving the reader an accessible entry point into contemporary Nietzsche interpretation and scholarship.

An alternative title for this book might be *Perspectives on Nietzsche*. Interpretation and perspectivism are both key Nietzschean themes, and Nietzsche's own work could well be used to explain why a book such as this is both possible and necessary. As Jacques Derrida writes,

[t]he closer one is to 'Nietzsche,' the more one is aware that there is no such thing as the Nietzsche-text. This text demands interpretation in the same way that it argues that there is no such thing as an entity, only interpretations – active and reactive – of that entity. (Derrida, 2002, p. 218)

Along with various other interpreters presented in this book, Derrida insists that no single and authoritative interpretation of the meaning of Nietzsche's writings is possible, and he draws on Nietzsche's own views of interpretation in general to argue his case. However, Nietzsche's perspectivism (itself open to interpretation from a variety of perspectives) certainly does not *need* to be invoked to justify a book such as this: one does not need a radical thesis on the irreducible plurality of interpretations to recognize the pluralism of Nietzsche's writings, and the simple fact that that he *has* been interpreted so differently, by so many important thinkers. Nietzsche's own views changed in quite significant ways between his different books. Many of his writings are ambiguous, even esoteric. Moreover, many of his notes were published posthumously, and whether or not these ought to be taken into serious account in understanding his thought remains a matter of debate. These are just a few of the reasons that the meaning of Nietzsche's work is plural, and that it is unsurprising that it has spawned so many strikingly different interpretations.

It is vital that students of Nietzsche's thought, especially those who seek to engage with and come to terms with its contemporary philosophical significance, read not only Nietzsche 'in-himself', but also those landmark interpretations which have shaped what Nietzsche means today. Nietzsche once famously wrote, 'I am all the names in history' (letter to Burkhardt, 6 January 1889). We are now in a position in which it would barely be an exaggeration to assert that all the names in history *since* Nietzsche – especially, but not just, in the history of European philosophy – have 'been Nietzsche'. That is, as Heidegger once put it, Nietzsche is the one in whose light or shadow everyone today thinks (Heidegger, 1998, p. 321). Many of the great thinkers of the twentieth century have felt the need to produce an interpretation of Nietzsche, to orient themselves in relation to the great event of his thought.

Of course, given the plethora of perspectives on Nietzsche, no book can take all – or even claim to take all of the most important – interpretations of Nietzsche into account. What this book *does* aim to do is to cover many of the indisputably influential interpretations of Nietzsche. The choice of interpretations is governed by this aim, which limits it to those which have to some degree stood the test of time. (There have been many interesting and important developments in Nietzsche scholarship since Alexander Nehamas's 1985 book, the most recent to be treated here, but not enough time has yet elapsed to determine which will remain 'classic' interpretations). The interpretations represented here have all been historically significant, and all retain some currency in contemporary scholarship. In accord with this last point, also excluded from representation here are some interpretations which were historically significant, but which for various reasons no longer enjoy currency. (For example, Ernst Bertram's Nietzsche (Bertram, 2009), which was the most influential in Germany between the two world wars, has today largely been passed over, likely because of its association with the infamous Nazi appropriation of Nietzsche's thought.) In addition to containing chapters on the widely known interpretations of Nietzsche by Heidegger, Deleuze, Nehamas, and others, the book includes chapters on readings of Nietzsche which have been catalytic in the European context, and which are now becoming increasingly recognized in anglophone scholarship, such as those of Pierre Klossowski, Wolfgang Müller-Lauter, and Gianni Vattimo.

Each chapter provides a clear introduction to a different major philosopher's interpretation of Nietzsche, and is written by a contributor with special expertise on the topic. Each chapter is appended with an annotated bibliography and suggestions for further study, giving a summary of the key primary and secondary literature on the topic. The chapters are arranged in roughly chronological order according to the publication date of each philosopher's major work on Nietzsche. However, the chapters are designed to be self-contained and independently readable. Each may be read on its own, or if one desires to read the entire book, the chapters may be read in any order. Thus, for example, a reader interested only in Muller-Lauter's interpretation of Nietzsche might consult only that chapter. Individual chapters might also be consulted for the light they shed not only on Nietzsche, by on the (frequently highly original) philosophy of the interpreter. For example, Robert T. Valgenti's chapter on Vattimo's Nietzsche – discussing as it does Vattimo's works which have not been translated into English – provides a useful introduction to, and overview of, the philosophy of Vattimo. The reader who reads the book from cover to cover will gain a good overview of the main images of Nietzsche which have appeared and which still form the bases of contemporary Nietzsche scholarship.

Studying these interpretations will often serve to introduce many key elements of Nietzsche's thought, and help the reader to gain a much deeper appreciation of Nietzsche's philosophy. However, this book is not intended as a first introduction to Nietzsche (there are many good such introductions already available). A certain basic familiarity with Nietzsche (including key ideas such as nihilism, the eternal return, and the will to power) is assumed, and readers coming to Nietzsche for the first time are advised to consult a basic introduction in combination with this book.

Finally, as with all books such as this, it is necessary to insist on the indispensability of reading original texts. As anyone who has read Nietzsche knows, there is absolutely no substitute for the pleasures (and perhaps also

the pains) of reading his own writing. The writings of many of his interpreters covered in this book similarly offer their own unique and irreplaceable
rewards. The chapters that follow are designed not to help the reader by-
pass such texts, but to aid and accompany the reading both of Nietzsche
and of his interpreters.

Bibliography

Bertram, Ernst (2009), *Nietzsche: Attempt at a Mythology*, trans. Robert E. Norton.
    Urbana: University of Illinois Press.
Derrida, Jacques (2002), Negotiations: Interventions and Interviews, 1971–2001,
    ed. and trans. Elizabeth Rottenberg. Stanford, CA: Stanford University Press.
Heidegger, Martin (1998), *Pathmarks*, ed. William McNeill. Cambridge: Cambridge
    University Press.
Nehamas, Alexander (1985), *Nietzsche: Life as Literature*. Cambridge, MA: Harvard
    University Press.

Chapter 1

Heidegger's Nietzsche

Sean Ryan

Interpretation as Confrontation

'Nietzsche destroyed me'. Such was Martin Heidegger's admission, reported to his former student Hans-Georg Gadamer before Heidegger's death in 1976 (Pöggeler, 2002, p. 16). What is remarkable about it is that Heidegger's philosophical encounter with Nietzsche, an encounter of extraordinary length and intensity, has proven to be perhaps the most influential of the last century, if also the most contested. And it is indeed a *philosophical* encounter, because from the decisive appearance of Nietzsche in the first hours of Heidegger's lectures of 1935 and through the next 25 war-interrupted years, in half a dozen lecture courses, two important essays (though the encounter left its mark on many others), and finally, in 1961, a two-volume book, Nietzsche is unreservedly announced to the world for the first time as a *philosopher*. With Heidegger's interpretation, Nietzsche no longer appears solely as a psychologist, moralist, and cultural critic, as he was to previous thinkers such as Wilhelm Dilthey, nor a precursor to the ideologues of National Socialism, as he was to official Nazi interpreters such as Heidegger's contemporary Alfred Baümler, but as a thinker of the same rank as Plato and Aristotle, Kant, and Hegel.

Yet Heidegger's later self-assessment sounds like a belated confession of failure, a final concession even of Nietzsche's superiority as a thinker. It sounds, in retrospect, as if the interpretation ventured by Heidegger was a contest with Nietzsche, a contest that Heidegger admits to have lost. And this is certainly the conclusion that many students of Nietzsche are quick to endorse, who find Heidegger's interpretation to be a singular misreading. And yet with this conclusion, however justified it might appear to be, we para-doxically find ourselves in the middle of the interpretation once more, an interpretation which, before all else, concerns the essence of interpretation itself. To understand why, we need to open the first pages of Heidegger's collection of lectures and essays on Nietzsche and read the first few lines of its foreword, a statement written in 1961 but one that clarifies what is already said – in anticipation – in the first hour of the first course in the collection, a lecture delivered in 1936.

'The matter of thinking', Heidegger states in the foreword, 'is in itself a confrontation' (Heidegger, 1979–87, Volume 1, p. xil). This definition, which appears to confirm the agonistic character of the interpretation, recalls an admission made by the young Nietzsche, who once claimed that '*Socrates*, to admit it simply, stands so near to me that I am almost always struggling in a struggle with him' (KSA 8, 6 [3]). The word translated here by 'confrontation', a word that Heidegger hyphenates to emphasize its literal meaning, is *Aus-einander-setzung*, literally a setting apart of one another, or as he explains in the revised text of the first lecture of 1936, 'genuine critique' (Heidegger, 1979–87, Volume 1, p. 4).

Yet genuine critique, for Heidegger, does not consist in criticism and refutation. His interpretation of Nietzsche does not seek to uncover falsehoods and contradictions in Nietzsche's philosophy, in order to surpass him as a thinker.[1] If Heidegger does not concur with Nietzsche's apparently contradictory claim that truth itself is an error, he does maintain that the traditional philosophical conception of truth, as the correctness of statements or beliefs, is only a derivative if necessary aspect of the full essence of truth. Genuine critique is not an attempt to surpass – in setting oneself apart from – the thought of another. Rather, it is the one who attempts the critique who is to be overcome; what a critical interpretation aims to overcome is one's own enduring thoughtlessness in the face of what needs to be thought, in order that one might finally be able to think for oneself. As Nietzsche also recognized, in his struggle with Socratic scepticism and idealism, the persistent difficulty in learning to think lies in gaining sufficient distance from what is altogether too close. Unlike Nietzsche, however, that proximity is for Heidegger historical rather than psychological; what is too near is not the type of the philosopher but the epoch of being in which we now find ourselves.

So it might be that Heidegger's admission has another, altogether different sense from that which first presents itself. The destruction wrought by Nietzsche on Heidegger might also have been the liberation of Heidegger's own thinking, its freedom from an insufficiently critical relationship both to the philosophical tradition and to the contemporary situation that is its outcome, a situation whose history includes those truisms that already surround the more recent arrival of Nietzsche's thought.

Although references to Nietzsche occur fairly frequently in Heidegger's earlier works – there is a notable reference to the untimely meditation on history in *Being and Time* (Heidegger, 1996, Section 76) – the critique of Nietzsche genuinely commences only in the mid 1930s. The generally positive tenor of the early commentaries indicates that the confrontation with Nietzsche has yet to begin and, as the more critical interpretation unfolds, we are witness to a marked shift in the tone of the encounter, from expressions of affinity with Nietzsche in the first lecture courses, to occasionally sharp disagreement throughout the following years, to the calm acknowledgment of respectful distance characteristic of the final writings.

Nietzsche and Metaphysics

The terms of the interpretation are laid down early in the summer semester lecture course of 1935 (Heidegger, 2000). In the middle of a discussion of the elusiveness of the experience and meaning of Being, which is almost like the Nothing, both an undiscoverable void and an empty word, Heidegger gives initial assent to Nietzsche's well-known criticism of philosophical concepts: 'So in the end Nietzsche is entirely right when he calls the "highest concepts" such as Being "the final wisp of evaporating reality"' (Heidegger, 2000, p. 38; see TI 'Reason'). The remark even appears to be a premonitory criticism of Heidegger himself, who in *Being and Time*, written nearly 40 years after *Twilight of the Idols*, will seemingly forget Nietzsche's admonition of philosophy and once again make the primary question of ontology, the question of the meaning of Being, *the* basic problem for philosophy. Being, Nietzsche continues – in praise of Heraclitus and against what he takes to be the Eleatic conception of Being, of being as permanence and substance – is a fiction, a philosophical addition to the sole reality, that of a world of becoming, of passing away, and alteration.[2] Heidegger willingly consents to Nietzsche's observation, because the tendency of Being to self-obscurity and self-oblivion is precisely what Heidegger at the time calls the *truth* of Being.

Yet Heidegger's ambivalence towards Nietzsche's assessment of the history of philosophy soon reveals itself: 'Does Nietzsche speak the truth? Or is he himself only the final victim of a long-standing errancy and neglect, but *as* this victim the unrecognized witness to a new necessity?' (Heidegger, 2000, p. 39). Though Nietzsche is somehow right about the self-oblivion of Being, an oblivion which makes possible that history but to which Nietzsche is nevertheless the first witness (despite his claiming to find a precursor in

Heraclitus), he too remains bound to a conception of Being that has already wandered some distance from its historical source. For by opposing to the concept of eternal Being the appearance of elusive becoming, and by construing the difference of Heraclitus and Parmenides in terms of this opposition, which is of more recent origin, Nietzsche simply signals how far is his own removal from the origins of philosophy. The initial experience of Being is one of *physis*, of the coming to presence of that which abides awhile in its passing away, an experience that has yet to come apart into the opposition of Being and becoming, even if it is given quite different interpretations by different pre-Socratic philosophers. The conception of Being as permanent and substantive presence, and its distinction from transience and illusiveness, on the other hand, is a later development, one that defines the onset of metaphysics in the thought of Plato and Aristotle.

This historical misunderstanding is not that to which Nietzsche is victim, however; nor is it the source of the new necessity to which he is witness. Still undeveloped in pre-Socratic philosophy, only emerging within and as metaphysics, is what Heidegger identifies as the difference of Being and beings, a difference that announces itself only at the end of the errant history of its neglect. Far from being grasped in its difference from beings, Being is itself traditionally conceived as a higher kind of entity – as a concept, for example, or as an ideal. This confusion is not due to any carelessness or thoughtlessness on the part of philosophy, but is a first and necessary response to the essential obscurity of Being. And Nietzsche too still grasps Being as an entity, albeit as a lie and a falsification. But just this is the new necessity of which Nietzsche is the still-unrecognized messenger, not just that the concept of Being comes to nothing, that the history of philosophy is one of metaphysical nihilism, but that this outcome has yet to be properly experienced, that its consequences have not yet been thought through to the end.

In subsequent lectures and essays, Heidegger will sometimes refer to Nietzsche as the last metaphysician, and to his thought as the end and consummation of metaphysics. Once again, these assessments are often read as Heidegger's attempt to surpass Nietzsche, to consign his thought to the wreckage of an ill-conceived past. But that is to misunderstand what the end of metaphysics means, for Heidegger. End certainly does not mean termination, and even the most cursory examination of the present state of philosophy shows that metaphysical thinking is not at an end, that it continues in a variety of reinventions and admixtures of past metaphysical positions. Nor of course does it mean perfection, in the manner of Hegel's teleological metaphysics. The end of metaphysics, for Heidegger, is the exhaustion rather than the culmination of its possibilities, and Nietzsche, the thinker who draws the line under those possibilities. Its character is not teleological but eschatological, which means that, in reaching its end, the history of metaphysics comes up for decision (Heidegger, 1975, p. 18). That decision, which is not one that any individual is free to make, Heidegger included, concerns whether the philosophical destiny of humanity is fulfilled in the masterful yet ultimately thoughtless knowledge of and control over beings, a mastery that seems to escalate ever more rapidly and become increasingly diffuse with the capitulation of science (and indeed of every field of activity, including, fatefully for Heidegger, that of the political) to the demands of technology, a mastery, which in the end is really a consummate form of enslavement. Or it concerns whether humanity might finally be capable of thinking through the origins and consequences of the nothingness of Being that makes such mastery possible.

The lecture courses that Heidegger devotes to Nietzsche during the following years, the outcome of which is summarized in the long, treatise-like essay of 1943, 'Nietzsche's Word: God is Dead', try to come to terms with the nihilistic history of metaphysics that is consummated – both exhausted and brought up for decision – in Nietzsche's thinking (Heidegger, 1977).[3] Heidegger chooses, for the names of his courses, the titles of four sections from *The Will to Power* – "The Will to Power as Art"; "The Eternal Recurrence of the Same" (only the first three words are Nietzsche's); "The Will to Power as Knowledge"; and "European Nihilism" – though he also discusses at length other published texts from the period of Nietzsche's philosophical maturity.

The decision to treat as pivotal a collection of notes not published during Nietzsche's lifetime is a refusal to take seriously neither Nietzsche's achievements as a writer nor the more general problem for philosophy of the question of style. An untranslated course that Heidegger began late in 1944, which was terminated by the evacuation of Freiburg in the face of advancing French forces, even sought to compare Nietzsche and Hölderlin, one a thinker whose philosophical expression was singularly poetic, the other a poet of extraordinary thoughtfulness (Heidegger, 1990). In fact, and to the contrary, the decision has everything to do with that question. A way of thinking, for Heidegger, is not a compilation of statements and an organization of concepts that might be written down in a philosophical text, but where it is that such thinking comes from, where it is that it goes, and the closer that a way of thinking approaches its matter, the sooner it assumes the poetic style of a telling silence (Heidegger, 1979–87, Volume 2, pp. 207–8). Nietzsche's notes for the unpublished *The Will to Power*, in which he struggles to find a form appropriate to the matter, which he abandons in order to resume his timely debates with both Wagner and Christianity (*The Case of Wagner, The Antichrist*), are for Heidegger a pointer to the unsaid centre of Nietzsche's thought, to that around which statements concerning the will to power, the eternal recurrence, and the revaluation of all values, endlessly circle.

Will to Power as Art, and the Eternal Recurrence of the Same

'The Will to Power as Art', the first of Heidegger's courses on Nietzsche, is that in which a critical sense of kinship is most evident (Heidegger, 1979–87, Volume 1). Will to power – that which answers to the traditional ontological question: 'What are beings?'– Heidegger begins, must be understood as the intrinsic unity of willing and empowering, and moreover not solely as a psychological state but as the self-transcendence of beings as a whole, their going beyond themselves in a continual movement of self-enhancement and self-recovery. Such transcendence is the openness of beings; it is the way in which they belong to the essence of truth, which means, for Heidegger, to the essence of unconcealment.

Yet will to power – which means, life, becoming, sensuousness – as belonging to truth? The idea seems to conflict with a central tenet of Nietzsche's thought, that the enhancement of life is best achieved not through truth but through art; art is worth more than truth. With this claim Nietzsche reverses the long-standing Platonic valuation of truth and art, of art as a thrice-removed mimesis of true being. For Nietzsche, art in the grand style, contra Wagner's understanding of art as a surrender to formlessness, is the rapturous formation and reformation of the sensuous. Truth, which fixes the transiency of life in relation to a non-existent ideal, is instead its stagnation and decline. Art is the essential counter-movement to the nihilistic belief in true Being; it is that which manifests the will to power in its incessant self-overcoming.

Nietzsche's reversal of Platonism in this way draws a line under the long history of metaphysics. And yet, Heidegger continues, it does not overcome its beginning. Instead, it returns us once more to Plato – whose thought must be distinguished from that of the subsequent history of Platonism – and to Plato's own experience of sensuous life in its relation to truth. Art, which concerns the realm of the sensuous, is a disclosure of the Being of beings. Thus Heidegger concurs with Nietzsche's estimation of the value of art, while refusing his rejection of the question of Being. For Plato, however, this disclosure of the truth of things is revealed not through art but through beauty, through the radiance that grants to the world of sensuous impermanence some insight into and recollection of true Being. The conflict between art and truth, between the aesthetic and the noetic, Heidegger concludes, is for Plato a felicitous discordance. For Nietzsche, on the other hand, whose overturning of the concept of truth nevertheless continues to grasp truth as the conformity of the transitory and sensuous with the eternal and supersensuous – who is removed from and so cannot bring into question the original (yet unexamined) experience of truth as unconcealment – that discordance is one which rages, which provokes holy dread. The lecture course ends hesitantly, with a question to which Heidegger as yet has no answer, the question whether or not Nietzsche has at least opened up the possibility of understanding anew the disclosure of the world of sensuous appearance, free of its opposition to the positing of a true world – the question, in other words, of the essence of truth.

If the lectures on art are Heidegger's critique of Nietzsche at its most brilliant, drawing not only upon passages from the *Republic* and *Phaedrus* but also weighing Nietzsche's conception of art against the aesthetic doctrines of Kant and Schopenhauer, the lectures on the eternal return are an extremely patient and close reading of Nietzsche's texts, including his unpublished manuscripts, and are perhaps the fruit of Heidegger's participation in a never-completed project for a historical-critical edition of Nietzsche's works (see Heidegger, 1979–87, Volume 2).

'The Eternal Recurrence of the Same' opens with the announcement that Nietzsche's most burdensome and difficult thought is indeed the fundamental thought (*Grundgedanke*) of his metaphysics; sometimes, in contrast, Heidegger will call the will to power Nietzsche's leading thought (*Hauptgedanke*). As a fundamental thought of metaphysics, eternal recurrence is neither simply a cosmological hypothesis, though it too concerns beings as a whole, nor a psychological experiment, though it also calls for thoughtful decision. It rests at the conjunction of both possibilities, as a thought about Being, and as a way in which thinking belongs to Being. Its form is itself inherently circular, a recoiling of the thought upon the thinker, and a drawing of the thinker into the thought – it has the form of what Heidegger calls, in *Being and Time*, a hermeneutical circle (Heidegger, 1996, Section 2). The difficulty of the circle of understanding, of that circle in which we already belong and yet into which we still must find our way, is that of entering into it in the *right* way.

Nietzsche's communication of the thought of recurrence entertains and rejects two ways in which the thought might be understood. The one possibility is that the thought is a representation of the whole – this is the perspective of the dwarf in the 'The Vision and the Riddle' section of *Thus Spoke Zarathustra*, a perspective from which the eternal recurrence is grasped too facilely, as an abstraction with no bearing on the existence of the one who propounds it. The other possibility is that of the one who willingly complies with it. This is the perspective of Zarathustra's totemic animals who treat the thought too lightly – though not in the manner of the over-man, who bears the thought lightly, but as a *burden* – who willingly yet thoughtlessly assent to its necessity and whose existence thoroughly con-forms to the eternal cycle of coming to be and passing away.

To enter into the circle in an appropriate way, which means neither to represent it abstractly nor to comply with it thoughtlessly, is to assent to one's own transitory passage and passing away, yet to do so in sufferance, to suffer willingly one's momentary belonging to the circle of becoming. Life, suffering, the circle: these are the three intertwined doctrines of which Zarathustra is the advocate.[4] The moment of entrance into the cir-cle, into the collision of past and future, is the posing of a decision con-cerning the nothingness of being; its domain is that of nihilism. And just as the domain of the decision is nothing at all, the language in which the decision is expressed is not one of assertoric or categorical disjunction (a decision between X and Y), because the decision is one that must be drawn from, and which reduces one to silence. It is a decision between two inex-pressibly different ways of understanding the single statement 'It is all alike', or alternatively 'Nothing matters', a choice between glib resignation and the sudden resolution that the Nothing matters profoundly.

Heidegger's interpretation of the figure of Zarathustra remains undecided to the last, and he will return to this essential figure of metaphysics in his final essay on Nietzsche some 16 years later. His reading of the doctrine of eternal recurrence is similarly undecided, for while he recognizes the singu-lar importance of Nietzsche's conception of the moment, of the groundless and unprecedented instant in which one becomes who one is, in which one becomes oneself, he finds that the doctrine of return is unable to pose the question of the very openness of the moment of decision. For Nietzsche, that moment is the inextricable interlocking of the opposition of being and becoming – the world *is*, in its becoming; one *becomes*, as the sole way of being. Nietzsche leaves no room for the nothingness of Being, which is utterly different from beings, which is no *thing*. Yet it is precisely this oblivion and obscurity of Being that grants to metaphysics its errant history, which begins with the positing and ends with the rejection of the conception of Being as permanent presence. Nietzsche is unable to do so, Heidegger maintains (and the harshness of this claim increases during the works that follow), because he still holds to a basic metaphysical distinction that first comes to clarity with Aristotle. If will to power is the 'what' of beings, their basic constitution or essence, the eternal recurrence is the 'how' of beings, their mode of being or existence; it is the way in which entities come to presence, as recurring eternally.

Will to Power as Knowledge, and European Nihilism

The third series of lectures now takes a direction seemingly at odds with that of the first course (see Heidegger, 1979–87, Volume 3). Will to power is the principle of a new valuation, the establishment of conditions for the preservation and enhancement of life. But while truth and knowledge are two such values, they are not supreme values, a place that is accorded instead to art. Not only is truth, the correctness of beliefs and statements, an error – albeit a necessary error, without which life would be impossible – it is the condition not of life's enhancement but only of its preservation, and the sheer preservation of life is already its decline.

Life: the concept, Heidegger insists, is for Nietzsche not biological but metaphysical, a last transformation of the initial experience of *physis*. To live, to be embodied and to go forth bodily into the world, is to confront and to seek to impose order upon the pandemonium of the whole, in order to compose oneself through and against that chaos. Truth and knowledge are necessary values, because their categories are schemata that impose order upon chaos, that bring order to disorder and so enable one to be. Nietzsche is here both following and transforming Leibniz's metaphysics of subjectivity: to live is to posses a perspective on the whole, one that answers to some practical need; what is true is what is held to be true, the belief in which preserves a particular form of life; and knowledge is a form of poetizing, the creation of stability amid the flux of becoming.

But this suggests that Nietzsche has an alternative conception of truth, Heidegger continues, one other than that which asserts truth to be an error. Both art and knowledge are creative, transfiguring activities, the one directed to the enhancement of life, the other to its preservation. As such, both are a harmonizing of life, a corresponding *with* life. Yet correspondence – of a lived perspective with the whole of life of which it is part, whether or not such correspondence is a creative fabrication – is the original metaphysical understanding of the essence of truth, and Nietzsche's bio-logic reveals itself to be perhaps the last transformation of that understanding. Of course, the idea that truth is not just a form of correspondence but also an artistic creation raises the suspicion that truth is not only subjective but arbitrary, that the truth can be whatever one likes. And so Heidegger identifies in Nietzsche's thought a third and final conception of truth, one that maintains its subjective character while removing from it any suggestion of arbitrariness. Truth is justice, which is to say, in Nietzsche's words, justice – it too is to be understood as a metaphysical and not an ethical or juridical concept – is the supreme representative of life itself. Will to power, as command and stability, self-overcoming and excelling, necessarily establishes only those conditions of life of which it is capable, and such positing of values in accord with one's abilities is for Nietzsche the very essence of justice.

Toward the end of 'The Will to Power as Knowledge', one senses a mounting disenchantment that will carry over into the fourth lecture course (the last in the Nietzsche volumes) and then into the essays Heidegger will write on or around Nietzsche in the early 1940s. That the will to power finds its essence in commanding and surpassing, and that truth is to be identified with justice, points to a fundamental anthropomorphism in Nietzsche's metaphysics, Heidegger concludes, whatever Nietzsche himself might have to say about the insignificance of the merely human from the perspective of the whole. If the doctrine of the eternal recurrence of the same is the consummation of Western metaphysics, then that of the will to power is the final possibility of the metaphysics of modernity, for which the human being is the ground of all Being, and Being a representation of human being. But where Nietzsche finds in the need for humanity to assume dominion over the earth a challenge of awesome and even divine momentousness, recent history has shown the actuality of that dominion to be one of planetary domination and exploitation. Heidegger's interpretation of Nietzsche in this regard leans towards the neo-Nietzschean writings of Ernst Jünger, for whom the experiences of the First World War demonstrated that the reality of the will to power shows itself in the total mobilization of all resources, and that the type of the overman, the one who is called upon to conform to that dominion, is to be identified with the *Gestalt* of the worker.[5] Thorough humanization is thorough dehumanization, and the task of self-legislation to which the overman is called is in truth the turning of all Being to the ends of human machination.

'European Nihilism' continues Heidegger's waxing critique of modern subjectivism and its relation to the end of metaphysics (Heidegger, 1979–87, Volume 4). Nihilism, Nietzsche is the first to see, is not simply the decline of religious faith but the collapse of all transcendent values, in the wake of which the will to power is to provide the principle of a new valuation. The former, classical nihilism, is unable to think the *nihil* that is its condition, both the valuing-as-nothing of the earthly and sensuous, and the vaporous nothingness of its highest values, of truth, Being, and other concepts. The latter, active nihilism, reverses this valuation – now it is the sensuous and transient that is to be esteemed above all else, and the supersensuous and permanent that is to be assessed as relatively worthless. Yet valuative thought is itself an essential mode of metaphysical thinking, Heidegger notes, and has its origins in Plato's positing of the idea of the good, which provides the conditions for Being. Valuation is the dispensation of measure; it allows any given thing to come to be and to persist within the limits that are allotted to it. The suspicion, then, is that Nietzsche too is unable to think the *nihil*, that valuative thought also prevents him from thinking through the nothingness of Being (which metaphysics understands as a particular relationship, that of negation, rather than the oblivion which is at the heart of the experience of Being), and that what is needed is a non-valuative understanding of the relationship of Being and human being.

That Nietzsche's valuative thought is a thorough humanization of metaphysics is evident, Heidegger continues, from his undertaking a critique of metaphysics in the form of a genealogy of morals. Humanization is commonly defined in terms of the saying of Protagoras, that 'man is the measure of all things', and takes comfort in the belief that the basic principle of humanism is not a mere modern contrivance but is as old as civil and enlightened discourse. The experience of Being that dictates the Greek statement, however, is utterly different to that of contemporary humanism. For Protagoras, the human being stands at the centre of a limited radius of unconcealment, which is dispensed to man in variable measure. For Descartes, with whom modern philosophical subjectivism first begins, the human being is the foundation for the representation of all beings, and it is man who provides the measure for the representedness of Being, with varying degrees of certainty. And although Nietzsche reverses the Cartesian prioritization of self-consciousness over bodily experience, it remains the case that all things are the representations of an underlying subject, that they are representations, for example, of a bodily affect or drive. Heidegger brings the course to an end with a meditation on the a priority of Being, noting that, for metaphysics, Being is the a priori – it is the idea, condition, or value that makes possible everything that is, a supposition that both presupposes and confuses the ontological difference of Being and beings.

Who Is Nietzsche's Zarathustra?

The 1940 lectures on nihilism mark for a time the end of Heidegger's direct engagement with Nietzsche's writings, and what follows over the next few years are essays and sketches summarizing Nietzsche's fundamental position and placing his thinking in relation to the preceding history of metaphysics.[6] After the abandonment of the course on Nietzsche and Hölderlin late in 1944, and Heidegger's post-war suspension from teaching by the French de-Nazification committee, he resumes lecturing in 1951, and once again returns to his interpretation of Nietzsche, though in a mood markedly different from that of ten years earlier (see Heidegger, 1968).

The primary insights of the later course are brought together in the 1953 essay 'Who Is Nietzsche's Zarathustra?'[7] What is of greatest importance to an understanding of this work is its title, which takes the form of a question, a question to which the essay in the end has no answer. As Heidegger notes, Nietzsche himself provides an answer to this question – Zarathustra is the teacher of the doctrines of eternal recurrence and the overman – to which response Heidegger proceeds to add others. Zarathustra is also a disciple of Dionysus and, more importantly, he is the teacher not of two disparate doctrines but of both these teachings together. In some way, he continues, not only is Zarathustra the teacher of the eternal return and the overman, somehow he *is* these two teachings, in their belonging together. And before these answers stands the one provided by the very title of the work in which the figure of Zarathustra appears, *Also sprach Zarathustra*, namely, that Zarathustra is a speaker, one who speaks forth and as an advocate of that which he teaches.

Are these answers, singly or jointly, a sufficient response to the question posed by the title of the essay? The last answer tells us that the figure of Zarathustra belongs essentially to the domain of language, though not merely to its abstract conception, which may be defined as significant expression. In speaking, Zarathustra gives utterance to the kind of word that needs to be heeded. Such speaking is not to be grasped as the mere transmission of information, nor is it an oblique communication that opens itself only to scholarly interpretation. Zarathustra may be understood not by piling up and memorizing statements and definitions but only by heeding the urgency of what it is that he advocates, and only in this way may we experience who it is that Zarathustra may be. And that means that the answer to the question of the title may properly be experienced only in silence.

And so the essay, the last of Heidegger's extended writings on Nietzsche, ends once again in ambivalence. Despite both its extraordinary breadth and its equally astonishing condensation of Nietzsche's wide-ranging thought into a handful of fundamental themes – will to power, eternal recurrence, revaluation of all values, nihilism, the overman – Heidegger's interpretation does not aspire to provide an exhaustive overview of Nietzsche. In the 1961 foreword to the *Nietzsche* volumes, he states that its aim is rather 'to think through those few thoughts that determine the whole' (Heidegger, 1979–87, p. xil). And perhaps the single most important expression of those determinative thoughts, for Heidegger, is a long aphorism from *The Will to Power*, to which he refers at decisive moments throughout his interpretation and which begins: 'To *impress* upon becoming the character of being – that is the *highest will to power*' (Nietzsche, 1968, Section 617; translation modified). One can certainly find in this aphorism (Heidegger usually quotes from the first three paragraphs) a remarkable summary of those fundamental themes listed above. Yet its importance for Heidegger seems to reside in what is unsaid in it, in what cannot be exhausted by a thematic presentation, the sole purpose of which is to provoke us to think.

Heidegger's Nietzsche is not the only or the last Nietzsche that we have. Nor is it always the most accurate, and it is hardly the most sympathetic. The greatness of an interpretation, however, resides in neither the subtlety of its scholarship nor the fidelity of its discipleship. It lies, rather, in its ability to open a new way to its topic, and that means, to confront those of us who would try to follow it, to challenge us to find our own way to Nietzsche, and to do so freely, critically.

Notes

[1] See the original text of the lecture: Heidegger, 1985, p. 5.

[2] This and the surrounding paragraphs of *Twilight of the Idols* are an interpretation of Heraclitus, fragment 7.

[3] The death of God marks the end of what Heidegger calls (in echo of a question Aristotle raises in his *Metaphysics*, whether first philosophy is ontology or theology) 'ont-theo-logic'. Ontology concerns beings as a whole; theology has to do with the highest being. Heidegger's 1943 essay takes its departure from Nietzsche's parable of the madman: see GS 125.

[4] These themes are pursued in the essay 'Who is Nietzsche's Zarathustra?' See 'The Convalescent' section of *Thus Spoke Zarathustra*.

[5] For a recapitulation, see Heidegger, 1998.

[6] Apart from the essay in *Nietzsche*, vol. 4, the essays placing Nietzsche in relation to the history of metaphysics appear in Heidegger, 1973.

[7] The essay is included in *Nietzsche*, vol. 2, but does not appear in the German edition.

Bibliography and Guide to Further Study

Heidegger's Nietzsche Interpretation

Heidegger, Martin (1968), *What Is Called Thinking?* trans. J. Glenn Gray. New York: Harper & Row. The first half of this volume contains the text of the 1951 course, which provides the seeds for the essay 'Who Is Nietzsche's Zarathustra?'

— (1973), *The End of Philosophy*, trans. Joan Stambaugh. New York: Harper & Row. Although the essays in this volume are not exclusively about Nietzsche, all but one appear in the German edition of *Nietzsche*, and were included there in order to place Nietzsche within the context of the history of metaphysics.

— (1977), 'The Word of Nietzsche: "God is Dead" ', trans. William Lovitt, in id., *The Question Concerning Technology and Other Essays*. New York: Harper & Row, 1977. A long essay from 1943 that ties together the themes from the lectures and essays of the previous years. The first of Heidegger's writings on Nietzsche to be made public.

— (1979–87), *Nietzsche*, 4 vols., ed. David Farrell Krell; trans. David Farrell Krell, Joan Stambaugh and Frank A. Capuzzi. New York: Harper & Row. Heidegger's two-volume German publication appears in four volumes in the English translation, with some additions and deletions. Volume 1, 'The Will to Power as Art', contains the course of 1936–7 of the same name. Volume 2, 'The Eternal Recurrence of the Same', contains the 1937 course of that name and the 1953 essay 'Who Is Nietzsche's Zarathustra?' Volume 3, 'The Will to Power as Knowledge and Metaphysics', contains the 1939 course, 'The Will to Power as Knowledge', two undelivered lectures from 1939 entitled 'The Eternal Recurrence of the Same and the Will to Power', and a 1940 essay, 'Nietzsche's Metaphysics'. Volume 4, 'European Nihilism', contains the 1940 course of that name and a 1944–6 essay, 'Nihilism as Determined by the History of Being'. Also important are the introductions and analyses in each volume by the editor, David Farrell Krell. Krell's unpublished 1971 doctoral thesis on Heidegger's Nietzsche interpretation was the first monograph on the topic.

Selected Works on Heidegger's Nietzsche Interpretation

The following texts are only suggested starting points for further reading. The literature is immense and yet uncannily incomplete.

Behler, Ernst (1991), *Confrontations: Derrida/Heidegger/Nietzsche*, trans. Steven Taubeneck. Stanford: Stanford University Press.

Derrida, Jacques (1989), 'Interpreting Signatures (Heidegger/Nietzsche): Two Questions', trans. Diane Michelfelder and Richard Palmer in, *Dialogue and Deconstruction: The Gadamer-Derrida Encounter*. Albany: State University of New York Press. Though Derrida often touches on the topic, this is one of the few texts that deal exclusively with Heidegger's Nietzsche.

Haar, Michel (1996), 'Critical Remarks on the Heideggerian Reading of Nietzsche', in Christopher Macann (ed.), *Critical Heidegger*. London and New York: Routledge.

Haar was one of the best French scholars of Heidegger's Nietzsche. Havas, Randall (1992), 'Who Is Heidegger's Nietzsche?', in Hubert Dreyfus and Harrison Hall (eds), *Heidegger: A Critical Reader*. Cambridge, MA: Blackwell.

McNeill, William (1995), 'Traces of Discordance: Heidegger–Nietzsche', in Peter Sedgwick (ed.), *Nietzsche: A Critical Reader*.Cambridge, MA: Blackwell.

Pöggeler, Otto (1987), *Martin Heidegger's Path of Thinking*, trans. Daniel Magurshak and Sigmund Barber. Atlantic highlands, NJ: Humanities Press. Perhaps the best account of Nietzsche within the context of Heidegger's overall thought. Pöggeler assisted Heidegger with preparing the *Nietzsche* volumes for publication.

— (2002), *Friedrich Nietzsche und Martin Heidegger*. Bonn: Bouvier.

Other Works Cited

Heidegger, Martin (1968), *The Will To Power*, ed. Walter Kaufmann; trans. W. Kaufman and R. J. Hollingdale. New York: Vintage.

— (1975), 'The Anaximander Fragment', trans. David Farrell Krell, in *Early Greek Thinking*. New York: Harper & Row.

— (1985), *Nietzsche: Der Wille zur Macht als Kunst*, Gesamtausgabe, vol. 43, ed. Bernd Heimbüchel. Frankfurt am Main: Vittorio Klostermann.

— (1990), *Nietzsches Metaphysik / Einleitung in die Philosophie: Denken und Dichten*, Gesamtausgabe, vol. 50, ed. Petra Jaeger. Frankfurt am Main: Vittorio Klostermann.

— (1996), *Being and Time*, trans. Joan Stambaugh. Albany: State University of New York Press.

— (1998), 'On the Question of Being', in William McNeill (ed.), *Pathmarks*. Cambridge: Cambridge University Press.

— (2000), *Introduction to Metaphysics*, trans. Gregory Fried and Richard Polt. New Haven: Yale University Press.

Chapter 2

Löwith's Nietzsche

J. Harvey Lomax

Loving, here, cannot have the common meaning of a desire for self-fulfilment through another human being, but . . . openness for the whole of what is and will continue to be.

Löwith, *Wissen, Glaube und Skepsis*

The Death of God

The death of God, most memorably proclaimed by Friedrich Nietzsche in *The Gay Science* and *Thus Spoke Zarathustra*, has moral and political consequences. Zarathustra's Shadow, the shadow of nihilism, paints the implications on a wall for all who have eyes to see: 'Nothing is true. All is permitted'. Nietzsche therefore regards himself and his writings as dynamite. Social earthquakes, bloodshed, wars, revolutions, and a new world order and disorder will as ineluctably follow him as night follows day. For human beings in community urgently need laws, and in order for any system of laws to warrant respect, it must appeal to standards, natural or supernatural, that transcend the merely human. In society the conviction that nothing is true and everything is permitted has the practical effect of liberating the most barbaric passions and of legitimating the right of the fastest, the cruellest, the strongest to rule. Yet Nietzsche paradoxically claims exactly not to degrade the human race or to foster decadence and nihilism, but on the contrary to redeem humanity from nihilism and to point the way to a new, unprecedented peak of human existence.

Karl Löwith,[1] a student of Martin Heidegger and one of the most learned and accomplished scholars of nineteenth-century intellectual history, demonstrates beyond a doubt that Nietzsche does not murder God. The death of God among thinking people in Europe has already occurred when

Nietzsche announces it.[2] 'When Montesquieu visited England in 1731, he reported that among the educated in that country, there remained no religion whatsoever' (Löwith, 1974, p. 7). 'Fichte was accused of atheism because he interpreted philosophically the Church's faith in revelation, as Kant did before him and Hegel and Schelling after him. Kant's religion "within the limits of reason alone", Hegel's "*philosophy* of religion",[3] and Schelling's *philosophy of mythology and revelation* all make faith as such superfluous' (*SS* 3, p. 299). This recent challenge to faith that ultimately undermines faith has roots going back not only to Descartes's atheistic proof of God based on radical doubt (*SS* 3, pp. 300–1) and to Hobbes's corporealism, but all the way to antiquity. 'The many ancient philosophers who were accused of impiety (*asebeia*) found themselves in conflict with the authority of their *polis*, which was simultaneously a religious institution; the post-Christian philosophers who were accused of atheism found themselves in conflict with the authority of the Church, which was at the same time a political power' (*SS* 3, p. 299). The anti-Christian Sermon on the Mount of Nietzsche's Zarathustra merely completes, as it were, the history of the long-standing tension between faith and philosophy.

In Löwith's interpretation not godlessness but the demand for a totally honest atheism distinguishes Nietzsche from his predecessors. To him previous German philosophers, including not only Kant, Fichte, and Hegel, but also Feuerbach and David Strauss, lack probity. He regards them as semi-priests and their philosophy as a decayed form of Protestantism (*SS* 3, p. 303). By contrast, Nietzsche's final work, *Ecce Homo*, concludes with a declaration of war: 'Dionysus contra the Crucified (ibid.)'. Nietzsche's critique of Christianity encompasses all its forms, emphatically going beyond theological dogmas to include social and humanitarian teachings and practices. Yet in the end, Löwith's Nietzsche cannot accommodate himself to a pure, unambiguous godlessness. Instead, disbelief and longing for the divine collide in Nietzsche. In Löwith's eyes Nietzsche longs not for the Scriptural God but for the Dionysian eternal recurrence of the selfsame, natural world. Thus the desire for the most intellectually honest atheism paradoxically culminates in a fundamentally religious aspiration (ibid.). In this sense Nietzsche's intellectual development as portrayed by Löwith seems to represent a great victory of faith over reason.

Löwith's Nietzsche grasps very well that he lives in a time of radical transition. Though modern European intellectuals no longer believe in either God or scriptural tenets, though they have begun even to question Christian values, nevertheless they continue to follow the old ways. Christian morality seems to hold them under its spell. The dread of nihilism is but another term for fear of the total collapse of the Christian way of life, of which move-ments for social justice or secular utopia are only expressions, in lieu of providence and the afterlife. Modern people may reject Christian self-denial, but they cannot openly affirm natural self-assertion. Though sophis-ticated folk no longer believe in Christian marriage or the Christian State, for the time being nothing stops them from giving marriage, birth, and death the appearance of Christian sacredness (Löwith, 1974, p. 8). They may still speak with bowed heads and in sombre tones of Christian love, but in everyday life they actually pursue honour or advantage (ibid., p. 9). As a result of such ambiguity, ambivalence, confusion, and phoniness, the whole world loses its credibility and meaning.

From the outset Nietzsche's dismantling of the traditional Platonic-Christian interpretation of existence has the positive goal of regaining the natural world. In place of God, who for thousands of years has been the highest being and *summum bonum*, Nietzsche substitutes the amorality and innocence of the empirical world of nature that subsists on its own excre-ment, the world that eternally comes back into being even as it passes away. The human being is just one ring in the huge, never-ending ring of the whole, natural universe. Devoid of its own purposes and indifferent to human ends, the natural world was not created and has no moral order. When man comes to understand the nature of the goalless, accidental world of nature, he liberates himself from guilt and duty. God can neither com-mand nor punish him. By freeing ourselves from God, we for the first time redeem the world and ourselves for the world (ibid., pp. 17–18). The ori-ginal title of *Thus Spoke Zarathustra*, 'Noon and Eternity', reflects the tri-umphant defeat of nihilism by the eternal recurrence, for the shadow of nihilism completely disappears at the declaration of the love for eternity that occurs in the bright sunlight of noon.

In the preface to *Zarathustra*, the titular hero sees the death of God as both a risk and an opportunity. Humanity risks sinking into the contempt-ible, self-satisfied, soulless condition of the Last Man. But God's passing also makes possible an ascent to the superman. Human beings can overcome themselves not by becoming divine or by imitating Jesus but by becoming fully themselves, by realizing their secular capacities and coming into their own. The superman at once gains victory over God and the nothing of nihilism. Rejecting metaphysical backworlds and otherworldly hopes, the superman will remain true to the earth (ibid., p. 10). The supermen will also become lords of the earth, and in that sense will replace God. God can no longer give orders, so the superman gives himself his own orders. Hum-ble obedience gets replaced by pride and sagacity (ibid.).

The Eternal Recurrence

If the superman believes in anything but himself, he has faith in the eternal order and periodicity of the cosmos, the endlessly turning hourglass of all existence. Cosmic necessity and eternal recurrence are not only inseparable but identical. The first express indication of eternal recurrence in Nietzsche's books occurs in *The Gay Science*, aphorism 341, shortly before the allusion to the death of God in 342 (see 343, 125). In 341 Nietzsche does not allege or affirm anything. He merely asks the reader how he or she would react to a demon who declared that literally every detail of one's life will forever occur over and over again in the future, in exactly the same sequence and context. The reader might react with either horror or delight. In any event the question of whether one desires the endless repetition of the selfsame life would make one conscious of a great gravity and seriousness in one's actions, and one might even find it necessary to cherish life and to live well (*SS* 6, pp. 418–19).

Löwith underlines that in *Zarathustra*, 'where eternal recurrence is the basic inspiration of the whole work', the recurrence appears not hypothetically but as a 'metaphysical truth' (*SS* 6, p. 419). The vision of eternity has the character of a 'supreme moment of fulfilment' (ibid.). After a great sickness and despair, the eternal recurrence has a decisive healing effect. Zarathustra rejoices in the freedom from all-too-human purposes in the eternal recurrence of all things. He thus transcends the hopes, fears, and regrets of ordinary life. The illusory idea of progress is also replaced by the eternal ring of being (*SS* 6, pp. 419–20).

The teaching of eternal recurrence combines creation and destruction, joy and suffering, good and evil. Therefore the lowest, most disgusting human types, not just the beautiful examples of the race, will return again and again without limit. Zarathustra first reacts to the idea with loathing and nausea. Only after his animals have persuaded him to accept the natural order as it is does Zarathustra overcome himself and become a kind of superman (*SS* 6, pp. 420–1). To him the world is now perfect. Zarathustra blesses and affirms it (ibid.). Zarathustra's soul and the eternal 'world' of Dionysus that it mirrors represent the highest kind of being (*SS* 6, p. 422).

By remaining attentive to Nietzsche's historical situation and carefully observing the link between the death of God and the eternal recurrence, Löwith sees the principal reason for Nietzsche's return to a kind of paganism. 'Placed at the final stage of an evaporated Christianity, he had to search for new sources of the future, and he found them in classic paganism. The death of the Christian God made him again understand the

Ancient World . . . Many scholars were familiar with the doctrines of eternal recurrence in Heracleitus and Empedocles, Plato and Aristotle, Eudoxus and the Stoics, but only Nietzsche perceived in it creative possibilities for the future' (*SS* 6, pp. 423–4).

Löwith's Nietzsche glorifies not only the superman's political will to power but also his will to affirm the eternal recurrence as a cure for the fundamental illness of the West, namely a weakness of will. The incapacity to rule and to impose one's will leads to a search for some sort of solid support, a search that culminates in faith in another will that commands what one must do. The less one knows how to give orders, the more urgently one desires a god, prince, doctor, confessor, dogma, or party conscience. Paralysis of the will gave birth both to Buddhism and Christianity. Both these religions propagated fanaticism to provide countless people something to hold onto and a new possibility of willing and delight in willing. As Nietzsche puts it, fanaticism is the only seeming 'strength of the will' of which the weak and uncertain are capable (Löwith, 1974, p. 11).[4] As soon as any human being desires to be commanded, that person becomes in principle a believer in Nietzsche's eyes. By contrast the free spirit parts ways with every faith and every wish for certainty, delights in perplexities and risks, and when he comes to the edge of abysses, dances (ibid.).

'Dionysus versus the Crucified' only formulaically encapsulates the crux of Nietzsche's writings and thought. At any rate Nietzsche thoroughly rejects the good news of the Christian gospels. To him Christianity is the enemy of life and sexuality, and the Christian God represents the greatest possible objection against existence. Moreover, he counts the strength of religious conviction and certainty of Christians over the ages as an argument against them (ibid., pp. 13–14). Zarathustra believes neither in old gods nor in new ones. Nietzsche himself speaks in the name of only one god, Dionysus, and he does so only because Dionysus is a symbol of the highest affirmation of the world and transfiguration of existence, namely the eternal recurrence. God on the Cross is a curse against life, whereas Dionysus is an auspicious promise and celebration of the sexual fecundity and eternal recurrence of this-worldly, natural life (ibid.). The world of nature is the highest power, and is *in that sense* divine (ibid., p. 14).

Löwith's Deconstruction of the Eternal Recurrence

Together, the death of God, the eternal recurrence, and the will to power comprise the single, unifying theme of Löwith's Nietzsche's whole system of aphorisms. However, Löwith does not stop at articulating the unity of eternal recurrence and will to power in the context of the expiration of Christianity. First, he pointedly asks whether, after Christianity, the natural world can again be revered as divine. If the world of nature is ungodly, immoral, inhumane, does the abolition of the distinction between the world of human ideals and the empirical world not force us to choose between what we venerate and ourselves? (ibid., pp. 14–15).[5] This query seems to leave us with a hopeless dilemma, the choice between self-debasement or suicide. Here Löwith appeals to Nietzsche's argument in *Twilight* that the abolition of the ideal world also implies the abolition of the mere apparentness of the apparent world, and therefore the world of appearances becomes the only real world (ibid., p. 15; *SS* 6, pp. 221–6). Löwith treats this brilliant account as a way of overcoming the aforementioned dilemma. Whether the argument suffices for the present purpose might have to remain a question for anyone who harbours aspirations beyond himself. But Löwith's Nietzsche concludes that the most thoughtful denier of ideal worlds will not hesitate to revere exactly himself and the eternally recurring world that will keep on bringing him back to life again (*SS* 6, p. 226; see BGE 287).

The second phase of Löwith's deconstruction of the eternal recurrence focuses on the origin of that scientific spirit of atheism that leads to rejection of otherworldly, Christian dogmas and to confidence in the empirical, natural world. Löwith echoes Nietzsche's insight that the scientific demand for intellectual honesty has its ultimate source in the Christian conscience (Löwith, 1974, p. 16). Whereas from the point of view of the eternal recurrence the will to truth might be seen as a natural expression of the will to power, Löwith's Nietzsche finally exposes the will to truth as the last hiding place and citadel of Christian faith (ibid.).

Third, Löwith's renown as a path-breaking, seminal Nietzsche-researcher rests above all on his critical distinction between two very different aspects of the eternal recurrence. On the one hand the teaching provides an atheistic replacement of religion. On the other hand it develops a physical metaphysics. Löwith calls the former the *anthropological* side of the eternal recurrence, and the latter the *cosmological* side. Under close examination the two aspects reveal themselves as discordant. The cosmological version of the eternal return represents Nietzsche's attempt to restore the pre-Socratic view of the world and thereby to overcome the modern division of the world into an inner world (*res cogitans*), an outer world (*res extensa*), and a backworld (*Hinterwelt*, which might be heaven, the Platonic ideas, or the thing-in-itself) (*SS* 6, pp. 220–2).[6] The cosmological eternal recurrence involves the world of self-willing destruction and creation. The anthropological recurrence, by contrast, saves man from nihilism. According to Löwith, however, the circle of the eternal cycle of the natural world will not serve to eternalize a human existence that has become gossamer and fleeting. The natural-scientific 'fact' of the goalless, autonomous being of the world of forces cannot provide the ethical gravity needed by the human being who has lost his goal and purpose (*SS* 6, p. 205). The cosmological teaching refers to a physical fact in the unwilled, necessity-bound physical world, and thus replaces ancient cosmology with modern physics. The anthropological teaching, on the other hand, establishes an ideal goal for willing, desiring man and thereby replaces the Christian teaching of immortality with the will to self-eternalization (*SS* 6, pp. 205–6).

Modern human beings do not know which way to turn, because they have no goal in terms of which to plan their lives. The teaching of the eternal return is therefore meant to provide a sketch of a new way to live. The image for this new way of life is the superman, the new lord of the earth (*SS* 6, pp. 206–7). The strength of will of the superman is inseparable from his highest ethical centre of gravity and his responsibility for the future. The new categorical imperative is to live in every moment in such a way that one could will that moment back again and again without end (*SS* 6, pp. 207–8). The model of the new man is Zarathustra, because he is the highest type of well-cultivated human being who gives himself his own orders. Other examples of people who climbed above themselves have occurred in antiquity and its renaissance. In the modern world such more-than-human human beings include Goethe and Napoleon (*SS* 6, p. 208). Thus the teaching of the eternal recurrence comprehends Nietzsche's plan for the future of European civilization (ibid.).

The practical maxim of the eternal recurrence in the anthropological sense simply involves living in a way that one would want to live again. The recurrence is neither a future event nor a mere recurring again and again of the same, but a *will to a rebirth*, to a new life. The good will toward life that characterizes the anthropological teaching of recurrence blocks the road to escapisms of all sorts, including metaphysical backworlds or suicide. The doctrine of recurrence overcomes the nihilistic, absolute scepticism that says nothing is true and everything is permitted (*SS* 6, p. 209). The emptiness of nihilism gets replaced by the iron necessity and redemption of self-made law.

This whole Nietzschean system collapses, as Löwith shows, over the inherent contradiction between the two forms of eternal recurrence. If the cosmological eternal recurrence of the selfsame is an unchangeable element of the physical world or indeed encompasses the whole of the physical world, it does not depend in any way on human willing, wishing, or believing. Nor would the imperative to live *as if* one would return eternally make any sense if the cosmological eternal recurrence were an ineluctable fact of nature (*SS* 6, p. 211).

Löwith acknowledges that Nietzsche does proffer arguments in favour of the cosmological eternal recurrence. All passing of the old amounts to the origin of the new, so the principle of preservation of energy requires the eternal return. Nietzsche speaks of it as the 'most scientific of all scientific hypotheses'. The world preserves itself precisely in its coming into being and passing away. Given endless time and a very large but finite number of possible states – situations, modifications, combinations, and developments – all possible occurrences must have already occurred. Each moment has to be a repetition of what once was and will be (*SS* 6, pp. 212–14). Even if one were to accept the validity of these far-from-apodictic 'proofs', however, Löwith rightly points out that Nietzsche has no logical or scientific warrant whatsoever to use the key term 'will to power' to refer to the interminable, goalless ebb and flow of nature (*SS* 6, pp. 216–18).

The fundamental fissure in Nietzsche's ethical-cosmological conception ultimately causes the doctrine of eternal recurrence to shatter into incommensurable shards. Consequently, in Löwith's interpretation, Nietzsche fails to overcome his central problem of nihilism. On the contrary, the shadow of nihilism plagues him to the bitter end. The albatross of nihilism explains why Nietzsche cannot bear his own wisdom (*SS* 6, p. 224 and, more generally, pp. 221–37).

Criticisms of Löwith's Nietzsche

Hardly anyone else even approaches Löwith's magisterial command of the Nietzschean *oeuvre*, his subtlety, thoughtfulness, and elegance and grace of expression. His interpretation of Nietzsche's whole system of aphorisms in terms of the eternal recurrence stands as a scholarly model and a monument in the intellectual history of the nineteenth century. Nevertheless, Löwith's reflections on Nietzsche stop short of developing the most illuminating comparisons and the most revealing question. At great length he measures Nietzsche against the pre-Socratics, the Bible and Christianity, and nearly every great philosopher from Descartes to Heidegger; but he fails even briefly to assess Nietzsche's relationship to Socrates, whom Nietzsche describes as the vortex of all history (see Dannhauser, 1974; Strauss, 1983; and Lampert, 2001). Löwith quite legitimately asks what doctrines Nietzsche *taught*, but he does not properly investigate what it means to Nietzsche to *be* a philosopher. But precisely that Socratic query is the decisive one: What is a philosopher?

Several passages from *Beyond Good and Evil* merit our consideration here: 'A philosopher: that is a human being who constantly experiences, sees, hears, suspects, dreams extraordinary things; who is struck by his own thoughts as from without, as from above and below . . . ' (292). Second,

> [t]he hermit does not believe that a philosopher . . . ever expressed his authentic and final opinions in books: does not one write books exactly to conceal what one harbors? Indeed, he will even doubt whether a philosopher *can* at all have 'final and authentic' opinions . . . Every philosophy is a foreground philosophy . . . 'There is something arbitrary about *his* stopping here . . . that he did not dig deeper there . . . ' Every philosophy hides a philosophy; every opinion is a hiding place, and every word is also a mask. (289)

Finally, 'I would take the liberty of ranking philosophers by the quality of their laughter . . . And assuming that gods, too, philosophize . . . I do not doubt that they also know how to laugh in a superhuman and new way – and at the cost of all serious things' (294). Philosophic thoughts that turn into doctrines or truths become 'pathetically decent and dull'. Only 'weary and mellow things' are immortalized by philosophers (296). Nietzsche presents himself here not as a teacher of wisdom but as a lover of wisdom (295). That even gods philosophize implies that even gods do not possess the ultimate truth about all things.

If Löwith does not entirely ignore Nietzsche's hints about his masks and his esoteric form of writing, he nonetheless gives them too little weight. Precisely with a view to the questionableness of the doctrine of eternal recurrence, Löwith does take note of Zarathustra's warning to his pupils that they should not remain his disciples. In sharp contrast to Jesus, Zarathustra wants no disciples and no believers. He urges them to lose him and find themselves. He also encourages his pupils to repudiate him. He indicates he may have deceived them (*SS* 6, p. 440). Löwith seems to take precious little account of numerous other passages where Nietzsche distances himself from his own or Zarathustra's teachings. When Zarathustra tells Life he will return, she demurs, exclaiming, 'You know that, Zarathustra? No one can know that!' Again, in the speech 'On Redemption', when Zarathustra relates how the creative backwards-willing of the past as one's own creation can redeem us from the past and from the spirit of revenge against the past, an astute hunchback challenges him. Löwith notices that the hunchback complains that Zarathustra speaks differently both to hunchbacks and to himself than he does to his pupils. But Löwith evidently fails to appreciate that of all people a clever hunchback seems least likely to fall victim to tall tales of the redemptive power of the creative, backwards-willing will.[7] The implication is that Zarathustra does not believe in the eternal recurrence. As for the superman who wills the recurrence, he gets replaced by the 'higher men' in Part IV of *Zarathustra*, which was written for Nietzsche's friends and not the public. To put it gently, Nietzsche mocks and ridicules the higher men. When they come to his cave, Zarathustra has to leave it because of the 'bad air'. The higher men worship the braying, yes-saying ass that represents the eternal return. They slumber while Zarathustra is awake. 'These are not my proper companions', he exclaims. At the very end of *Zarathustra*, he overcomes his pity for the higher men and leaves them behind without even bidding them adieu (Lomax, 2003, p. 125). In *The Antichrist* 54 Nietzsche says, 'One should not be misled: great minds are sceptics. Zarathustra is a sceptic'.[8]

Regarding Löwith's deconstruction of the will to truth, suffice it for present purposes to observe that that will long predates Christianity and need not disappear even if, as seems unlikely, Christianity in all its forms should die out within the next few centuries. In at least one Platonic dialogue, the lie in the soul or self-deception gets described as a terrible illness. Socrates's assertion in Plato's *Apology* that the unexamined life is not liveable for a human being makes little sense apart from a will to truth, albeit a very self-interested will to truth. Even if one posited that the will to truth derives from the desire for self-preservation or the will to power, which is by no means self-evident, the utility of the truth for achieving good life, however understood, certainly need not undermine philosophic aspirations, but on the contrary would tend to feed the love of wisdom.

Löwith's Critique of Heidegger's Nietzsche

No decent treatment of Karl Löwith's Nietzsche could conclude without addressing Löwith's reaction to Heidegger's Nietzsche (*SS* 8, pp. 193–227 and pp. 241–57). Löwith has two principal, far-reaching complaints about Heidegger's interpretation. Rather than drawing the meaning of Nietzsche's writings primarily from the text, Heidegger insinuates his own formidable system of thought into his exegeses. By selecting isolated passages and by concentrating on what is unsaid and developing the ostensible implications thereof, Heidegger gives himself free rein to employ his own history of Being to interpret Nietzsche (*SS* 8, p. 193; *SS* 6, pp. 381, 383). Second, Heidegger seems to protect himself against his critics by presenting reason itself as the most stubborn opponent of true thinking (*SS* 8, p. 198; see Heidegger, 2002). Unabashed and perhaps even amused, Löwith does not hesitate to confront the Master at length while relying exactly on reason.

A condensed version of Löwith's incisive critique appears at the end of the appendix to *Nietzsche's Philosophy of the Eternal Recurrence of the Same* (pp. 225–8; *SS* 6, pp. 381–4). Heidegger correctly sees the teachings of superman, eternal recurrence, and will to power as a unity. But he fails to grasp the grave contradiction, discussed above, between the being of the world and the existence of man. Consequently he does not properly conceive the reversal of the will to the nothing into the willing of the eternal recurrence and the revaluation of all values (*SS* 6, pp. 381–2). For Heidegger the reversal and revaluation are merely negative. For Nietzsche, however, they entail a new beginning and a noon (*SS* 6, p. 382).

According to Heidegger, despite Nietzsche's efforts to overcome the nihilism of metaphysics, namely, Christian Platonism, he remained entangled in it, because he never understood the heart of nihilism, namely, the hiddenness of the truth of Being. Löwith replies that the (cosmological) idea of eternal recurrence as the eternal law of all that is and becomes transcends nihilism (ibid.).

Heidegger also characterizes Nietzsche's philosophy as a metaphysics of values. Löwith rejoins that Nietzsche explicitly states that the total character of life *cannot* be assessed or evaluated (*SS* 6, p. 383). Life as will to power cannot be devalued because in every moment it is wholly what it is and remains the same in all change. Similarly, Heidegger interprets the noon as a transitoriness brought to a halt. In fact Nietzsche describes the noon, which equals the return, not as a

'securing of continuance' but as an eternal recurrence of flux, i.e. of the same coming into being and passing away.

Löwith seems to regard as particularly forced Heidegger's imposition of the distinction between will to power as *essentia* (essence) and eternal recurrence as *existentia* (existence) into Nietzsche's philosophic conception. Heidegger then unpersuasively concludes that Nietzsche, by following these traditional metaphysical categories, does not really devise anything new but only brings to completion the previous metaphysics, which, without genuinely thinking, defined Being in terms of unexamined essence and existence (ibid.). Löwith freely concedes that Nietzsche thinks of eternity as the lasting presence of a becoming that always has the same type, power, and meaning. But he asks whether such a conception really exposes, as Heidegger believes, a deficiency on Nietzsche's part and a failure to reach Being. Löwith contends, to the contrary, that an ultimate reliance on the eternal truth of nature is a sign not of any personal shortcoming but of wisdom (*SS* 6, p. 384).

Concluding Thought on Christianity and Philosophy

Löwith closes his last essay on Heidegger's Nietzsche with a few final reflections on Christianity and the death of God. He notes the significance for the history of philosophy that Christianity did not remain confined to a sect but spread across the Roman Empire. Only thanks to Christianity does the West and Western philosophy exist. The Greek beginning did not suffice to create the West, and indeed modern philosophy is replete with concepts engendered or modified by Christian theology, from Descartes's proofs of God to Hegel's philosophy of religion to Nietzsche's anti-Christianity. It is biblical religion, too, that gives man his special status in the whole of being (*SS* 8, p. 256). Löwith might have added that the philosopher has need of the challenging dialogue with religion for purposes of self-justification and self-understanding (see Meier, 1998 and 2006). Today we live in a liberal time when the Church is manifestly not a tyrannical monolith and when home-grown, Western fanaticism has largely been tamed. In such circumstances one sometimes wonders, even while admiring the depth and beauty of Nietzsche's seductive writings, whether it would not be better to tend to the harvest than to destroy the plowshare.

Notes

This chapter is dedicated to Werner J. Dannhauser. The University of Memphis generously provided a grant and leave that made this and other research possible. Special thanks are due Matthias Kaelberer, Linda Bennett, and Henry Kurtz. Ruediger Völkel and the University of Heidelberg Library earned gratitude and acknowledgement for making available research materials on Löwith that were otherwise inaccessible. Earlier grants from the Earhart Foundation, the National Endowment for the Humanities, and the Bradley Foundation also contributed mightily to this long-term project.

[1] For general articles on Löwith, see Gadamer, Anz, Barash, Habermas, Hosowya, Lutz, Riedel, and Sass. See also Cho, Del Caro, Flahiff, Gornisiewicz, Hafkesbrink,

Kuhn, Marcuse, Mitchells, Niebuhr, Schneider, and Seward. Scholars have cited Löwith's writings on Nietzsche hundreds of times, and his *Nietzsche's Philosophie der ewigen Wiederkehr des Gleichen*, translated as *Nietzsche's Philosophy of the Eternal Recurrence of the Same* (Löwith, 1965), is widely regarded as a classic. As Bernd Magnus has remarked, 'In many, many ways, Löwith's Nietzsche established the framework within which much Anglophone Nietzsche scholarship has moved in the past three decades and is likely to continue to move . . . ' (1997, xviii). In this chapter all translations and paraphrases from Löwith and Nietzsche are my own. Löwith's collected writings, the *Saemtliche Schriften,* will be cited as *SS* followed by the volume and page numbers.

² *Von Hegel zu Nietzsche* (*From Hegel to Nietzsche,* translated as Löwith, 1965) in *SS* 4; *Nietzsches Philosophie* (*Nietzsche's Philosophy*) in *SS* 6; and *Gott, Mensch und Welt* (*God, Man and World*) in *SS* 9.

³ See *SS* 4, 56. 'Hegel's completion of Christian philosophy' is 'a last step before a big reversal and a break with Christianity'. See also *SS* 4, 25: Hegel speaks of the 'common enemy' of Goethe and himself. Compare *SS* 4, 33: one can 'speak only in a very attenuated sense of Hegel's and Goethe's Protestantism'. They deal with Christian images in a meta-Christian way.

⁴ Löwith cites GS 347 and GM II, 22.

⁵ Löwith refers to GS 346.

⁶ Nietzsche errs in attributing backworlds to Plato (as opposed to the exoteric surface of the Platonic writings). See Cropsey (1977) and (1995).

⁷ See Lomax (1997), p. xxv and, more generally, pp. xix-xviii.

⁸ See A 126 for a comparison to the Platonic cave.

Bibliography and Guide to Further Study

Works by Löwith

Löwith, Karl (1965), *From Hegel to Nietzsche: The Revolution in Nineteenth-Century Thought,* trans. David E. Green. London: Constable.

— (1974), 'Nietzsche's Vollendung des Atheismus' ('Nietzsche's Completion of Atheism'), in Hans Steffen (ed.), *Nietzsche: Werk und Wirkungen.* Göttingen: Vandenhoeck & Ruprecht.

— (1981–6), *Sämtliche Schriften* (*Complete Writings*), vols. 1–9. Stuttgart: J. B. Metzslersche Verlagsbuchhandlung.

— (1995), *Martin Heidegger and European Nihilism,* ed. R. Wolin; trans. Gary Steiner New York: Columbia University Press.

— (1997), *Nietzsche's Philosophy of the Eternal Recurrence of the Same,* trans J. Harvey Lomax. Berkeley: University of California Press. Löwith's classic work on Nietzsche boldly challenged the Nazi interpretation and quickly went out of print as a consequence. It was not republished in German until the 1950s, and this 1997 translation is the first English edition.

Works on Löwith

Barash, Jeffrey Andrew, (1998), 'On the Political Implications of Karl Löwith's Concept of Secularization'. *History and Theory*, 37, (1), 69–82. An interpretation of Löwith's writings as primarily an effort to discover and clarify the relationship between intellectual developments and totalitarian movements.

Del Caro, Adrian (1999), '*Nietzsche's Philosophy of the Eternal Recurrence of the Same*. By Karl Löwith'. *Monatshefte*, 9, (4), 562–63. A brief review of *Nietzsche's Philosophy* in English.

Flahiff, G. B. (1950), '*Meaning in History. The Theological Implications of the Philosophy of History*. By Karl Löwith'. *The Catholic Historical Review*, 36, (1), 73–4.

Gornisiewicz, Arkadiusz (2010), 'Karl Löwith and Leo Strauss on Modernity, Secularization, and Nihilism', in Paweł Armada and Arkadiusz Górnisiewicz (eds) *Modernity and What Has Been Lost. Considerations on the Legacy of Leo Strauss*. South Bend, IN: St. Augustine's Press. A comparison of Löwith to a friend, comrade Jewish-German emigrant, and fellow student of Heidegger who focused on many of the same philosophic issues.

Habermas, Jürgen (1985), 'Karl Löwith's Stoic Retreat from Historical Consciousness', in *Philosophical-Political Profiles*. Cambridge, MA: MIT Press. A critique by a colleague and a leader of the Frankfurt School.

Hafkesbrink, Hanna (1941), '*Von Hegel zu Nietzsche*. By Karl Löwith'. *Philosophy and Phenomenological Research*, 2, (2), 257–9.

Heidegger, Martin (2002), 'Nietzsche's Word: "God is Dead"', in *Off the Beaten Track*, trans. Julian Young and Kenneth Haynes. Cambridge: Cambridge University Press. (See the chapter in the present book on Heidegger's Nietzsche for a more extensive treatment with further citations.)

Kuhn, Helmut (1949), '*Meaning in History. The Theological Implications of the Philosophy of History*. By Karl Löwith'. The Journal of Philosophy, 46, (25), 822–26.

Lomax, J. Harvey (1997), 'Translator's Introduction', in Löwith, 1997.

— (2003), *The Paradox of Philosophical Education. Nietzsche's New Nobility and the Eternal Recurrence in Beyond Good and Evil*. Lanham, MD: Rowman and Littlefield/ Lexington.

Magnus, Bernd (1997), 'Preface', in Löwith, 1997.

Marcuse, Herbert (1942), '*Von Hegel zu Nietzsche*. By Karl Löwith'. *The Philosophical Review*, 51, (6), 630–33. A radical, neo-Marxist critique by another student of Heidegger.

McKnight, Stephen A. (1990), 'The Legitimacy of the Modern Age: The Löwith-Blumenberg Debate in Light of Recent Scholarship'. *Political Science Reviewer*, 19, (1), 177–195.

Mitchells, K. (1966), '*From Hegel to Nietzsche: The Revolution in Nineteenth Century Thought*. By Karl Löwith'. Philosophy, 41, (155), 91–93.

Niebuhr, Reinhold (1949), '*Meaning in History*. By Karl Löwith'. *The Journal of Religion*, 29, (4), 302–03. An insightful, informed reflection on Löwith's interpretation of history by the famous theologian.

Seward, G. (1943), '*Von Hegel zu Nietzsche.* Karl Löwith'. *The Journal of Philosophy*, 40, (2), 47–9.
Wolin, Richard (2001), *Heidegger's Children.* Princeton: Princeton University Press. Chapter 4, 'Karl Löwith: The Stoic Response to Modern Nihilism'.

Other Works Cited

Cropsey, Joseph (1977), 'Plato's *Phaedrus* and Plato's Socrates', in id., *Political Philosophy and the Issues of Politics.* Chicago: University of Chicago Press.
— (1995), *Plato's World. Man's Place in the Cosmos.* Chicago: University of Chicago Press.
Dannhauser, Werner J. (1974), *Nietzsche's View of Socrates.* Ithaca, NY: Cornell University Press.
Lampert, Laurence (2001), *Nietzsche's Task; An Interpretation of* Beyond Good and Evil. New Haven: Yale University Press.
Meier, Heinrich (1998), *The Lesson of Carl Schmitt: Four Chapters on the Distinction between Political Theology and Political Philosophy.* Chicago: University of Chicago Press.
— (2006), *Leo Strauss and the Theologico-Political Problem.* Chicago: University of Chicago Press.
Strauss, Leo (1983), 'Note on the Plan of Nietzsche's *Beyond Good and Evil*', in id., *Studies in Platonic Political Philosophy.* Chicago: University of Chicago Press.

Chapter 3

Bataille's Nietzsche

Yue Zhuo

Considered by Michel Foucault as one of the most important writers of his century, Georges Bataille (1897–1962) was the chief representative of what the French philosopher Vincent Descombes calls the 'second French moment of Nietzsche',[1] a period covering the late 1930s up until the years of the Second World War. Compared to the 'third French moment of Nietzsche', beginning in the early 1960s, and marked particularly by the famous Royaumont conference dedicated to Nietzsche in July 1964, this second moment remains relatively unknown to anglophone readers. Bataille's reading of Nietzsche dialogued closely with those of his friends, Pierre Klossowski and Maurice Blanchot; collectively, they inspired the next generation of interpreters such as Michel Foucault and Gilles Deleuze.

Nietzsche was a major source of influence throughout Bataille's life. 'Except for (a few) exceptions', the latter wrote, 'my company on earth is mostly Nietzsche . . . ' (cited in Lotringer, 1992, p. viii). Bataille discovered Nietzsche in 1922–3, when he collaborated with the Russian émigré philosopher Lev Shestov on the French translation of his book: *L'Idée de bien chez Tolstoï et Nietzsche* (*The Idea of the Good in Tolstoy and Nietzsche*). His writings on him are abundant, and they can be divided into three periods. The first one occurred during the years of Acéphale (1936–9), a secret society he founded with Georges Ambrosino, Pierre Klossowski, and Patrick Waldberg in 1936, which, along with the journal bearing the same title, aimed at an anti-Christian, Nietzschean 'religious war' against the politics of the time. The second period corresponds to the years of what he called his 'inner experience' (1939–45), resulting in an intensely personal study of Nietzsche published in 1945: *On Nietzsche* (Bataille, 1992). The third period covers the early years of the 1950s, during which Bataille wrote a series of articles on Nietzsche in the context of a reflection on sovereignty and on Stalinist communism. These articles became part of his posthumously published book *Sovereignty* (Bataille, 1993).

This chapter will introduce Bataille's writings on Nietzsche on the basis of a broad chronological divide: first the prewar public 'reparation'[2] to Nietzsche's political views through the activities of Acéphale, then a personal, passionate, and in-depth 'moral' investigation of Nietzsche's philosophy during and after WWII, which was expressed through what I would call a constant desire to 'wrestle with' or to 'surpass' the philosopher. All along, Bataille's concerns for community (and for its impossibility) remain central to his reading of Nietzsche.

The 'Depoliticization' of Nietzsche: *Acéphale*

The first half of the 1930s was for Georges Bataille a period of leftist political experiments. He first joined Boris Souvarine's anti-Stalinist Democratic Communist Circle in 1931, and contributed non-conformist writings on fascism and on the danger of State hegemony in the circle's house journal, *La Critique Sociale* (*Social Critique*). In 1935, he co-founded, with André Breton, the anti-fascist group Contre-Attaque (Counter Attack), which attempted to turn the popular energies that fascism had released among the masses *against* fascism. Bataille had been greatly inspired by the mobilization of the masses during the Popular Front: on 12 February 1934, thousands of workers, joined by crowds from different left-wing parties, held a general strike throughout France to demonstrate their opposition to fascism. Bataille described this 'ALL-POWERFUL multitude', this 'HUMAN OCEAN' (his capitals), as an effervescence that went beyond professional politicians' desire to seize power (Bataille, 1985b, p. 168). He saw in the organic movement of the workers an antithesis to Hitler and Mussolini's use of mass energies: having remained a spontaneous *defence* organization, it lacked a clear political goal beyond resistance. Yet it was precisely this 'IMPOVERISHED MAJESTY' (Bataille, 1985b, p. 163), or what Maurice Blanchot later called the 'declaration of powerlessness' (Blanchot, 1988, p. 31), that slowed down the spread of fascism in France.

Bataille's first immersion into Nietzsche's thought was framed by this context. Occurring mostly during the activities of Acéphale (headless) but extending to the period of the College de Sociologie,[3] it consisted of a double 'distancing' from politics that took the form, first, of the experience of 'retreat' into some utopian revival of a Dionysian 'religion', then, of a theoretical clearing of Nietzsche's thoughts from the fascist and Nazi appropriations. In both instances, Bataille's chief concern was the question of community. Through Nietzsche, he attempted to disassociate what he called the 'sacred' from the exercise of power. If in *The Birth of Tragedy* Nietzsche presented the Dionysian principle as an experience involving intoxication, excess, and the collapse of the '*principium individuationis*', Bataille fantasized the revival of this *tragedy* in real life, thinking that human beings could be assembled around a spectacle of sacrifice, mutilation, and death, instead of under the power of a religious or military leader.

With Acéphale, Bataille hoped to create such a community whose energies would precisely escape the control of any head or leader. The cover of the first issue of the journal featured a drawing by André Masson, representing a headless man ready to carry out a human sacrifice, and the group's most well-known ritual consisted of a secret 'appointment' in the forest, during which each of its members would take a silent oath to the community by trying to find on his own a mysterious tree that had been struck by lighting. In Bataille's view, the acephalic man shared many characteristics with Nietzsche's 'super-man'[4]: 'The *acephalic man* mythologically expresses sovereignty committed to destruction and the death of God, and in this the identification with the headless man merges and melds with the identification with the superhuman, which IS entirely "the death of God"' (Bataille, 1985d, p. 199).

Indeed, the very formation of the secret society was inspired by Nietzsche's call for a more 'aristocratic reign' through the retreat to a contemplative life, in art and religion. For individuals of the 'noble lineage', writes Nietzsche in *Beyond Good and Evil*, religion can be used 'as a means of securing calm in the face of the turmoil and tribulations of the *cruder* forms of government, and purity in the face of the *necessary* dirt of politics' (Nietzsche, 2002, p. 54). The Nietzschean 'religion', here, is distinctively anti-Christian. It is the religion of Dionysos, god of the Earth, of passions and contradictions, of mysteries and ecstasies, of destruction and defiance.

Bataille, however, saw in the figure of Dionysos not so much an opposition to Christianity per se, but to the forms of sovereignty tied to the 'narrow tradition' of the past:

THE CRITICAL PHASE OF A CIVILIZATION'S DECOMPOSITION IS REGULALY FOLLOWED BY A RECOMPOSITION, WHICH DEVELOPS IN TWO DIFFERENT DIRECTIONS: THE RECONSTITUTION OF RELIGIOUS ELEMENTS OF CIVIL AND MILITARY SOVERIGHTY, TYING EXISTENCE TO THE *PAST*, IS FOLLOWED OR ACCOMPANIED BY THE BIRTH OF FREE AND LIBERATING SACRED FIGURES AND MYTH, *RENEWING* LIFE AND MAIKING IT "THAT WHICH FROLICS IN THE *FUTURE*," "THAT WHICH ONLY BELONGS TO A *FUTURE*". (Bataille, 1985e, pp. 206–7)

The world of mythic Greece that the Nietzschean Dionysos conjures up represents for Bataille an opposite pole not so much to 'properly religious movements' (Osirian, Christian or even Buddhist), but to the concentration of power taken on by a monarchical figure, whose unique goal is its self-solidification. Dionysos is above all a *mythical* figure of 'tragic freedom', breaking down the traditional religious order that encourages submission to civil and military sovereignty. Springing up from an ancient past, it looks ahead into the future, announcing the possibility of new forms of the sacred that would 'release life from servitude' (Bataille, 1985e, p. 27). The goal of Bataille in the 1930s, as Klossowski recalls in an interview with Bernard-Henri Lévy, was to 'create a religion . . . A religion without God' (Klossowski, 1991, p. 170). Acéphale waged a 'religious' war against capitalist production, modern civilization and the political dead-end of the 1930s; Nietzsche became both the mainspring and the weapon of this war.

One of Bataille's opening gestures in this war was to free Nietzsche from his political instrumentalization. The entire second issue of *Acéphale* sought to disengage the philosopher from the fascist and Nazi 'falsifications'. It was a time when Mussolini fed himself regularly on the expression 'Will to Power'. After Hitler's 1933 visit to Elisabeth Förster-Nietzsche, Nietzsche's vocally anti-Semitic sister, Nietzsche's work began to be appropriated by National Socialist theoreticians such as Alfred Rosenberg and Alfred Bäumler. Bataille insisted that Nietzsche's freedom of thought resisted all appropriations: 'Whether it be anti-Semitism, fascism–or socialism–there is only *use*. Nietzsche addressed *free spirits*, incapable of letting themselves be used' (Bataille, 1985c, p. 184).

Bataille's central piece in the issue, 'Nietzsche and the Fascists', aimed at more than simply rejecting the Nazi and fascist misuses of Nietzsche's works. It attempted to understand what in the deep structure of Nietzsche's political thought had allowed such appropriations. One of the questions that fascinated Bataille was why, among all political movements posterior to Nietzsche's death, fascism was the one that consciously and systematically appropriated his criticism of modern society. Nietzsche denounced the egalitarian humanist models such as socialism and advocated an 'aristocratic rule', but he himself kept a distance from all political parties of his day. What was the element that both drew fascism and Nietzcheanism together and yet made them 'violently mutually exclusive' (Bataille, 1985c, pp. 185–6)? Bataille's answer was that while the philosophy of Nietzsche mobilized the 'great will' and the vital experience, the 'aggressive instincts' it released remained 'unemployed' (Bataille, 1985c, p. 185). Fascist and Nazi readings of Nietzsche, on the contrary, focused on the concept of the will to power and converted it into a force to master and to conquer. In doing so, they transformed what in Nietzsche was purposeless into something useful; they instrumentalized Nietzsche's thought in order to benefit their own enterprises.

Bataille further elucidated the specific nature of Nietzsche's political thinking by quoting Karl Jaspers.[5] According to the latter, Nietzsche's originality lies in his refusal to define the scope of the political, leaving the notion of the political somewhat open. Neither a systematization in relation to God (Hegel), nor a *praxis* in relation to the reality of man (Machiavelli), Nietzsche's political concern embraces the condition of man 'without possessing a complete substance': 'it establishes the origin of the political event without immersing itself methodologically into the specific concrete realities of political practices, as we see everyday in man's struggle for power' (cited in Bataille, 1980, p. 28). On the one hand, the lack of specificity of Nietzsche's language was what made it open to fascist and Nazi appropriations; at the same time, the latter feared its 'free air'; they quickly produced a world where 'life is tied down and stabilized in an endless servitude' (Bataille, 1985c, p. 186).

The dive into Nietzsche during the Acéphale period, as Bataille later recalled, was less about a philosophical interest in Nietzsche's thinking as such than about what he saw as the 'agreement of this thinking to a reality that is set in motion' (Bataille, 1973, p. 472). The years leading to the Second World War were, according to Bataille, a period of political confusion. Nietzsche 'accompanied' him in his reflections on fascism, on religion, and on the 'post-monocephalic'[6] social structures. Bataille and the Acéphale group redeemed the freedom of Nietzsche's thinking from the professional politicians' use, but by the same token this freedom did not yield to concrete suggestions for a lasting model of community. Following Nietzsche's claim that human existence oscillates between two possibilities, an eternal integration into God (unity) and an eternal disintegration that annihilates God, Bataille saw in fascism a closed form of organization that 'produced God', namely, monocracy and hegemony, and in social revolutions a 'decomposition' of social structures reaching the opposite extreme. What he searched for in the 'recomposition' of social structures was a utopian equilibrium, neither unitary nor anarchic, a community that could somehow sustain itself through its exposure to danger, to exaltation and to death, through its desire for self-dissolution. 'The only society full of life and force, the only free society, *is the bi- or poly-cephalic* society that gives the fundamental antagonisms of life a constant explosive outlet, but one limited to the richest forms' (Bataille, 1985d, p. 199). Inspired by the Popular

Front but also sensing its imminent failure, Acéphale was another attempt of protest against unitary communities, be it fascism, Nazism, or Stalin's socialism. If the anti-fascist movement was a vast mass temporarily held together only by what they refuse, Acéphale sought to mythologize this headless community outside the world of politics.

The 'Surpassing' of Nietzsche: *On Nietzsche* and *Sovereignty*

Originally intended for the centenary of Nietzsche's birth (October 15, 1844), *On Nietzsche* was published several months later, in February 1945. After *Inner Experience* (1943) and *Guilty* (1944), it constituted the third volume of an unfinished project Bataille had conceived under the title of *The Atheological Summa.* The French title *Sur Nietzsche,* suggests Allan Stoekl, can be read as a word play on *surnietzsche,* which means 'over Nietzsche' (Stoekl, 1979, p. 63). Described by Bataille himself as a 'chaotic book', which he wrote in order to overcome the 'fear of going crazy' (Bataille, 1992, pp. xxvi, xiv), *On Nietzsche* is composed of heterogeneous parts, including an important preface, a rewrite of conference notes, many quotations from Nietzsche, aphorisms and journal entries. It is best read in conjunction with *Memorandum* (1945), Bataille's collection of quotations of Nietzsche, as well as two conferences he delivered during the same period, 'Nietzsche's Laughter' (1942) and 'Discussion on Sin' (1945).

Bataille's approach to Nietzsche is driven by 'moral concerns' and his book intends to 'pose and solve intimate problems of morality' (Bataille, 1992, pp. xix, xxv). In particular, he wants to see if morality can be conceived *outside* action, rising from and returning to nothingness without 'objectifying' itself into practical conducts, staying within what he calls the realm of 'immanence'. Bataille's chief concern at that time was the dilemma which Nietzsche's concepts of the *Übermensch* and of the will to power had failed to solve: how would an 'inner experience' of 'sovereignty' be possible? What would be the new forms of sovereignty after the death of God?

Nietzsche himself already outlined this conundrum in the preface of *On the Genealogy of Morals,* where he posited morality as the 'culprit' and the 'danger of dangers', preventing what he perceived as the moral summit – the possibility of the '*highest power and splendor* of the human type' – from ever being reached (Nietzsche, 1996, p. 8). Bataille's 'wrestling with' Nietzsche and his attempt to 'surpass' him consisted of delineating this very moral summit, which he called sometimes 'the whole human being' (*l'homme entier*), sometimes 'evil' (*le mal*), and later, in the 1950s, the 'sovereign' (*le souverain*).

In *On Nietzsche*, Bataille identifies 'the whole human being' as an experience Nietzsche himself lived but which his philosophy failed to elucidate. Nietzsche proposed an ultimate form of *free man*: 'An extreme, unconditional human yearning was expressed for the first time by Nietzsche *independently of moral goals or of serving God*' (Bataille, 1992, p. xx), but his image remains vague:

'The majority of people,' [Nietzsche] wrote, 'are a fragmentary, exclusive image of what humanity is; you have to add them up to get humanity. In this sense, whole eras and whole peoples have something fragmentary about them; and it may be necessary for humanity's growth for it to develop only in parts. It is a crucial matter therefore to see that what is at stake is always the idea of producing a synthetic humanity and that the inferior humans who make up a majority of us are only preliminaries, or preparatory attempts whose concerted play allows a *whole human being* to appear here and there like a military boundary marker showing the extent of humanity's advance'. (*The Will to Power*, p. 881; cited in Bataille, 1992, p. xxvi)

What is unclear for Bataille in such a passage is whether Nietzsche's 'whole human being' refers to distinct individuals, or to humanity as a whole. To put it differently, one does not know if the term 'total human being' refers to a few 'higher men' or to a 'higher kind of man' (*Übermensch*). Nietzsche proposed a 'new humanness', a totally free mankind, but it is never more than metaphorically defined as a 'rope fastened between animal and over-man–a rope over an abyss' (Nietzsche, 2006, p. 7). 'Nietzsche had no desire to define such a free and sovereign humankind, halfway between modern humanity and a super-humanity, that is, superman. Appropriately, he thought when something is free, you can't define it' (Bataille, 1992, p. 170).

Bataille takes on the challenge to define the 'impossible'. The moral summit, or 'entirety', according to him, has for its essence freedom, not the struggle toward a freedom, but a pure practice of freedom without a goal. Bataille names this purposeless freedom *evil*, which, far removed from any Christian connotation associated with original sin, could be best understood in terms transgression: 'evil is the opposite of a constraint, which is exercised, in principle, with a view toward a good. Evil is surely not what a hypocritical series of misunderstandings wished to make it out to be: at bottom, is it not a concrete *freedom*, the uneasy breaking of a taboo?' (1992, p. xxv, translation modified). To use Bataille's own language of expenditure

or consumption of energy, *evil* is also defined as exuberance and loss, sur-
plus energy, or what he had called in his 1933 article 'The Notion of Expenditure', the 'nonproductive expenditure' (*la dépense improductive*): human
activities that have no end beyond themselves and that cannot be reinte-
grated into the capitalist economy of production and conservation (Bataille,
1985a, p. 118). 'Only in empty longing, only in an unlucky desire to be
consumed simply by the desire to burn with desire, is entirety *wholly what it
is*. In this respect entirety is also longing for laughter, longing for pleasure,
holiness, or death. Entirety lacks further tasks to fulfill' (Bataille, 1992,
p. xxvii–xxviii).

Bataille's Nietzsche, contrary to the dominant reception, is more a philosopher of *evil* than one of 'will to power', whose fundamental concern is
not ascension to power but transgression. This can be confirmed, according to Bataille, when one examines *The Will to Power* more carefully. This
collection of unfinished notes, compiled by Nietzsche's sister to propagate
the idea of a 'superior race', and at the time considered by many as
Nietzsche's philosophical *magnum opus* and definite system, does not in fact
offer clear propositions for activities nor any attempt to define the goal of
politics. Nietzsche's last completed work, *Ecce Homo*, on the other hand,
'affirms absence of goals as well as the author's insubordination to all plans'
(Bataille, 1992, p. xxxi, translation modified). Bataille consequently questions the use value of Nietzsche's moral philosophy. Considered from the
practical standpoint of political action, it is an excess dissolving into nothingness, radically incompatible with any type of practical conduct or politics that lends itself to the principle of the 'will to power'.

At the same time, Bataille, paradoxical thinker as he is, criticizes Nietzsche's
'failure' in providing any real guidance for action. The oddity of Nietzsche's
doctrines is that they cannot be followed. 'In the end, the only knowledge
Zarathustra's students gain is to repudiate their master. For it is said to them
they should hate him and "raise their hand against his crown"' (Bataille,
1992, p. 87). The risk of becoming Zarathustra's disciple, in other words, is
not so much in answering the call of the prophet for 'living dangerously',
but in not having 'something to do in this world'. Nietzsche's philosophy
creates a deep sense of dead end: it invites its followers to a divine and solitary dance (of Zarathustra), but it is a dance that leads nowhere – 'we have
nothing more to do, no more exit, no more goal, no more meaning!'
(Bataille, 1973, p. 219).

How to make the 'useless' philosophy of Nietzsche useful, especially during the period of Occupation when Bataille saw himself sapped by sickness
and solitude,[7] while the war was real and outside him? If by definition the

man of action cannot be the 'whole human being', can the 'whole human being' nonetheless retain the possibility of action? Bataille suggests that Chance may be the only way to bring Nietzsche's philosophy beyond its own limits: 'Chance, as it turned out, corresponded to Nietzsche's intentions more accurately than power. Only "play" gave me the possibility of exploring the far reaches of possibility and not prejudicing the results, of giving to the *future* alone and its free occurrence the power usually assigned to choosing sides (which is only a form of the past)' (Bataille, 1992, p. xxvi). During the months immediately preceding the Liberation,[8] Bataille did not define Chance more than the spark of an erotic experience, the desire for communication, and a secret waiting for a new Time to arrive. His dialogue with Nietzsche and his questioning on the problem of 'intimate morality', temporarily 'suspended' by the Liberation, would resume several years later, after a period of intense public activities.

Bataille's postwar writings on Nietzsche are collected in *Sovereignty*, which is the last volume of *The Accursed Share*, his trilogy on general economy. In the beginning of the 1950s, Bataille devoted a series of articles to Nietzsche in the context of his reflections on Stalinist communism, which he named the 'most active contradiction' of sovereignty (Bataille, 1993, p. 261). The fact that Bataille needed Nietzsche to think about communism, and communism to measure the 'limits' of Nietzsche, shows the persistence of Bataille's need to 'wrestle' with the philosopher on the question of morality. After the war, Nietzsche continued to provide Bataille 'company' for his reflections on transgression and interdiction, and on the (im)possibility of community. With writers such as Franz Kafka and the Marquis de Sade, he became one of the important voices to define the space of literature, 'protesting' against the totalitarian Communist regime that excludes artistic freedom.

In Nietzsche's work, Bataille finds the basis of what he calls, in an article entitled 'Nietzsche and Jesus', the 'sovereign thought', that is, a thought both of protestation and of affirmation:

Apparently the moral problem took 'shape' in Nietzsche in the following way: for Christianity the good is God, but the converse is true: God is limited to the category of the good that is manifested in man's utility, but for Nietzsche that which is sovereign is good, but God is dead (his servility killed Him), so man is morally bound to be sovereign. Man is thought (language), and he can be sovereign only through a sovereign thought. Now, just as the original sovereign (that of the gods and kings) is tragic (before the reduction of tragedy to morality), but only at the end, *sovereign thought* is boundless tragedy. That triumph which it basically is, is first of all a collapse; it is the collapse of what which it is not. In its immediacy, sovereign thought is 'off its hinges'; it exceeds the bounds of knowledge; it destroys the world that reassures, that is *commensurate* with man's activity. (Bataille, 1993, p. 381)

Working here against Hegel's totalizing system of 'absolute knowledge', Bataille identifies in Nietzsche's philosophy an opening-up that at the same time raises a problem. God being cleared off; all interdictions are lifted. Nietzsche's world resembles a 'deserted beach' where an immensity of freedom (nothingness) reigns and where a phantom being (a child?) 'plays' without becoming a philosophical subject or object. Nietzsche never seeks to *objectify* that immensity, turning it into the world of 'things', a sense of seriousness or a duty (Bataille, 1993, pp. 376–7). Contrary to Hegel, who captures subjectivity in the identity that subject and object attain in discourse, Nietzsche's philosophy does not objectify language; subjectivity, if there is such a thing, is situated in the object's fading and disintegration. 'I am talking about the discourse in which thought taken to the limit of thought requires the sacrifice, or death, of thought. To my mind, this is the meaning of the work and life of Nietzsche' (Bataille, 1993, p. 370). Nietzsche's 'problem' is therefore a problem of 'immanence', of a hanging subjectivity without objectification. In a world that nothing objectifies, who will be responsible for defining the laws of interdiction?

Bataille's personal development on the 'sovereign' or sovereignty is rich, complex, and sometimes elusive. It ranges from traditional, objective forms of sovereignty such as kings, the Church or the State, encompassing all institutions as well as leisure classes that do not work but consume the production of others, to more 'subjective' experiences such as confrontation with nothingness, affirmation of the right to death, and renunciation of 'absolute knowledge'. Essentially a negative concept, sovereignty is an 'aspect that is opposed to the servile and the subordinate' and points to the 'life beyond utility' (Bataille, 1993, pp. 197–8). Temporally and spatially unstable, it cannot be achieved in an objective or systematic way. Sovereignty occurs as a 'miracle', or Chance, partaking 'at once of the divine, of the sacred, of the ludicrous or the erotic, of the repugnant or the funereal' (Bataille, 1993, p. 201).

Nietzsche's main flaw, according to Bataille, is 'in having misinterpreted the opposition of sovereignty and power' (Bataille, 1993, p. 453, note 1). In Nietzsche's thought, traditional sovereignty as oppressive morality has been shattered, becoming independent of 'its mired forms' such as Christianity.

But the 'aristocratic morality' that comes to replace it, that is, the necessity of active and ruthless self-affirmation, still expresses itself through the aspiration for a divine power and an attachment to the feudal hierarchical bond of master and slave. Zarathustra, the prophet of *Übermensch*, is the perfect example. Nietzsche transposes the expression of his own subjectivity onto a fictional figure from the sacred world: *Zarathustra* is the 'plagiarism of sacred literature' (Bataille, 1993, p. 420). Nietzsche's philosophy anticipated an intimate morality based on individual transgression, but it did not fully take on the form of what Bataille calls the 'sovereign subjectivity', that is, an 'immanent' subjectivity completely separate from the world of things and from objective activity, free from the desire for privilege or power and indifferent to the question of social rank.

In the 1950s, Bataille identified the best embodiment of this 'sovereign subjectivity' with the figure of the writer or artist banished from the world of Communism, which he named also the 'man of sovereign art'. 'In Soviet society', he writes, 'the writer and the artist are *in the service* of leaders who are not sovereign . . . except in the renunciation of sovereignty' (Bataille, 1993, p. 411). The Soviet system, by reducing art and artists to things and tools and by wiping out all cultures from the past, forces the subject into a free zone where he can exercise his 'inner' freedom without seeking recognition from the official party, or identifying himself with any kind of social function. Art and literature, becoming now decisively an 'abdication' (*démission*) of power, are on their own, moving to the sphere outside authority and 'paternal' law. The 'man of sovereign art' is a man of 'destitution', low in social standing (a *déclassé*), and lives in society as an outsider (Bataille, 1993, p. 423).

The intense dialogue that Bataille engaged himself in with Nietzsche during and after the war was not truly motivated by challenge, but rather by companionship. At the centre of his 'wrestling' with the philosopher was the question of community. 'My life in the company of Nietzsche is a community', Bataille writes in *On Nietzsche*, '[m]y book is this community' (Bataille, 1992, p. 9, translation modified). If Nietzsche's 'companionship' during the Acéphale years gave the members of the secret society the temporary impression that a concrete community was still possible *outside* the real world, after September 1939, it replaced the dispersing members of that community to become itself the secret society. Through Nietzsche, Bataille began to build a notion of community that will be based on its very impossibility.

Bataille sees the problem of community as deeply unsolved in Nietzsche. Unable to provide a satisfying description of the nature of the moral summit,

Nietzsche remains a philosopher of 'ardour', who leaves the faces of his potential disciples featureless:

> . . . [Nietzsche] must have known he failed, and in the end knew he was a voice crying out in the wilderness. To be done with obligation and *good*, to expose the lying emptiness of morality, he destroyed the effective value of language. Fame came late to him, and as it did, he thwarted it. His expectations went unanswered.

> Today it appears that I ought to say his readers and his admirers show him scant respect (he knew this and said so). *Except for me?* (I am oversimplifying). Still . . . to try, as he asked, to follow him is to be vulnerable to trials and tribulations similar to his. (Bataille, 1992, p. xxi)

'Intimacy with great thinking', writes Nietzsche in *Thus Spoke Zarathustra*, 'is unbearable. I seek and call out to those to whom I can communicate such thinking without bringing out their deaths' (cited in Bataille, 1992, p. 8). Such a harmless 'star friendship',[9] according to Bataille, is no longer possible if one wishes to experience the moral limit and the 'sovereign' freedom. True communication requires the opening of oneself to the outside and to others to the point of fissure and death. It requires one to be defenceless to the forces of destruction: ' "Communication" cannot proceed from one full and intact individual to another. It requires individuals whose separate existence in themselves is *risked*, place at the limit of death and nothingness' (Bataille, 1992, p. 19).

It was through this 'exposing' of himself that Bataille hoped to redeem Nietzsche from his 'powerlessness', his fall into madness. There where he collapsed, that was where Bataille would 'draw on the ruins' and continue to write (Bataille, 1973, p. 429). For whom? For a 'negative community': the community of those who have no community (cited in Blanchot, 1988, p. 24). 'The community I am talking about is the one that existed virtually because of the existence of Nietzsche (who is its exigency) and which each of Nietzsche's readers undoes by slipping away – that is to say, by not resolving the stated enigma' (cited in Blanchot, 1988, p. 22). Such a community is a 'literary', or what Blanchot calls the 'unavowable' (*inavouable*) community: not a social organization where the sharing of belles-lettres and of glorification of 'work' takes place, but the experience of a 'nocturnal communication' where the reader is abandoned to himself to confront the magnificence and inaccessibility of thought and the limit of his own individuality. The members of this literary community do not know each other, but they 'recognize' each other through their willingness to confront the unknown and experience loss. 'Nietzsche wrote "with his blood," and criticizing or, better, *experiencing* him means pouring out one's lifeblood' (Bataille, 1992, p. xxiv).

Conclusion

Bataille's reading of Nietzsche, especially in *On Nietzsche* and in *Sovereignty*, was intensely personal. As Albert Camus pointed out, Bataille had 'too much personality for not having taken from Nietzsche what suited him, and that part only' (Bataille, 1976a, p. 614). Bataille, who considered Nietzsche his 'main company on earth', did not contest this 'criticism': 'For a long time, it seemed to me that my thinking had no other meaning than to continue that of Nietzsche' (Bataille, 1976b, p. 640). Speaking like Nietzsche, or speaking after Nietzsche, however, was for him a way to address the whole 'negative community' of free spirits. If Bataille placed the question of 'intimate morality' at the centre of his inquiry of Nietzsche, it was because the moral integrity of the subject was always for him the basis of all sovereignty.

Bataille's early focus on the concepts of the *Übermensch* and of the will to power was linked to the history of Nietzsche's reception before and during the 1930s. An avid reader of the translations and interpretations by Henri Albert, Charles Andler, Daniel Halévy, Geneviève Bianquis, and Thierry Maulnier, Bataille inherited, on the one hand, a free philosophical style that emphasized the biographical, the literary, and sometimes the unsystematic approach, and on the other hand, a sociological reflex of relating Nietzsche's philosophy to contemporary politics. Little known to the anglophone world during these years, Bataille's passionate reading of Nietzsche broke new ground on various fronts: its dissociation of the *Übermensch* and of the will to power from the uses of National Socialist propaganda predated Walter Kaufmann's pivotal *Nietzsche, Philosopher, Psychologist, Antichrist* (1974), which was credited for refuting all the Nazi misappropriations of Nietzsche; his inquiry into the possibility of a 'moral summit' raised the same question that, 17 years later, Gilles Deleuze would focus on in the beginning of *Nietzsche and Philosophy*, namely, the ambiguity of the origin of 'the value of values'; his original take on the notion of community became the basis of a memorable exchange between Jean-Luc Nancy and Maurice Blanchot, on their respective approaches to the 'inoperative community' and the 'unavowable community'. More broadly, his 'alliance' with Nietzsche against the totalizing system of Hegel was a major inspiration for the next generation of philosophers of 'difference' such as Jacques Derrida and Gilles Deleuze.

Notes

[1] Vincent Descombes describes three 'moments' in the French reception of Nietzsche: the first was associated with writers of the end of the nineteenth-century, the second with a group of 'non-conformist' intellectuals of the interwar years (mainly the members of the Collège de Sociologie but also Maurice Blanchot) and the third with a generation of philosophers (later known as the 'post-structuralists') who became active in the 1960's and 1970's. See Descombes (1997).

[2] The second issue of the journal *Acéphale* (January 1937), titled 'Reparation to Nietzsche', sought to 'rectify' the misappropriations of Nietzsche by National Socialism.

[3] Collège de Sociologie (1937–1939) is a group Bataille founded with Roger Caillois and Michel Leiris in November 1937 in an attempt to reinvigorate the modern world with a 'science of the sacred', a science that would replace the narrow functionalist Durkheimian and Maussian sociology with one that would include various forms of 'expenditure'.

[4] In Bataille's lifetime, '*Übermensch*' was unanimously translated in French as *surhomme* (superman). For the sake of textual consistency, I keep the usage of 'superman' instead of a more contemporary and accurate translation of *Übermensch* as 'overman'.

[5] Bataille reviewed Jaspers's *Nietzsche: An Introduction to his Philosophical Activity* (1936) in the same issue of *Acéphale*. Juxtaposed with Klossowski's review of Karl Löwith's *Nietzsche's philosophy of the Eternal Recurrence of the Same* (1935), the two reviews were titled of 'Deux interpretations récentes de Nietzsche'. See Bataille (1980).

[6] 'Monocephalic' (with one head) is Bataille's term to describe monocracy, as an opposition to 'bi- or poly-cephalic', society governed by more than one leader.

[7] Affected by tuberculosis, Bataille had to quit his job as a librarian at the Bibliothèque Nationale in 1942. He lived in a small provincial town in Burgundy, Vézelay, from 1943 to 1949.

[8] The second dairy of part III of *On Nietzsche*, dating from April to June 1944, is titled 'Position of Chance'. The English translation did not keep the title.

[9] For Nietzsche's famous notion of 'Star friendship' based on the affinity of souls and distance, see GS 279.

Bibliography and Guide to Further Study

Bataille's Nietzsche Interpretation

Bataille, Georges (1973), *Mémorandum* in *oeuvres complètes*, VI. Paris: Gallimard. Aphorisms of Nietzsche, collected and presented by Bataille. Paris: Gallimard, 1945. Untranslated.

— (1980), 'Deux interpretations récentes de Nietzsche', in *Acéphale: Religion, sociologie, philosophie, 1936–1939*. Paris: Jean-Michel Place. Bataille's review of Jaspers' Nietzsche juxtaposed with Klossowski's review of Löwith's Nietzsche, in *Acéphale* 2 (January 1937). Untranslated.

— (1985c), 'Nietzsche and the Fascists', in *Visions of Excess* (*Acéphale* 2, January 1937). Key text of Bataille in this special issue dedicated to Nietzsche and the fascists.

— (1985d), 'Propositions', in *Visions of Excess* (*Acéphale* 2, January 1937).

— (1985e), 'Nietzschean Chronicle', in *Visions of Excess* (*Acéphale* 3–4, July 1937). This piece emphasizes the tragic and mythical aspect of Nietzsche's Dionysos.

— (1992), *On Nietzsche*, trans. Bruce Boone. St. Paul, MN: Paragon House [1945]. Bataille's Major Work on Nietzsche. Bataille, Georges, (1993), *Sovereignty*, in id., *Accursed Share, an Essay on General Economy*. Volume II, *The History of Eroticism*; Volume III, *Sovereignty*; trans. Robert Hurley. New York: Zone books [1976, posthumous]. Part four of *Sovereignty*, 'The Literary World and Communism', includes subchapters on Nietzsche that are rewrites of previously published articles, such as 'Nietzsche à la lumière du marxisme' (1951), 'Nietzsche et Jésus selon Gide et Jaspers' (1950), and 'Nietzsche et Thomas Mann' (1951).

— (2001a), 'Nietzsche's Laughter', in Stuart Kendall (ed.) *The Unfinished System of Nonknowledge*, trans. Michelle Kendall and Stuart Kendall. Minneapolis and London: University of Minnesota Press [1942]. A dialogue with Nietzsche's 'inner experience'.

— (2001b), 'Discussion on Sin', in id., *The Unfinished System of Nonknowledge* [1945]. A presentation given by Bataille followed with discussions. The second chapter of *On Nietzsche*, 'Summit and Decline', is based on this presentation.

Other Works by Bataille

Bataille, Georges, (1976a), Notes of 'Les problèmes du surréalisme', in *Oeuvres complètes*, VII. Paris: Gallimard.

— (1976b), Notes of *La Souveraineté*. 'Albert Camus ou la défaite de Nietzsche', in *Oeuvres complètes*, VIII. Paris: Gallimard.

— (1985a), 'The Notion of Expenditure', in Allan Stoekl (ed), *Visions of Excess: Selected Writings 1927–1939*, trans. A. Stoekl, Carl R. Lovitt and Donald M. Leslie Jr. Minneapolis: University of Minnesota Press.

— (1985b), 'Popular Front in the Street', in *Visions of Excess*.

Works on Bataille's Nietzsche

Hollier, Denis (1985), 'Bataille's Tomb: A Halloween Story', trans. Richard Miller. *October*, 33, 73–102.

Lotringer, Sylvère (1992), 'Introduction', in Bataille, 1992.

Smith, Douglas (1996), *Transvaluations: Nietzsche in France, 1872–1972*. Oxford: Clarendon Press. Part of Chapter 3: '(De)nazifying Nietzsche: Appropriations and Counter-Appropriations'.

Stoekl, Allan (1979), 'The Death of *Acéphale* and the Will to Chance: Nietzsche in the text of Bataille'. *Glyph*, 6, 42–67.

Nietzsche Translations Cited

Nietzsche, Friedrich (1967), *The Will to Power*, trans. Walter Kaufmann. New York: Vintage Books.
— (1996), *On the Genealogy of Morals*, trans. Douglas Smith. Oxford: Oxford University Press.
— (2001), *The Gay Science*, ed. Bernard Williams; trans. Josefine Nauckhoff and Andrian Del Caro. Cambridge: Cambridge University Press.
— (2002), *Beyond Good and Evil*, ed. Rolf-Peter Horstmann; trans. Judith Norman. Cambridge: Cambridge University Press.
— (2006), *Thus Spoke Zarathustra*, ed. Adrian Del Caro and Robert. B. Pippin; trans. Andrian Del Caro. Cambridge: Cambridge University Press.

Other Works Cited

Blanchot, Maurice (1988), *The Unavowable Community*, trans. Pierre Joris. Barrytown: Station Hill Press.
Descombes, Vincent (1997), 'Nietzsche's French Moment', in *Why We Are Not Nietzscheans*, ed. Luc Ferry and Alain Renault; trans. Robert de Loaiza. Chicago, Ill.: University of Chicago Press.
Klossowski, Pierre (1991), 'Cette drôle de société secrète', in Bernard-Henri Lévy, *Les Aventures de la liberté*. Paris: Grasset.

Chapter 4

Kaufmann's Nietzsche

David Rathbone

In *Ecce Homo*, Nietzsche envisioned a day in which chairs in philosophy would be endowed in universities devoted to the interpretation of his work. Half a century later, Nietzsche's vision materialized at Princeton in the shape of Walter Kaufmann, a brilliant multi-lingual German-born Jew, who explained how the invasions worked by the Nazis included not only the occupation of neighbouring countries, but also of Nietzsche's works, forcing him into an unwilling collaboration with their insidious plans. In postwar America, Walter Kaufmann led the effort of liberation necessary to emancipate Nietzsche from this outrage, showing how the awful collaboration began through the efforts of Nietzsche's sister Elizabeth, and continued through the influence of Bäumler, Heidegger, and others. A crucial aspect of Kaufmann's work consisted in disentangling Nietzsche from this morass of proto-Nazi foment.

Born in Freiburg and raised in Berlin as a Lutheran Christian, Kaufmann reports in *Faith of a Heretic* that he converted to Judaism at the age of 12, only later to discover through the Nazi's genealogical hunt for Jewish bloodlines that he actually was of Jewish descent. Kaufmann fled Nazi Germany in 1939 at the age of 18, planning to become a rabbi in the UnitedStates. Midway through his PhD in philosophy at Harvard the war intervened, and Kaufmann first joined the US Air Force, then movied into Allied Military Intelligence. He returned to Harvard at the end of the war with a dissertation almost finished on 'Nietzsche's Theory of Values', which he submitted as his PhD in 1947, and rewrote and published as *Nietzsche: Philosopher, Psychologist, Antichrist* in 1950. This significant work earned him a job at Princeton, where he remained a professor until his sudden death by heart attack in 1982 at the age of 61 (Kaufmann, 1959b, pp. 3–4). Kaufmann's Nietzsche-interpretation was thus quite literally shaped by his experiences during the second world war, and he aims to establish not only that the Nazi's 'use' of Nietzsche was in fact an *abuse*, but further, that it is only in Nietzsche's thought, understood as a whole that we find the resources necessary to root out the deeper problem of which the Nazis were but a symptom: the human desire for revenge, which Nietzsche calls *ressentiment*. The ultimate theatre of struggle is not so much the battlefield as the human mind, and it is on the psychological front Kaufmann believes Nietzsche makes his greatest gains.

Alongside the successive editions of his *Nietzsche* (1956, 1968, and 1974), Kaufmann published translations of almost all of Nietzsche's works, beginning with the *The Portable Nietzsche* in 1954, collaborating with Reg Hollingdale on translations of the *Genealogy of Morals* and *The Will to Power* in 1967, in 1968 publishing a second anthology of translations called *The Basic Writings of Nietzsche*, and then finally in 1974, *The Gay Science*. This meant that together with Hollingdale's translations of *Dawn* in 1982, *Untimely Meditations* in 1983, and *Human, All Too Human* in 1986, Hollingdale and Kaufmann between them had succeeded through their trans-Atlantic friendship in making all of Nietzsche's published works, and some of his unpublished notebooks and letters, widely available in English translation.

In his preface to *The New Nietzsche*, David B. Allison wrote that 'until the Colli-Montinari edition of Nietzsche's complete works appears in English, the principal translation will continue to be that of Kaufmann' (1985, p. x). In the late 1990s, that project began with the publication of the first two of the twenty projected volumes in the Stanford University complete edition. Just as these volumes appeared in the United States, Cambridge University Press also began publishing a new series of translations of Nietzsche edited by Karl Ameriks and Desmond Clarke, now numbering nine volumes, and two new translations of Zarathustra appeared. Does this mean that Kaufmann's translations have become redundant? Not at all. With other authors, new translations of a work often do supplant older ones. But this is not the case with Nietzsche, for his writing is sufficiently multiple, subtle, and nuanced that a reader can only ever benefit from comparing different translations. Far from competing, the various translations now available in English complement one another, throwing each other's strengths and the weakness into relief, and also forming an invaluable aid to those attempting to learn to read Nietzsche in German. The comparative study of all seven English translations of *Thus Spake Zarathustra*, for example, is also a fascinating exercise in the hermeneutics of perspectivism. As Kaufmann put it in *Tragedy and Philosophy*, '[c]onfronted with art, "linear thinking" breaks down. What is needed is multidimensional thinking' (1968, p. 113).

Kaufmann's Nietzsche interpretation continued to develop alongside his translation work, through the essays he collected under the title *From*

Shakespeare to Existentialism (1959a), as well as through his books *Critique of Religion and Philosophy* (1958), *The Faith of a Heretic* (1959b), *Hegel: Reinterpretation, Texts and Commentary* (1965), *Tragedy and Philosophy* (1968), *Without Guilt and Justice* (1973) and 13 more essays published under the title *Existentialism, Religion and Death* (1976a). Kaufmann then used his thought to frame his own creative endeavours as a photographer, with his pair of volumes, *Religions in Four Dimensions* (1976b), and *Man's Lot* (1978), which intersperse text with hundreds of Kaufmann's own photographs. And then finally, in 1980, Kaufmann published a trilogy of works, at the center of which Nietzsche still stood (*Discovering the Mind*; Volume 1, Goethe, Kant, Hegel; Volume 2, Nietzsche, Heidegger, Buber; Volume 3, Freud, Adler, Jung). In *Beyond Good and Evil* 6, Nietzsche says that every philosophy has been 'a kind of involuntary and unconscious memoir' of its author. As Kaufmann had read and reflected upon this work of Nietzsche's from an early age, his philosophizing must be understood as a kind of *conscious* and *voluntary* memoir which aimed to blend philosophical erudition with existential honesty in a lucid prose style.

The Systematic Perspective

It is equally fatal for the mind to have a system, and to have none. It will simply have to decide to combine the two.

Friedrich Schlegel, *Atheneum Fragments* 53, in Wheeler, 1984

This insightful aphorism of Schlegel's is a helpful starting point in understanding Kaufmann's Nietzsche interpretation. Nietzsche's highly original use of aphorism and mytho-poetic prose, creatively interwoven with the more traditional philosophical genres of essay and monograph, has led some interpreters to deny that there is any systematic core to Nietzsche's way of thinking at all. As Kaufmann points out in his *Nietzsche*: 'In a sense, the present book as a whole represents an attempt at a *constructive* refutation of this view' (1974, p. 3). Kaufmann recognizes a kind of system in Nietzsche's thought, while also insisting that to see Nietzsche's thought as *nothing but* this system is to fall into an error which Kaufmann calls 'reductionism' (1980, Volume 2, p. 106). In order to avoid this pitfall, the systematic perspective needs not only to be explicated, but also to be embedded in an appreciation of Kaufmann's way of seeing the *whole* of Nietzsche's work and life.

In Kaufmann's interpretation, Nietzsche's method is to return systematic-ity to its place as a means, and not an end. As he puts it, 'systems are neither unqualifiedly good nor entirely bad. When we consider them as a whole, we become aware of both their *Nutzen und Nachteil*, their usefulness and their disadvantages' (1974, p. 81). So although Nietzsche does warn us against taking systems too seriously (see D 318, GS 322, and TI 'Maxims' 26), he is no less wary of 'looting readers' (HAH 137), approaching his texts unsys-tematically, pulling out quotable quotes with no sensitivity for their context. Nietzsche teaches us 'to read *well*, that is to say, to read slowly, deeply, look-ing cautiously before and aft, with reservations, with doors left open, with delicate eyes and fingers' (D preface 5). Thus Nietzsche's objection is not to systematicity as such, but to *systematizers* – to those who mistake the sys-tematic aspects of philosophical method for the whole of philosophy itself. From Hegelians to logicians, Nietzsche is deeply suspicious of the will to formalization, and of the reduction of thinking to 'nothing but' a formal system – 'a subtle corruption and disease of the character' says Nietzsche, adding 'I am not bigoted enough for a system – not even for *my* system' (cited by Kaufmann, 1974, p. 80).

With these provisos in mind, we can say that Nietzsche's 'system' revolves around a triangulation of the three rubrics of the eternal return, the *Übermensch*, and the will to power. In Kaufmann's interpretation, these three central themes are related as follows. The eternal return and the *Übermensch* are myths, deliberately created by Nietzsche as allegories for ideas which we cannot literally express. Just as little children cannot directly apprehend the value of generosity, but can appreciate it indirectly through the myth of Santa Claus, we humans are from one perspective still children who stam-mer and stutter when we try to put our highest values into words in so-called moral theory and metaphysics, which are really kinds of myths. So instead of offering a moral or metaphysical system, which would be to treat us like slaves by merely dictating commands for us to follow, Nietzsche forces us back upon our own autonomy by offering us nothing more than two myths, which we must decide how to interpret for ourselves. On the one hand, the myth that our lives return over and over in an endless repetition of the same existence; and on the other, the myth of the *Übermensch*, teaching us that we are a link in a chain, a bridge to a higher kind of existence, a rope stretched between our ancestors and our descendants.

It must be firmly borne in mind that the eternal return and the *Übermensch* appear primarily in *Zarathustra*, and that this is a mytho-poetic work, necessarily requiring allegorical interpretation. Early stirrings of both the eternal return and the *Übermensch* can be found throughout

The Gay Science (pp. 143, 341, 382), and Kaufmann traces both 'visions' back to the second *Untimely Meditation* (1974, pp. 317–9). The *Übermensch* re-emerges briefly in Section 4 of *The Antichrist*, before both 'visions' return with Zarathustra-like intensity in *Ecce Homo*, both *Zarathustra* and *Ecce Homo* resonating to the 'logic of the dream' (HAH I, 13) more than the clear 'net of communication' (GS 354), which the less poetic works represent. Thus to ask, 'Do our lives really recur?' or 'What species will *homo sapiens* evolve into, and how can I tell if I'm one of them already?' is about as insightful in Kaufmann's view as asking 'Do eagles ever really fly with snakes coiled around their necks?' or 'Where exactly in Germany is the town called The Mottled Cow?' All of these myths, images, and parables require allegorical interpretation in order for their meaning to be apprehended and experienced.

So for Kaufmann, it is not surprising that 'the two conceptions have seemed contradictory to many readers', (1974, p. 307), for interpreted too literally, these two thoughts do indeed contradict. In a world of deterministic cyclic repetition, there can be no real evolution (which might be thought necessary for the production of the *Übermensch*), for the very idea of evolution entails the creation of genuinely new forms of life, the likes of which have never before been seen. But interpreted figuratively, this tension lessens into an orienting contrast, for if the *Übermensch* is an allegory for that perspective on existence we call freedom, and eternal return is a symbol for thinking time as a finite whole, then the two allegories in conjunction figure an autonomy possible only on the basis of finitude. Freedom must not be made to depend upon a hypothetical other-worldly transcendence going on to an unknown extent in the background ('the soul superstition'), but must be built upon a dynamic and finite existence willing and able to see itself as a whole. Kaufmann points out that the *Übermenschen* of GS 143 (that is, gods, demigods, and heroes) 'appear as symbols of the repudiation of any conformity to a single norm: antitheses to mediocrity and stagnation' (1974, p. 309) and exactly the same can be said of the 'fortunate accidents' of *Antichrist*, Section 4. This indicates that the allegory of the *Übermensch* is a way to think the revaluation of the traditional triad of values *liberté, fraternité, egalité* (freedom, fraternity, equality), as the new triad *liberté, fraternité, difference*. For the value of equality is actually incompatible with the other two values: to be free means *not* having to be 'the same' and conform, and to fraternize means to seek out interactions with *others*, who are interesting only in so far as they contrast with you, and are not 'the same'. Thus in Kaufmann's interpretation, what is overcome by the overman are the old assumptions of uniformity and conformity, and their tacit condescension and implicit levelling violence along with them. For him, a new era of autonomy is now arriving for those who can understand it.

Kaufmann thus argues strongly against the evolutionary interpretation of the *Übermensch*, maintaining that this is too literal a reading of Nietzsche's poetic motif (1974, p. 310). For Kaufmann, the meaning of the thought of this mythical creature is entirely existential – a way for us to speak indirectly about how we ourselves can change our own lives, and not those of our distant descendants in future generations. The way in which we can change our own lives is by asking ourselves with each decision we face: 'would I be willing to make the same choice again, not only once or twice, but over again eternally?' If our answer is to that question is 'yes', then that is a sign that this decision points to the path which leads us to the *Übermensch*, a higher direction in which we can head if we embrace our own difference and repudiate conformity. But it must be noted that Zarathustra never actually *finds* the *Übermensch* for whom he spends the whole of *Zarathustra* searching, the 'Higher Man' and the 'Last Man' being the two figures actually appearing in that narrative.

This symbolizes the regulative nature of the *Übermensch* myth, such that any individual claiming to *be* the *Übermensch* (as Nazis thought possible) does not understand the crucially symbolic nature of the idea. But just as we can make clear the meaning of 'heading north' without being tied to the thought that we are going to a place called 'North', but merely to a more *northerly* location, we can likewise make symbolic sense of the myth of becoming freer (more or less 'over' our human selves), without submitting to the naive assumption that we can literally 'be' an *Übermensch*:

> [The *Übermensch*] is the 'Dionysian' man who is depicted under the name of Goethe at the end of *Twilight of the Idols*. He has overcome his animal nature, organized the chaos of his passions, sublimated his impulses, and given style to his character – or, as Nietzsche said of Goethe: 'he disciplined himself to wholeness, he *created* himself' and became 'the man of tolerance, not from weakness but from strength,' 'a spirit who has become free'. (1974, p. 316)

On this interpretation, says Kaufmann, 'the conception [of the *Übermensch*] does not only not conflict with the doctrine of the eternal recurrence, but the essential connection between the two ideas becomes clear' (1974, pp. 316–7) – namely, that 'they suggest the possible infinite value of the moment and the individual' (ibid., p. 319). Kaufmann in fact maintains that, far from contradicting each other, 'the conception of the overman is inseparable from that of the recurrence' (ibid., p. 321), for together they balance the finitude of human freedom with the infinite value of the individual, whose actions begin infinite chains of consequence, but whose existence goes no further than death. Our 'new infinite' (GS 374) is no longer the imaginary infinite of life after death, but now rather the perspectival nature (or 'depth' in the language of 'The Second Dance Song' in Book 3 of *Zarathustra*) of our this-worldly life. 'Thus we can live several lives at various speeds', as Kaufmann puts it (1968, p. xvii), just as multiple as we are whole (BGE 212).

The doctrine of the will to power, in contrast to the myths of eternal return and the *Übermensch*, is in Kaufmann's presentation a direct attempt by Nietzsche to make explicit his most basic insight into the psychological structure of experience, and the nature of reality 'viewed from inside' (BGE 36).[1] Kaufmann thus locates the will to power doctrine at the heart of his Nietzsche interpretation, as the key to understanding Nietzsche's work as a whole. Kaufmann divides Nietzsche into 'early' and 'late', describing Nietzsche's early work as dualistic, revolving around the Apollo–Dionysus opposition, and his late work as monistic, revolving around the 'single basic principle' of will to power (Nietzsche , 1974, p. 178).[2] Kaufmann demonstrates in the sixth chapter of his *Nietzsche* how the emerging doctrine of will to power dawned upon Nietzsche as the difference-preserving common root holding the Apollo-Dionysus opposition together in tension, which provided the focus necessary for Nietzsche to divine the way forward in his attempt to fathom both himself and his world as a whole.

It is crucial to appreciate that Nietzsche's will to power doctrine is not equivalent to merely saying, as one early uncomprehending anarchist put it, 'might is right'.[3] This type of simplistic misunderstanding of Nietzsche's doctrine as a mere apology for brutality is debunked in Chapters 6–9 of Kaufmann's *Nietzsche*, and summarized succinctly in *The Discovery of the Mind*, Volume 2, Chapter 20. For although Nietzsche does anchor the complicated phenomenon of the will in the feeling of being obeyed (BGE 19; GM II 10, 12, 22), the notion of will *to power* should not be confused with a mere will to dominate: 'We need to keep in mind that not all power is power over other people; there is also the power to help others, to restore the sick, to revive some of the dead, to do ever so many things' (Kaufmann, 1980, Volume 2, p. 91). To be thoughtful, to be helpful, to be kind and careful: these are higher forms of the will to power than mere violence, cruelty, and greed, precisely because to be loved and respected is a higher form of life than to be reviled, feared, and despised. Nor should will to power be confused with the mere will to survive. Will to power is a will to expenditure, for life can only find and modify its limits through exhaustion. As every athlete knows, staying home and resting for months before a big competition will make you weak, not strong, for power cannot be accumulated except by being spent. Training means exhausting yourself on a daily basis, for our limits (such as level of fitness) can be moved only gradually through 'the history of every day' (GS 308).

One of the main psychological discoveries following upon Nietzsche's doctrine of will to power is indicated, says Kaufmann, with a deliberate obscurity and subtlety by Nietzsche, as required by his philosophy of masks (as elaborated in BGE, Part 9). This is Kaufmann's interpretation of Nietzsche's sense of an esoteric/exoteric division in philosophy – not that there is a secret cabal who know some hidden truth of Nietzsche's philosophy, but rather that there are some thoughts which are on the horizon of human thinkability, and the sensitive few are united by their ability to divine the significance of Nietzsche's most subtle themes (Kaufmann, 1980, Volume 2, pp. 153–4) in a way akin to that in which animals sense approaching storms long before humans do (GS 316). This is the theme of *sublimation*. Nietzsche borrowed the word from Goethe, who had taken it from chemistry. A sublimation in chemistry occurs when a substance goes from one phase to another, skipping an intermediary step: under certain conditions, for example, water can go from solid ice to gaseous steam without going through a transition to a liquid phase as water (carbon dioxide or 'dry ice' does this at room temperature). Nietzsche saw how the ancient Greeks had discovered conditions for what can metaphorically be called psychological 'sublimations', or phase-jumps of the mind, turning anger into victory, without having to go through an intervening phase of war, with the invention of sport; or turning grief into wisdom, without having to go through a long phase of struggle, with the invention of the tragic theatre; or turning the strife of a disagreement into the conciliation of insight, without having to undergo a phase of actual fighting, through the invention of the philosophical dialogue by Socrates. Nietzsche's own thoughts on sublimation open his aphoristic phase (HAH 95), but swim so deep that the bubbles only surface occasionally (D 202 and 248; BGE 189; WP 677) until the theme returns in full in the *Genealogy of Morals*.[4]

The Perspective of the Whole

Nietzsche saw himself as the first great psychologist among philosophers, and his whole philosophy is relevant to our question . . .

Kaufmann, 1978

Both eternal return and the *Übermensch* are for Kaufmann symbolic expressions of Nietzsche's attempt to see the whole: the eternal return, a way to think time as a whole, and the *Übermensch*, a way to think our own existence in terms of life as a whole, and not as an end or crown of creation set apart from nature (A 13–14). Thus in the spirit of Goethe, Kaufmann's way of reading Nietzsche can be summed up in one imperative: 'see the whole'. He argues that 'life does indeed reside in the whole of Nietzsche's thinking and writing, and there is a unity which is obscured, but not obliterated, by the apparent discontinuity in his experimentalism'. And again: 'In the end, it is not so much a matter of balancing one text against another, as it is a question of gaining a whole and coherent view' (Kaufmann, 1980, p. 229). As David Pickus puts it,

> [t]he key issue with Kaufmann is not simply that he wrote one of the first serious full-length philosophical studies of Nietzsche to appear in America. It was that Kaufmann was openly a contender for the right to interpret Nietzsche as a whole. (2003, p. 231)

To appreciate Kaufmann's imperative to see the whole of Nietzsche, a simple distinction between the concepts of 'all' and 'whole' first needs to be clarified. You are currently situated in front of a book, for example. But you do not see *all* of this book. One side of it (the cover) is facing away from you; then there are all the pages other than this one. But further, if you look at it under a microscope, every page contains a world of detail – the microstructure of the paper, the ragged edge of the ink stain constituting each letter, the tangled chains of polymers in the glue of the binding. A comprehensive catalogue of each and every detail of the physical structure of the book would consist of a massive amount of data requiring a library of volumes to record it all, were the *total* catalogue of all possible facts about this book possible. But it is not at all clear as a matter of principle whether such a catalogue is even possible. Upon reflection, you must admit that you never actually see *all* of the book.

But here you are, with the *whole* book in your hands. Of course, your *seeing* of the whole of the book comes in degrees, as you get to read it more and more. But as you turn the last page, it is still the same whole you picked up at the shop or the library – you saw the whole superficially then when you looked at its cover; you are gradually seeing the whole in greater depth right now; and, depending on the depth of the book, you may or may not decide at some future point that you have exhausted the whole book (Kaufmann, 1958, pp. 84, 263). The point is that our 'seeing the whole' of anything is always provisional, and permanently open, in principle, to revision. But such revision does not make us doubt that there *is* a whole; on the contrary, it reinforces that way of thinking, with the thought 'I hadn't yet seen the *whole* whole'.

Nietzsche's aphoristic style is thoroughly holistic, although it might seem to be the opposite: thus Nietzsche asks rhetorically, '[d]o you think this work must be fragmentary because I give it to you (and have to give it to you) in fragments?' (HAH I 128). Nietzsche's aphorisms are not at all mere snippets of incomplete ideas. Each and every aphorism is a polished and self-contained whole, in which Nietzsche tries to say more in a few lines than other philosophers can say in entire books – in fact, each aphorism reflects his whole philosophy, for the whole of Nietzsche's works form the ultimate horizon for each aphorism (the Greek etymology of the word 'aphorism' indicates this: *apo* – *orizo* means 'out of' or 'from' a horizon). Like Leibniz's monads, each and every aphorism is a representation of the whole of Nietzsche's thought from one particular perspective; but *unlike* Leibniz's monads, there is no one perspective of all perspectives for Nietzsche, no one key perspective seeing into all others.[5]

This is how Nietzsche's systematicity connects to his holism: each new aphorism that is read and appreciated subtly changes the interpretation of all others read before it, along with the interpretation of the mytho-poetic themes. This is clearly an open-ended process of becoming, and not a teleological quest to arrive at a conclusion presenting one ultimate truth of Nietzsche's being. 'Absolute consciousness' may not be an obviously absurd idea, but an 'absolute aphorism' certainly is, and Nietzsche should be appreciated as always *showing* in his style what he often says in his content, namely, that in metaphysics (i.e. GS 'God is dead' 125), as in philosophical psychology (i.e. '[w]e must also put an end to the atomism of the soul', BGE 12), we must come to see that we are wholes, despite being neither unities nor totalities. As Nietzsche says in *Twilight of the Idols*: '[t]oday the individual still has to be made possible by being pruned: possible here means *whole*' (TI 'Improvers' 41).

The imperative to see the whole in studying Nietzsche divides into two projects: firstly, the pursuit of a principle of modesty preventing us from making premature claims to have seen the whole of Nietzsche's thought, when in fact we appreciate it only partially (see Kaufmann, 1974, p. 230). And secondly, the pursuit of a principle of pragmatism which prevents us from undertaking unrealistic projects, ignoring the crucial existential imperative that knowledge remain in the service of life, rather than life becoming enslaved to mere learning. 'This volume wants to be read as a whole', Kaufmann says in the preface to his *Faith of a Heretic* (1959b, p. ix), and not only Kaufmann's *Nietzsche* but his own works as a whole also need to be studied in the same spirit, philosophizing 'full time' (1958, p. xiii), yet proving that such 'taking seriously' does not have to be devoid of play and joy (GS 327).

For philosophers of what Kaufmann calls the 'existential persuasion', being a philosopher is thus a question of the whole of life, and not just a 'job', one possible career among others in a nine-to-five working life (1958, pp.15–44). The kind of 'mere scholars' that Nietzsche attacks in *Beyond Good and Evil*, Section 211 see only parts, and see philosophy only as a part of their life, and their life as part of a university department, which is part of a university which is part of a city, a country, and so on (TI 'Germans' 3). In contrast, the 'philosophers of the future' Nietzsche sees coming are 'just as multiple as whole' (BGE 212), in other words, able to see the whole, and themselves as wholes in that whole, without mistaking it or themselves for *all*. As Nietzsche puts it, 'one belongs to the whole; there is nothing which could judge, measure, compare, or sentence our being, for that would mean judging, measuring, comparing, or sentencing the whole. But there is nothing besides the whole' (TI 'Errors' 8). This new perspective has far-reaching consequences in many social, political and personal contexts.

Existentialism

Heidegger interprets Nietzsche as the *last* of the metaphysicians, but Kaufmann insists on the contrary that he must rather be read as the *first* of several things, including the first of the existentialists. While it is true that 'to detect only the existential dimensions in [Kaufmann's] *Nietzsche* is to miss the real innovation as well as the historical significance of his work' (Ratner-Rosenhagen, 2006, p. 268), it is also true that to ignore the existential element is also to fail to see the whole. In the *Critique of Religion and Philosophy* Kaufmann points out that existentialism 'is not a philosophy but a label for several different revolts against traditional philosophy' (1958, p. 19). He writes that

[i]n many ways Nietzsche is close to what one might call the temper of existentialism. He fused philosophy and psychology, he took a special interest in what Jaspers later called *Psychologie der Weltanschauungen*, he wrote of the death of God, he discussed nihilism and alternative attitudes toward an absurd world, he was a penetrating literary critic, and he

mobilized the resources of literature to communicate his philosophy'. (1974, p. 422)

There are three main senses in which Kaufmann's Nietzsche can be called existentialist. The first is the sense in which Nietzsche's work was his life, his biography and his bibliography inseparably entwined in one work of *Bildung*; and the second, the sense in which the reader's experience also becomes bound up in Nietzsche writings, for reading Nietzsche is never a mere academic exercise. Nietzsche's texts cry out to be tested in attempts and experiments in the reader's own life. As Kaufmann puts it, '[e]xperimenting involves testing an answer by trying to live according to it' (1974, p. 89; see Ratner-Rosenhagen, 2006, p. 251). Thus Kaufmann insists on the importance of getting to know Nietzsche's works first hand: 'Nietzsche's philosophy has to be studied and evaluated on the basis of his books' (1974, p. 450). With a robust common sense, Kaufmann aims to steer his readers between the extremes of the dilettante and the pedant.[6]

So on the one hand, Kaufmann asks us to please do Nietzsche the courtesy of actually reading his dozen published books from *Birth of Tragedy* to *Ecce Homo* before deciding upon an 'interpretation'. But on the other, he warns us not to drag Nietzsche back into the academy and imprison him there, his thoughts pinned like dead butterflies in a museum case. For although Kaufmann was a respected and successful academic, it was not primarily in the form of college text-books that his translations made Nietzsche so well known to the post-war generation in the United States. His translations spread far and wide as the paperbacks which the beat generation took on their journeys, the post-war existentialists read in their cafés, and from which freethinkers of all sorts drew inspiration during the turbulent decades of the 1960s and 1970s (see Ratner-Rosenhagen, 2006, p. 268, note 72).

The third sense in which Kaufmann's Nietzsche is an existentialist is the technical philosophical sense, meaning that he thinks that our existence *precedes* our essence. Existentialists maintain that it is our free decisions which determine what we become, and not some pre-existing soul, genetic programming, or social conditioning. There is a common anxiety that this putative existentialism on which Kaufmann's interpretation focuses obscures the many other aspects of Nietzsche's rich *oeuvre*. However, this anxiety is allayed by Kaufmann's avoidance of reductionism: for although according to him Nietzsche was in several senses an existentialist, he was not in any sense 'merely' or 'nothing but' an existentialist. This holds for Kaufman's so-called humanist emphasis too (see Ansell-Pearson, 1991, p. 311, note 5). Existentialist and humanist themes do indeed run through Kaufmann (for example, ' "human-istic education" is really a tautology', Kaufmann, 1958 p. 292), but to reduce Kaufmann's Nietzsche to 'nothing but' an existentialist, or a humanist, is to do injustice to his extensive and subtle reading.[7]

Conclusion

It is in depth of erudition that Kaufmann shines brightest. Like Nietzsche himself, he has read Shakespeare, Swift, and Sterne, as well as Kant, Goethe, Schiller, Schelling, Hegel and the Schlegels, Feuerbach, Schopenhauer, and Max Stirner – *actually* read them, and not just the secondary literature *about* them. Students are thus oriented by these stars of the philosophical firmament as they read Kaufmann, introduced to each, and directed by a standard of scholarship second to none. This is not to say that either Kaufmann or Nietzsche ought to be followed unquestioningly; on the con-trary, this is precisely what Nietzsche warns us against. Perhaps there is even a sense in which hostile critics might have appealed to Nietzsche, afraid as he was of sycophants and disciples and always challenging his readers to think for themselves. But the theme of friendship runs deep in Nietzsche, and he often addresses his readers as his friends, and this good will is a sig-nificant aspect of most appreciative readers' experiences of Nietzsche. Although in places he does distance himself from his friend Friedrich,[8] no one has devoted more energy to loyally defending Nietzsche from ill-informed and judgemental critics, and rebutting groundless gossip and smear campaigns. Kaufmann's unwillingness to accept any silence concern-ing the abuse of Nietzsche by the Nazis drives his retrieval of a Nietzsche 'just as multiple as he is whole' (BGE 212), just as radically pacifist (for example HAH 284) as he is selectively belligerent (for example EH 'Wise' 7). The work of Walter Kaufmann can be said to continue to add new dimen-sions to our possibilities for thinking about, with, and through the inex-haustible works of Friedrich Nietzsche.

Notes

[1] The doctrine of the will to power has its roots in chapter six of HAH I, and develops through D 124 and 262, GS 13 and 310, and Z II 'On Self-overcoming' and 'On Human Cleverness'. It is elaborated most fully throughout BGE and GM.

[2] See also op. cit. chapter 6: 'The Discovery of the Will to Power', passim.

[3] Arthur Desmond (1859–1918, aka Ragnar Redbeard) wrote *Might is Right* in Australia in 1892-3, a notorious work appropriating aspects of Stirner and

Nietzsche and proclaiming 'death to the weakling, wealth to the strong'. See Redbeard (2008).

[4] Hollingdale's translation of *Aufhebung* as "sublimation" (D, Preface 4, and 248) confuses matters, and this is further complicated by Carol Diethe's translation of both *Sublimirung* in 7 and *Aufhebung* in 10 of GM II as 'sublimate', and both *Aufhebung* and *Sublimieren* as 'sublimate' in GM III 27. Nietzsche calls morality and dissimulation sublations precisely because these degenerate into mere systematicity, unlike sublimations. A liar covering their tracks must be systematic, and only those whose only concern is to appear moral (such as when ethics becomes nothing more than a public relations issue in the corporate world) are satisfied with a merely algorithmic moral code.

[5] See Kaufmann's comments on Nietzsche's 'monadology' in (1974), pp. 263–4.

[6] Both forms of a fear of autonomy Kaufmann later characterized as 'decidophobia': see Kaufmann (1973), p. 25.

[7] As does Ratner-Rosenhagen, when she speaks of Kaufmann's 'retreat into monism' (p. 267). Much more problematic, however, is Kaufmann's willingness to partition off Nietzsche's misogyny as 'philosophically irrelevant' (Kaufmann, 1974, p. 84 and p. 222; Kaufmann, 1980, volume 2, pp.145–7). This is a serious lapse in Kaufmann's otherwise holistic approach.

[8] In *Discovering the Mind* volume 2 Kaufmann says of Nietzsche 'I love him although my disagreements with him are legion' (1980, p. 6).

Bibliography and Guide to Further Study

Kaufmann's Nietzsche Interpretation

Kaufmann, Walter (1958), *Critique of Religion and Philosophy*. New York: Harper.

— (1959a), *From Shakespeare to Existentialism*. Princeton: Princeton University Press. Collected essays, vol. 1. The Faber & Faber UK edition is entitled, *The Owl and the Nightingale*. Revised ed. 1980.

— (1959b), *The Faith of a Heretic*. New York: McGraw-Hill.

— (1965), *Hegel: Reinterpretation, Texts and Commentary*. New York: Doubleday.

— (1968), *Tragedy and Philosophy*. New York: Doubleday.

— (1973), *Without Guilt and Justice*. New York: Peter H. Wyden Inc.

— (1974a), *Nietzsche: Philosopher, Psychologist, Antichrist*, 4th edn. Princeton: Princeton University Press. [1st edn 1950]

— (1976a), *Existentialism, Religion and Death*. New York: New American Library.

— (1976b), *Religions in Four Dimensions*. New York: Reader's Digest/McGraw-Hill.

— (1978), *Man's Lot*. New York: Reader's Digest/McGraw-Hill.

— (1980), *Discovering the Mind*, 3 vols. New York: McGraw-Hill.

— (ed.) (1975), *Existentialism from Dostoevsky to Sartre*. New York: Meridian. [1st edn 1956]

Kaufmann's Nietzsche Translations

Nietzsche, Friedrich (1954), *The Portable Nietzsche*. New York: Viking Press. Contains Z, TI, A, and NW, selections from EH, and various letters.

— (1968a), *Basic Writings of Nietzsche*. New York: The Modern Library. Contains GM co-translated with Hollingdale, along with Kaufmann's own translations of BT, BGE, CW, and all of EH.
— (1968b), *The Will to Power* (trans. with R. J. Hollingdale). New York: Vintage Books.
— (1974b), *The Gay Science*. New York: Random House.

Works on Kaufmann

Pickus, David (2003), 'The Walter Kaufmann Myth'. *Nietzsche-Studien*, 32, 226–58.
— (2007), 'Wishes of the Heart: Walter Kaufmann, Karl Jaspers and Disposition in Nietzsche Scholarship'. *Journal of Nietzsche Studies*, 33, 5–24.
Ratner-Rosenhagen, Jennifer (2006), 'Dionysian Enlightenment: Walter Kaufmann's *Nietzsche* in Historical Perspective'. *Modern Intellectual History*, 3, 239–96.

Other Works Cited

Allison, David B. (1985), *The New Nietzsche: Contemporary Styles of Interpretation*. Cambridge, MA: MIT Press.
Ansell-Pearson, Kieth (1991), 'Who Is the *Übermensch?* Time, Truth and Woman in Nietzsche'. *Journal of the History of Ideas*, 53, 309–41.
Nietzsche, Friedrich. (1997), *Daybreak*, ed. Maudemarie Clark and Brian Leiter; trans. R. J. Hollingdale. Cambridge: Cambridge University Press.
Redbeard, Ragnar (2008), *Might is Right*. Indiana: Zem Books [1892].
Wheeler, Kathleen M. (ed.) (1984), *German Aesthetic and Literary Criticism: The Romantic Ironists and Goethe*. Cambridge: Cambridge University Press.

Chapter 5

Deleuze's Nietzsche

Jon Roffe

Gilles Deleuze was one of the foremost French philosophers of the twentieth century. Crossing over a good number of traditional boundaries, he wrote quite traditional books on the history of philosophy, but also challenging works (co-authored with the psychiatrist and political activist Félix Guattari) on contemporary existence and socio-political reality that push against most of the genre conventions of philosophical writing. Formidable volumes of technical, philosophical examinations of reality, time and language sit side by side in his *oeuvre* with extended analyses of cinema and literature, painting and music. Deleuze's reading of Nietzsche itself emphasizes all of these trajectories. For Deleuze, Nietzsche is at once a formidable metaphysician, a thinker of the most concrete and pressing issues of life and society, and a subtle analyst of the dynamics of aesthetic experience (in the broadest sense).

Historically speaking, Deleuze was an instrumental figure in the broad revival of interest in Nietzsche's thought in France after the Second World War.[1] While thinkers like Georges Bataille and Jean Wahl had already challenged the association of Nietzsche's thought with National Socialism, the generation of thinkers after the war, including Deleuze, went further, establishing him once again as a decisive figure in Western thought. An inaugural member of the French Society for Nietzsche Studies, established in 1946 with Jean Wahl as its president, Deleuze was also involved, with Maurice de Gandillac and Michel Foucault, in the project to publish the entirety of Nietzsche's works in French translation. He organized an early conference on Nietzsche at Rouyamont in 1964, and was a participant in the famous Nietzsche event at Cerisy-la-Salle in 1972. While Nietzsche's influence can be found, implicitly or explicitly, in almost all of Deleuze's work, it is particularly concentrated in his early studies in the history of philosophy, and in his key work, *Difference and Repetition* (Deleuze, 1994). The locus of the engagement, however, is to be found in the 1962 *Nietzsche and Philosophy* (Deleuze, 1983), and it is this book on which the current chapter will focus.[2]

Before doing so, it is worth registering the fact that a simple explication of Deleuze's Nietzsche is something of a difficult task, for two reasons in particular.

On the one hand, all of Deleuze's texts on other philosophers present a peculiar kind of difficulty to the reader. Put simply, it's often difficult to know exactly *who* is speaking. In the case of *Nietzsche and Philosophy*, for example, is it Nietzsche himself (that is, is Deleuze merely presenting Nietzsche's own views)? Is it Nietzsche refracted through a Deleuzean lens? Or perhaps Deleuze's own views, dressed in a Nietzschean framework? This kind of ambiguity that attends much of Deleuze's work is not something that arises by chance, and Deleuze himself is fully aware of it. Indeed, when speaking of his work, he sometimes notes that it is just such a *free indirect discourse* that he is looking to embody. This term, taken by Deleuze from Pasolini, is meant by Deleuze to characterize a mode of writing in which he adopts a fluid point of view, or creates a diagonal trajectory, which runs between the positions of 'Deleuze' and 'Nietzsche' without being reducible to either. At the same time, Deleuze is adamant that this way of reading philosophers does not falsify them, and indeed requires a great deal of fidelity to their work. In an (infamous) text, he likens it to a kind of buggery or immaculate conception, which gives rise to a strange offspring. He adds, however, that '[i]t was really important for it to be his own child, because the author had to actually say all I had him saying. But the child was bound to be monstrous too, because it resulted from all sorts of shifting, slipping, dislocations and hidden emissions that I really enjoyed' (Deleuze, 1995, p. 6). Rather than seeing the task of the historian of philosophy as one of simply 'reporting the facts', the goal is to tease out certain lines of development that are only explicable from a certain point of view. This approach is also quintessentially Nietzschean, emphasizing as it does the irreducibility of the mode of existence of the one who interprets in the act of interpretation. While this is not the place to explicate the detailed workings of Deleuze's peculiar mode of address, this point is important to keep in mind when reading his reading of Nietzsche.

On the other hand, there is a difficulty specific to Deleuze's reading of Nietzsche. Above all, if Deleuze's Nietzsche is hard to summarize in a few words, this is because his reading revolves around two of the most formidably complex (interpretively, conceptually, textually) Nietzschean themes: the doctrines of the will to power and the eternal return. The goal of this chapter, in light of these difficulties, will be to present a skeletal outline of Deleuze's main claims in his Nietzsche book, drawing on occasion from *Difference and Repetition* in order to illuminate the former.

The Completion of the Critical Project

Unlike some other readings of Nietzsche, which cast his philosophy as a *critique of metaphysics*, Deleuze takes Nietzsche to be presenting a *critical metaphysics*, which is to say that he remains (broadly speaking) within the tradition inaugurated by Kant. Rather than attempting to do away with or entirely replace the Kantian moment in thought, Deleuze reads Nietzsche as the thinker who completes this trajectory, finally presenting a mature and fully elaborated critical philosophy: 'Nietzsche thinks that the idea of critique is identical to that of philosophy but that this is precisely the idea that Kant has missed, that he has compromised and spoilt, not only in its application but in principle' (p. 88).[3]

Deleuze takes Nietzsche to be completing the Kantian project in a number of respects. He is, in the first instance, interested in the renovation he brings about in the notion of critique itself. For Kant, the project of a critique of pure reason is not principally negative in nature. Instead, the goal is to discover the nature and legitimate role of reason, in order to properly assess the part it plays in the acquisition of knowledge. The famous Kantian claim, of course, is that human thought cannot legitimately extend beyond the scope of experience, and that all knowledge must be formed on the basis of sensible encounters.

Now, Deleuze will cast Nietzschean thought as completing the Kantian critique by extending it beyond the bounds of epistemological judgements. The problem with Kant is simply that he took knowledge as such to be of neutral, homogenous and intrinsic value. According to Deleuze, what Nietzsche introduces into critical philosophy is the decisive import of the question of *values*, this or that value that underpins a given claim or point of view: 'One of the principal motifs of Nietzsche's work is that Kant had not carried out a true critique because he was not able to pose the problem of a critique in terms of values' (p. 1).

Put another way, the problem with the Kantian viewpoint is that it assumes every knowing subject occupies not just the same neutral social and historical space, but are in themselves essentially identical to every other. Behind the Kantian question 'by what right do we assert that we know something?' lies the more profound Nietzschean challenge: not simply 'why is truth valued?' but 'who wants *this* truth, and why do they want it?'

Correlatively, there is great significance for Deleuze in the radical role played in Nietzsche's thought by history and genealogical analysis. Kant's critique is essentially ahistorical in nature. It is only by grasping historical reality as the unfolding of various interrelated formations of the will to power (something discussed in what follows) that we are in a position to answer the *diagnostic* question: 'Who wants this or that truth? What, in this individual, is invested in seeing the world in this way?' This is because the answer to such questions cannot be derived a priori or even via the Kantian sense of transcendental reasoning (though we will see that there is for Deleuze a genuinely transcendental aspect to Nietzsche's philosophy), but must always take into account the genuine socio-historical conditions in which such investments are operative.

In other words, Deleuze argues that Nietzsche's critical approach to the question of truth reveals that, beneath the model of thought that revolves around the distinction between true and false, and even the Kantian distinction between legitimate and illegitimate, lie the true genetic conditions for both thought and reality. These conditions are, for Nietzsche nothing other than the irreducibly multiple formations of the will to power.

We have already arrived at the fundamental structure underlying Deleuze's reading of Nietzsche. On his account, the Nietzschean project aims to attack the patina of normality with which a certain conception of the relationship between thought and truth is presented in Western philosophy – a conception he calls, here as elsewhere, the *dogmatic image of thought.* However, this is in order to advance a positive project characterized by an historically and socially sensitive diagnostic approach to life and thought. At the same time, this diagnostic is not itself in the service of some higher or more correct form of knowledge, but oriented towards the creation of new ways of thinking and feeling. This is indeed what Deleuze considers the highest achievement of Nietzsche's extension and reformulation of the Kantian critique: the insistence that the current form of human existence should itself be subject to critical attention in order to open up new ways of living. He writes that 'the point of critique is not justification but a different way of feeling: another sensibility' (p. 94). Or, as he says elsewhere, 'Nietzsche reinvents [. . .] total critique which is at the same time a creation, total positivity' (Deleuze, 2004c, p. 139): Zarathustra's destructive lion and creative child embodied in a single philosophical *oeuvre.*

The Genetic Conditions of Reality

As we have just noted, Kant begins by taking knowledge itself as both intrinsically valuable and the natural goal of thinking.[4] He then proceeds, on Deleuze's account, by extrapolating from particular cases of experience in order to establish a formal and universal set of conditions that every experience must presume in order to be possible as an experience. This is the famous transcendental method of reasoning used to such powerful effect in the *Critique of Pure Reason*.

However, from Deleuze's point of view, this formulation is triply mistaken. It is mistaken, first of all, insofar as it asserts that these conditions are unchanging, which Nietzsche's thorough-going genealogical analyses reveal to be false (social and historical context being for him irreducible). Kant also asserts that transcendental conditions are homogenous and universal, which Nietzsche shows to be untrue not just across history but within a given milieu. Indeed, even within each individual there is for Nietzsche not one thinker but a multiple set of combating impulses, struggling for supremacy (as famous passages in *Daybreak* demonstrate). Finally, by conceiving of the conditions for experience in terms of *possible* experience, Kant (as his contemporary and critic Solomon Maimon had already pointed out) does not provide any reason to think that these conditions of possibility are the conditions for *actual* experience.

In contrast, the will to power provides Nietzsche with a theory of conditions that are 1) socially and historically specific, 2) only as 'large' as what they condition, entirely singular and local, and 3) the conditions for actual reality and our experience of it. In other words, to arrive at what Deleuze thinks is most striking about Nietzsche's thought, we need to invert the Kantian account: Nietzsche's philosophy is an attempt to reveal the historically determined, culturally specific and truly *genetic* conditions that structure and really produce existing modes of life and thought.

Quantity, Quality and the Will to Power

What, then, on Deleuze's account, is the will to power, and how does it operate in this fashion? The first thing to note is that there can be no question, given this approach, of conceiving the will to power as some kind of superior subjective state, manifested in a kind of egomaniacal self-regard. For Deleuze, this is the most serious misreading of the concept of the will to power possible, one which obscures everything important in Nietzsche's own account. In contrast, the will to power must be considered to be at once an *ontological* concept and a *transcendental* concept, which is to say that the will to power on Deleuze's account is that element in reality (not in the mind of a person) which provides the real conditions for the advent of particular states of affairs.

To see exactly what these points mean, the most straightforward approach is to follow the order of Deleuze's explication in the key chapter of *Nietzsche and Philosophy*, entitled 'Active and Reactive', where he lays out the basic elements of his reading of Nietzsche's philosophical account of reality.

Deleuze begins by noting that for Nietzsche nature, reality as such, consists of multiplicitous forces engaged in mutual relations: quoting *The Will to Power*, he states that 'all reality is already quantity of force. What exists is nothing but quantities of force in mutual "relations of tension"' (p. 40). This landscape of force-relations is also, on Deleuze's account, irreducibly unequal, meaning that there exists no natural parity between any two forces: in a memorable passage, he states that 'to dream of two equal forces, even if they are said to be of opposite senses is a coarse and approximate dream, a statistical dream' (p. 43), a dream that Nietzsche believes science often participates in. As a result, given any relation between forces, there will always be a dominating force and a force dominated; in turn, every complex of forces engaged in mutual relations of domination and subordination constitute a body (of every kind and degree of complexity), structured according to a hierarchy of these force relations.

Deleuze immediately adds that, according to Nietzsche, to insist on the level of *quantity* alone would overlook the equally significant role played in force relations by *quality*. In short, the quality of a relation between forces expresses the character of the relation itself: 'Quality is distinct from quantity but only because it is that aspect of quantity that cannot be equalised, that cannot be equalised out in the difference between quantities' (pp. 43–4). Every time there is a relation between forces, we are dealing with a quantitative relation expressed qualitatively.

Now, whereas the quantitative relations between forces are properly thought in terms of the relative domination of one over the other, the quality of these relations we must speak of in terms of *active* and *reactive*. The priest, for example, as Nietzsche discusses this type in *The Genealogy of Morals*, may be in the dominant position in relation to his subordinate flock, but he nonetheless embodies a reactive mode of being which leeches a capacity for genuine action from not only himself but those whom he dominates. The subordinate can always express their full measure of capacity, even if it is in service of the goals of the dominator: such a situation remains a case of an active hierarchy of relations, as in the case of a healthy human body, for example. The reactive, on the other hand, have been separated from their capacity to act, subordinated not to another end – as in the case of merely physical slavery – but separated from the direct act-end relationship, rendered to some degree incapable.

Even more profoundly, Deleuze notes, we must speak of a process of becoming-reactive of active forces in situations like this. A reactive quality of this or that relation or individual is not some kind of equal but opposed contrasting reality that exists in a tenuous balance or struggle for supremacy. This is because only active forces struggle for supremacy in this way. Reactive forces do not function by striving to outstrip active forces, to dominate them – if they did this, they would be active forces – but rather operate by undermining the capacity manifest in active forces.

Deleuze's way of writing about this entropic effect of reactive forces should put us in mind of something like a wasting disease. The problem is that active forces have no natural immunity to this kind of disease, which is what leads Deleuze to the following sentiment in Nietzsche's work: 'inferior forces can prevail without ceasing to be inferior in quantity and reactive in quality, without ceasing to be slaves in this sense. One of the finest remarks in *The Will to Power* is: "The strong must be protected from the weak"' (p. 58). It remains to give a name to this wasting disease itself: *ressentiment.*

It is important to note that Deleuze insists upon the essentially *active* nature of all forces, whether they are dominated or dominating. Despite the fact that dominated forces are subordinate to ends not their own, they remain in the final analysis active, a striving constitutive, in part, of a body. This is important for two reasons. On the one hand, we must always keep in mind that reality in general for Deleuze's Nietzsche is at root positive and active in nature. Negativity and reactivity are characteristics of certain force relationships – the analysis of which constitutes some of Nietzsche's most famous texts – but we must not be led into thinking that there is any kind of *primordial* negativity. On the other hand, Deleuze insists that Nietzsche's genius lies in the capacity to distinguish between merely dominated forces (which have no intrinsic status with respect to activity and reactivity) and genuinely reactive set-ups, which, even if dominating others, are no less passive and insidious in nature. This is the situation of the priest once again: a 'leader' who subordinates his flock to his conception of life, but who remains entirely expressive of a passive and inferior relation to the world.

With quantity and quality of force relations (which, as we have seen, are irreducibly entwined notions) having now been considered, we can finally turn to the Deleuzean account of the will to power. For Deleuze, what is the will to power? His answer, reminiscent once more of Kant's transcendental philosophy, is that the will to power is the genetic condition of force relations; it is what grounds and gives rise to particular ensembles of quantity and quality:

Nietzsche calls the genealogical element of force the will to power. Genealogical means differential and genetic. The will to power is the differential element of forces, that is to say the element that produces the differences in quantity between two or more forces whose relation is presupposed. The will to power is the genetic element of force, that is to say the element that produces the quality due to each force in this relation. (pp. 52–3)

The will to power is the reason for the existence of this or that quantitative and qualitative relation between forces: this is the sense we must give to the term 'genetic' here. The will to power is not just a necessary condition for any given arrangement of force relations, but, like the grain of sand in the oyster that gives rise to the pearl, the genuinely productive element that is expressed through those relations. We could say it is the *ground* for the relations of force, except that the idea of a ground has the ring of generality and neutrality that we have seen problematized by Nietzsche's rewriting of the critical project. This is why Deleuze uses the term 'differential': we must realize that the will to power is neither homogenous nor general, but is and is expressed locally through specific relations of force. Deleuze frequently emphasizes the significance of this point: 'the will to power is a good principle [. . .] because it is an essentially *plastic* principle that is no wider than what it conditions, that changes itself with the conditioned and determines itself in each case along with what it determines' (p. 50).

At the quantitative level, forces are either dominating or dominated; at the qualitative level, relations of forces are either active or reactive; but the will to power is characterized as either *affirmative* or *negative*. Again, though, we would be mistaken if we were to think of this difference in the character of the will to power in terms of an originary, quasi-Manichean struggle between affirmation and negation. The will to power itself is essentially affirmative and productive in nature. Deleuze writes:

> The will to power is not force but the differential element which simultaneously determines the relations of forces (quantity) and the respective quantities of related forces. It is in this element of difference that affirmation manifests itself and develops itself as creative. (p. 197)

For Deleuze, interactions at the level of forces are fundamentally governed by chance: *this* meal, *this* friendship, *this* way of looking at the world have no necessity but arise according to the order of aleatory encounters. The will to power, as the genetic and determinative element in these relations, does not act like an iron-clad causal structure, but provides these chance encounters with their internal *meaning* or *sense*. The lamb and *its* eagle form a chance compound of force relations, but the will to power which is expressed in these relations gives this event its proper *sense*, its affirmative character: this is good.

Just as with the advent of reactive qualities of force relations, the negative modality of the will to power must be accounted for in terms of particular cultural and historical developments, through which the sense of the will to power has been inverted. And, where the advent of the reactive quality of force relations manifests itself in the wasting disease of *ressentiment*, the advent of the negative form of the will to power also goes under another name, *nihilism*:

> Nihil *in "nihilism" means negation as a quality of the will to power*. Thus, in its primary and basic sense, nihilism signifies the value of nil taken on by life, the fiction of higher values which gives this value and the will to nothing-ness which is expressed in these higher values. (p. 147)

The seeds of this negative modality of the will to power were to be found in the resentful glint in the eye of the lamb, the slave, but in its elaborated form, it means that the very sense and value of living itself has been under-mined through the course of human history. Life, once fundamentally affirmed in all of its forms, has depreciated in value; affirmation has been inverted. The artist, the legislator, the noble type, separated from what they can do by the multiplication of reactive forces, no longer express a funda-mental affirmation of living, but instead a negative and devalued mode of being: they become the ascetic (who denies the sensuous), the perpetual accuser (for whom everyone is necessarily guilty), the slavish type (for whom life is suffering).

Quantity of force, quality of force, will to power: this tripartite structure forms the backbone of Deleuze's reading of Nietzsche. With it in hand, he goes on to demonstrate how even very complicated moments in the latter's thought can be made sense of in terms of the diagnostic categories it affords the analyst of history, society and thought, the crowning achievement per-haps being the impressive way in which, as we have just seen, it allows Deleuze to tackle even the most complex and important themes in Nietzsche, such as nihlism itself.

Equally important however is the systematic account Deleuze gives of some of Nietzsche's key terms. Unlike some perspectives on Nietzsche's work, which conceive of him as a thinker hostile to any and all systematic viewpoints, Deleuze treats him as a thinker whose system is highly coherent.

The Eternal Return of Difference

It remains to discuss the central role that the doctrine of the eternal return plays in Deleuze's reading of Nietzsche, which is arguably its most controversial aspect. In *Nietzsche and Philosophy*, Deleuze circles around this infamous concept, returning to it in each of the book's five chapters, sometimes more than once. This process of a repetitive circling around leads Deleuze to the following conclusions.

In the first instance, the eternal return is equated by Deleuze with the *affirmation* of *chance*. While encounters between forces, as we have already seen, happen according to chance and not some pre-determined program, the eternal return is the affirmation of the ensemble of these chance encounters. To this initial point, Deleuze adds the following claim: that the eternal return is the universal affirmation of *change* and *difference*. Every (chance) encounter brings about changes in the bodies that engage in them (my body with a glass of wine or the *Genealogy of Morals* no less than the body of the lamb when it is consumed by the eagle). These changes arise, once again, on the basis of chance encounters. If the eternal return is an affirmation of chance, this is because it is *through* such chance encounters that changes, differences, novelty arise in the world. This is the fundamental reason that Deleuze increasingly characterizes the eternal return, against the letter of the Nietzschean text in some cases, as the eternal return of *difference*.

How does this affirmation *operate*? Deleuze puts it best when he poses to himself the following question: 'How does the thought of pure becoming [change unbound by any higher law] serve as a foundation for the eternal return?' (p. 48). His answer directs us to consider the eternal return as a claim about the nature of reality at the basic level:

All we need to do to think this thought is to stop believing in being as distinct from and opposed to becoming or to believe in the being of becoming itself. What is the being of that which becomes, of that which neither starts nor finishes becoming? *Returning is the being of that which becomes.* (p. 48)

Despite the perplexity that Deleuze's terminology might give rise to, this cuts to the heart of the matter. First of all, we need to reject the idea that beneath particular bodies and the relations of forces that constitute them there exists a more fundamental, stable, and homogenous level of reality.

Put in a positive sense, what the doctrine of the eternal return asserts is that *nothing* is immune to change, to the metamorphoses that arise through chance encounters. The most comprehensive thing that we can say about being as such is that it is nothing other than the reality of this unbounded movement of change. Everything is perpetually becoming something else, something different, according to the order of encounters, and there is *nothing besides*. In *Difference and Repetition*, Deleuze puts the point like this: 'The eternal return is a force of affirmation, but it affirms everything of the multiple, everything of the different, everything of chance except what subordinates them to the One, to the Same and the Necessary' (Deleuze, 1994, p. 115). This is precisely because the One, the Same, and Necessity play no foundational role in Neitzsche's account of reality.

While this version of the account has an ontological character – that is, it seems to be a claim about Being – this is supplemented with the emphasis that Deleuze puts on its *temporal* character. Deleuze, making use in particular of remarks in the *Will to Power* notebooks, insists that we misunderstand Nietzsche's intentions with the doctrine of the eternal return if we reduce it to the hypothesis of the cyclical nature of time (pp. 47–8). If what has already occurred returns again, then the eternal return is in fact an agent of stability that reveals an underlying natural order – that state of things which comes back each time around. Time, however, is precisely the agent that disallows this vision of the world, since it is what makes possible the arrival of something radically new and unexpected. In fact, Deleuze will not hesitate to assert in *Difference and Repetition* that the eternal return is the 'form of time' (Deleuze, 1994, p. 88) as such.

In other words, the belief in the cyclical nature of the universe – with which Nietzsche radically breaks, for Deleuze – is not a philosophical claim about time at all but a claim about Being. If the path of the universe is cyclical, there is no time, and what we call time makes no difference. Once we conceive of the eternal return as the elemental fact of both time and reality, we can see that it subordinates every identity, everything which currently exists, to the possibility of being radically altered, even destroyed – not by what is here and now, but by what is yet to come. Thus the eternal return, as the form of time itself, subordinates current reality to a 'centrifugal force' (Deleuze, 1994, p. 90), not directly bringing about change, but integrally affirming the future possibility of a radical otherwise.

The final point to make with respect to the eternal return on Deleuze's account is that it is fundamentally *selective* in nature. Rather than being the eternal return of the same state of affairs, it is 'on the side of' the future; it affirms what changes. It functions as a guarantee that whatever dominant state of things currently holds – a reactive and nihilistic mode of existence, for example – is not vouched for by time, which is on the side of what is yet to come. Consequently, every existing arrangement of forces, every body which clings to the present or the established order as if to an unquestionable foundation, is 'selected out' by the inexorable arrival of the new that is figured, for Deleuze, by the eternal return.

Conclusion

While we have not been able to examine many of the fascinating riches of Deleuze's reading of Nietzsche here, the skeleton of his account should be clear. For Deleuze, Nietzsche's philosophy constitutes a completion of the critical project inaugurated by Kant, insofar as it questions the remaining dogmatic assumptions in Kant's own philosophy, and extends the critique to the level of *values*.

Nietzsche's 'completed' critical philosophy is at once systematic and metaphysical, presenting us, on Deleuze's account, with a rigorous, clearly composed view of reality in terms of the chance interactions between forces, which give rise in turn to bodies or hierarchically organized ensembles of force relations. At a diagnostic level, every force relation can be thought in terms of its quantity (in each case, one force is dominated and the other dominates) and its quality (the relation can be either active or reactive). Reactive forces are not, on Deleuze's account, merely contrary active forces, but forces which have been cut off from what they can do, introducing a new, regressive, modality into human bodies and the social bodies they form a part of in particular.

The *sense* or *meaning* of any given force relation is provided for it by the will to power, conceived of as the genetic force that provides the relation with its raison d'être, its orientation with respect to its activities. The will to power is primordially affirmative in character, but a negative mode of the will to power has arisen, through the course of human history, that gives a nihilistic cast to the value of life expressed by particular individuals and particular cultures.

Finally, the doctrine of the eternal return is a key element of Deleuze's reading of Nietzsche. He conceives of this as at once a claim about the nature of reality (there is no fundamental and neutral level of reality beyond the play of forces), a claim about time (insofar as it is the bearer of chance and the new, time tends to evacuate normality and identity), and as a result a claim about selection as an ontological process (the eternal return selects in favour of the different and against the same). It is this Nietzsche, the far-seeing diagnostician and critical metaphysician, who stalks the pages of each of Deleuze's books.

Notes

[1] A useful summary of the key aspects of Deleuze's reading of Nietzsche, along with illuminating historical detail, can be found in Dosse (2010), pp. 129–35.

[2] Unless otherwise specified, all page numbers cited refer to this text.

[3] In this same passage, Deleuze declares that 'If we stop thinking that the organization of [its] three essays is fortuitous we must conclude that Nietzsche, in *The Genealogy of Morals*, wanted to rewrite the *Critique of Pure Reason*'.

[4] It is important to note, however, that Deleuze also salutes Kant for being the first to challenge the assumption that the failure of thought only takes the form of error and simply arises through interference at the level of external encounters, insofar as he introduces the category of transcendental illusion, a tendency towards the illegitimate operation of thought within thinking itself (see Deleuze, 1994, p. 136).

Bibliography and Guide to Further Study

Deleuze's Nietzsche Interpretation

Deleuze, Gilles (1983), *Nietzsche and Philosophy*, trans. Hugh Tomlinson. New York: Columbia University Press [1962]. Deleuze's first and major work on the philosophy of Nietzsche.

— (1994), *Difference and Repetition*, trans. Paul Patton. New York: Columbia University Press. The primary part of Deleuze's doctoral thesis, *Difference and Repetition* (originally published in 1968), is at once the most systematic and the most historically engaged of the books he wrote. Presenting a striking metaphysics oriented by the categories indicated in the title, Nietzsche's influence is explicit throughout. Much of the sense of the work can be realized by rewriting the title as *The Will to Power and the Eternal Return*, something that Deleuze himself intimates at points.

— (1995), *Negotiations*, trans. Martin Joughin. New York: Columbia University Press. An excellent collection of interviews and short essays covering the latter part (from the early seventies onwards) of Deleuze's work.

— (2001), 'Nietzsche' in Deleuze, *Pure Immanence: Essays on a Life*, trans. Anne Boyman. New York: Zone Books. This small book was written in 1965 to be included in a series of short introductory texts to philosophy. It covers the same general territory as *Nietzsche and Philosophy*, while also including a long discussion of Nietzsche's life and a 'Dictionary of the Main Characters in Nietzsche's Work'.

— (2004a), 'Conclusions on the Will to Power and the Eternal Return', in Deleuze, *Desert Islands and Other Texts*, ed. David Lapoujade; trans. Michael Taormina. New York: Semiotext(e). This is the text of a summary Deleuze presented at the end of the 1967 Royaumont conference that he himself organized, which presents in outline the contributions of the various speakers. Deleuze orients his remarks, as the title suggests, around the two themes of the will to power and the eternal return in particular.

— (2004b), 'Nietzsche's Burst of Laughter', in *Desert Islands and Other Texts*. An extract from a longer 1967 interview, this short text discusses the project, then underway, of a collected works of Nietzsche, and Nietzsche's contemporary significance.

— (2004c), 'On Nietzsche and the Image of Thought', in *Desert Islands and Other Texts*. Like the previous text, the occasion for this 1968 interview was the re-edition by Gallimard of Nietzsche's complete works in new translations. This longer interview also discusses *Nietzsche and Philosophy*.

— (2004d), 'Nomad Thought', in *Desert Islands and Other Texts*. This slightly later text shows the marks of the general changes in Deleuze's philosophy undergone through the process of writing *Anti-Oedipus* with Félix Guattari. In this text, the piece he presented at the famous 1972 Cerisy-la-Salle conference on Nietzsche's work, Nietzsche appears no longer as a key figure in the development of critical philosophy, but a genuine exception to the philosophical cannon, a thinker outside metaphysics, a philosophical 'nomad'.

Works on Deleuze's Nietzsche

Ansell Pearson, Keith (1997), *Viroid Life: Perspectives on Nietzsche and the Trans-Human Condition*. New York: Routledge. Ansell Pearson's hydra-headed work on Nietzsche is from start to finish a not unambiguous running debate with Deleuze's Nietzsche and the broader Nietzschean strains in the rest of Deleuze's philosophy.

— (2007), 'Overcoming the Weight of Man: Nietzsche, Deleuze, and the Possibilities of Life'. *Revue Internationale de Philosophie*, 61, (3), 245–59. An excellent summary of the ethical content of Deleuze's reading of Nietzsche.

Borradori, Giovanna (1999), 'On the Presence of Bergson in Deleuze's Nietzsche'. *Philosophy Today*, 43, (4), Supplement, 140–6.

— (2001), 'The temporalisation of difference: Reflections on Deleuze's Interpretation of Bergson'. *Continental Philosophy Review*, 34, (1), 1–20. In both of these pieces, Borradori traces the implicit connections between Deleuze's account of Bergson and the presentation of Nietzsche's philosophy as a metaphysics of affirmative difference.

Descombes, Vincent (1997), 'Nietzsche's French Moment', in Luc Ferry and Alain Renaut (eds), *Why We are Not Nietzscheans*, trans. Robert de Loaiza. Chicago: University of Chicago Press. This text, one among many published in the latter quarter of the twentieth century, takes Deleuze's reading of Nietzsche to task for, among other things, undermining the responsibility of human beings for their moral choices. Similar lines of argument are pursued by the editors of this collection in a number of other places.

Hardt, Michael (1993), *Gilles Deleuze: An Apprenticeship in Philosophy*. Minneapolis: University of Minnesota Press. See the chapter, 'Nietzschean Ethics: From

Efficient Power to an Ethics of Affirmation'. Hardt's book, one of the earliest studies of Deleuze in English, includes a now-classic discussion of Deleuze's Nietzsche.

Norman, Judith (2000), 'Nietzsche contra Contra: Difference and Opposition'. *Continental Philosophy Review*, 33, (2), 189–206. This article gives a summary of the important difference between Nietzsche's critique of negation and an oppositional metaphysics as it is argued for in Deleuze's book.

Sinnerbrink, Robert (1997), 'Active Slaves and Reactive Masters? Deleuze's Anti-dialectical Nietzsche'. *Social Semiotics*, 7, (2), 147–60. This article argues that Deleuze's book-length antagonism with Hegel's philosophy of history in *Nietzsche and Philosophy* is undermined by the remnants of a dialectical theory that feeds, on Deleuze's own account, into nihilism.

Other Works Cited

Dosse, François (2010), *Gilles Deleuze and Félix Guattari: Intersecting Lives*, trans. D. Glassman. New York: Columbia University Press.

Chapter 6

Klossowski's Nietzsche

Ashley Woodward

Along with Gilles Deleuze, Pierre Klossowski (1905–2001) was one of the key figures associated with the 'Nietzsche revival' in France in the 1960s and 70s. Klossowski's interest in Nietzsche began in the 1930s. His first writings on Nietzsche were published in Georges Bataille's review *Acéphale*. Klossowski translated Nietzsche's *The Gay Science* and some of his posthumous writings (*Nachlass*), as well as Heidegger's lectures on Nietzsche, into French. His most important and influential contributions to Nietzsche scholarship, however, began with the 1957 essay 'Nietzsche, Polytheism, and Parody', hailed by Maurice Blanchot as one of the most important writings on Nietzsche in French (cited in James, 2007, p. 210). This was followed by a series of papers collected in 1969 in the book *Nietzsche and the Vicious Circle* (Klossowski, 2005). Michel Foucault called this collection '[t]he greatest book of philosophy I have ever read, on a par with Nietzsche himself' (Foucault, 1985, pp. 85–8; cited in Smith, 2005, p. vii).

While Klossowski's reading of Nietzsche has received comparatively little attention in the anglophone world, it is an important source of many of the ideas which were developed by other French philosophers of his generation, and which in the English-speaking world came to be associated with 'poststructuralism' and 'postmodernism'. As such, it deserves greater attention if the French Nietzscheanism of this generation, which sometimes remains baffling, is to be better understood. However, Klossowski's interpretation of Nietzsche is challenging in itself, being often surprising, bizarre, frustrating, and perhaps even frightening.[1] This chapter will introduce Klossowski's Nietzsche by focusing on three main aspects of his interpretation: the relationship between the body and thought, the dissolution of subjectivity in the experience of the eternal return, and the idea of conspiracy in Nietzsche's political thought.

The Semiotic of Impulses

The second chapter of *Nietzsche and the Vicious Circle* is titled 'The Valetudinary States at the Origin of a Semiotic of Impulses'. This chapter gives the most focused treatment of one of Klossowski's central themes, Nietzsche's radical reformulation of the traditional philosophical view on the relationship between thought and the body. Unpacking the title of this chapter will give us an abbreviated understanding of Nietzsche's method, and his new idea of the body–thought relation. 'Valetudinary sates' are the states of health or sickness of the body. With the phrase 'semiotic of impulses', Klossowski refers to the way that, for Nietzsche, thought has its origin in the impulses of the body, but these impulses are distorted or inverted by the time they reach consciousness. In order to understand these impulses, we therefore need a 'semiotic', a method of interpreting signs, which will allow us to trace thoughts back to the bodily impulses from which they originate. According to Klossowski, Nietzsche researched this theory of the body–thought relation by using his own sick body as a kind of experimental laboratory.

As is well known, the most prominent philosophers both ancient and modern (for example, Plato and Descartes) have elevated thought and denigrated the body. Perhaps surprisingly, given the torment to which his own body subjected him, of all philosophers Nietzsche has been one of the most critical of the 'despisers of the body' (see Nietzsche, 1961, pp. 61–3) and one of the most influential in revaluing the body's philosophical significance. He pointedly asks, 'Can one go more dangerously wrong than by despising the body?' (Nietzsche, 2003, p. 244).

Nietzsche's sickness is well-known, though its cause remains a matter of speculation and controversy.[2] The frightening severity of his illness, which plagued him in cyclical bouts throughout most of his adult life, is indicated by the following excerpt from a letter, dated early January 1880, to Doctor O. Eiser:

To dare write a letter, I have to wait four weeks for a tolerable moment – after which I still have to pay for it! . . .

My existence is a *dreadful burden*: I would have rejected it long ago, had I not been making the most instructive experiments in the intellectual and moral domain in just this condition of suffering and almost complete renunciation – this joyous mood, avid for knowledge, raised me to heights where I triumphed over every torture and all despair. On the whole, I am happier now than I have ever been in my life. And yet, continual pain; for many hours of the day, a sensation closely akin to seasickness, a semi-paralysis that makes it difficult to speak, alternating with furious attacks (the last one made me vomit for three days and three nights, I longed for death!). I can't read, rarely write, visit no one, can't listen to music! I keep to myself and take walks in the rarefied air, a diet of eggs and milk. No pain-relieving remedies work. The cold is harmful to me. . . .

My only consolation is my thoughts and perspectives. (quoted in Klossowski, 2005, pp. 15–16)

Perhaps even more striking than Nietzsche's description of his suffering here is his claim to happiness in spite of it, predicated on the 'most instructive experiments' that his condition afforded him.

More than any other interpreter, Klossowski takes Nietzsche's sickness and his own attitude towards it as a key to understanding his philosophy. Nietzsche's illness afforded him access to an unusual and privileged perspective on the body that Klossowski calls *lucid delirium* – a lucid awareness of the impulses of the body, produced when the mind is so overwhelmed by them that it can't carry on its usual, rational functioning. According to Klossowski, Nietzsche exploited his illness for philosophical ends, using it as an opportunity to carry out a kind of phenomenological research on the nature of the body, of thought, and of their relationship. In the periods when his health improved, Nietzsche was then able to translate his reflections into rational thought and express them in written language, and this very process of translation afforded further insight into the body–thought relation. In explaining and developing the theory Nietzsche devised, Klossowski draws on his own, original concepts: *impulses, phantasms, simulacra*, and *the code of everyday signs*.

According to Klossowski, Nietzsche presents an image of the body as composed of heterogenous *impulses*. Klossowski's term 'impulses' refers to various expressions used by Nietzsche, such as 'drives', 'instincts', and 'affects', and has resonances with these terms as used in psychoanalytic theory. Impulses have *intensity* and *tonality*. Intensity is the magnitude or degree of force of an impulse or impulsive state, referring to its rise or fall, its manic or depressive state. Tonality expresses the quality of an impulsive state, its tone, timbre, amplitude, for example, 'aggressiveness, tolerance, intimidation, anguish, the need for solitude . . . the forgetting of oneself', and so forth (Klossowski, 2005, p. 5). Significantly, impulses are not just constitutive of the body, but of all reality; in Klossowski's terms, Nietzsche's will to power is composed of fluctuating impulses in relation with each other. (Nietzsche himself equates the forces of the body with the forces that constitute all reality in BGE 36.)

At its most fundamental level, the body is only the relations of random, fluctuating, heterogenous impulses, in conflict and tension with each other. Klossowski asserts that the impulses which constitute the body are *fortuitous*, meaning that they occur by chance, without rhyme or reason governing them. Following Ian James, we can therefore refer to Klossowski's image of the body as the 'fortuitous body' (James, 2001). Klossowski describes it as follows:

> *The body is a product of chance*, it is nothing but the *locus* where a group of individuated impulses confront each other so as to produce this interval that constitutes a *human life.* (Klossowski, 2005, p. 21)

At this fundamental level of the body, there is *no coherent individuality.* Our sense of self – the 'ego' – is composed of a certain ordering of the impulses under the direction of the impulse which happens to be dominant. There are many impulses within us which all contend with each other for dominance, and beneath the apparent unity of the dominant impulse is a multiplicity of fluctuating impulses. Most of these impulses remain beneath the level of conscious awareness. Moreover, the body as we usually perceive it – as 'organized' according to its parts and their functions (limbs, internal organs, etc.) – is itself a product of particular orderings of the drives, under dominant impulses stabilised through the habits of culture and the values of medical knowledge. (Klossowski's fortuitous body thus bears similarities to Freud's 'infantile body', Lacan's 'fragmentary body', Deleuze and Guattari's 'body without organs', and Lyotard's 'libidinal body'.)

Klossowski then explains how Nietzsche *revalues* the body–thought relation, elevating the body and denigrating conscious thought, in direct opposition to mainstream philosophical tradition. Klossowski makes the claim – which might initially strike the reader as gratuitous and bizarre – that Nietzsche took the side of his nervous system against his own brain. He writes that Nietzsche

> would destroy the person out of a love for the *nervous system* he knew he had been gifted with, and in which he took a certain *pride*. By studying the reactions of his nervous system, he would come to conceive of himself in a *different manner* than he had previously known – and indeed, in a manner that will perhaps never again be known. (Klossowski, 2005, pp. 19–20)

We can understand this claim as follows. Nietzsche revalues the body–thought relation by 'naturalizing' thought as part of the body, then ascribing values to different parts of the body and its powers according to an evolutionary schema: conscious thought is a product of the brain, and is the *most imperfect* part of the human animal because it is that part which has developed latest (see GS 11). Klossowski insists that to understand Nietzsche, we must understand his inversion of the brain/body hierarchy: one organ – the weakest – has come to dominate the organism. While Nietzsche employed this evolutionary argument, his valetudinary states also provided a 'phenomenological' basis for this revaluation, since his own rational mind was often overwhelmed by painful bodily impulses, which he gave his nervous system credit for being able to bare.[3]

Moreover, Nietzsche associates the brain not only with consciousness, rationality, and thought, but with the habitual representations of the world we call 'culture'. Klossowski uses the phrase *the code of everyday signs* to designate everything of this order; it indicates everyday language and the habitual, representational categories the brain uses to structure the world. One of Klossowski's most striking contentions in his reading of Nietzsche is that not only does thought arise from the body (an unsurprising claim today), but that conscious thought *falsifies* the impulses of the body: that is, there is a kind of 'mistranslation' which occurs when bodily impulses pass into conscious thought. Thought *filters and inverts* the impulses of the body. (For Nietzsche's own claims to this effect, see in particular GS 354.) Klossowski describes the process as follows:

> The body wants to make itself understood through the intermediary of a language of signs that is fallaciously deciphered by consciousness. Consciousness itself *constitutes this code of signs* that inverts, falsifies and filters what is expressed through the body.

> Consciousness is itself nothing other than a deciphering of the messages transmitted by the impulses. The deciphering is in itself an inversion of the message, which is now attributed to the individual. (Klossowski, 2005, pp. 20–1)

Why is this translation a falsification? Because in themselves, the impulses of the body are meaningless. Klossowski distinguishes the *intensity* of bodily impulses from the conscious *intention* which underlies and structures meaning. At bottom, fluctuating impulses constitute an 'unintelligible and unexchangable depth', which – despite their immanent, bodily nature – Klossowski sometimes indicates with the term 'soul', drawing on mystical Christian theologians such as Meister Eckhart and Teresa of Avila for whom the soul is unintelligible and incommunicable (Smith, 2005b, p. 9).

It is at this level of the soul that Klossowski also locates his concept of the *phantasm*: phantasms are 'obsessional images' which arise from the relations of impulses, which drive and motivate us, but which in themselves are opaque and inexpressible. The singularity and resistance to categorization of each individual person is given by the fact that everyone has their own unique phantasms (for example, according to Klossowski one of Nietzsche's primary phantasms was the eternal return). Phantasms, opaque in themselves, are made intelligible through 'willed reproductions' which Klossowski calls *simulacra*. Simulacra draw on the code of everyday signs to translate phantasms into forms that can be consciously recognized and understood, but at the expense of an inevitable falsification (see Smith, 2005a, p. x). Klossowski sees Nietzsche's attempts to teach the eternal return through his philosophy as simulacral: he presents the doctrine in a variety of ways (as existential thought, as cosmological principle, etc.), but none of these fully capture the *lived experience* of the eternal return itself.

The upshot of all this is that we have to treat ideas as *signs* of the impulses they originate in and falsify (hence Klossowski's phrase 'semiotic of impulses').[4] With this theory, Nietzsche is able to develop a *bodily* critique of thought and culture. The ideas of a tradition of thought or of a particular thinker may be seen as originating in certain impulses and 'tonalities of the soul'. (For example, science may be seen as driven by the desire for security.) According to Klossowski, Nietzsche thus attempts to develop a mode of doing philosophy *adequate to the body*. There is no 'true' interpretation of impulses, since the impulses themselves have no meaning, and every interpretation will of necessity evince a degree of falsification. However, there are more or less 'authentic' interpretations – authenticity residing, for Klossowski, in the acceptance of the very 'opacity' of our 'selves' as collections of bodily impulses, or more generally, 'adhesion to that which is in becoming' (Klossowski, 2005, p. 67). Although, according to him, Nietzsche sides with the body, we neither can nor should entirely renounce 'the code of everyday signs'. Klossowski writes:

> We cannot renounce language, nor our intentions, nor our willing; but we could evaluate this willing and these intentions in a *different* manner than we have hitherto evaluated them – namely, as subject to the 'law' of the vicious Circle. (Klossowski, 2005, p. 41)

In raising the spectre of the eternal return – the vicious circle – this quotation brings us to a consideration of this second major theme in Klossowski's interpretation of Nietzsche.

The Eternal Return as Vicious Circle

It is common for interpreters of Nietzsche to select one of his ideas as the central theme of all his works, and for Klossowski this central theme is undoubtedly the eternal return. This is indicated in the title of Klossowski's book (*Nietzsche and the Vicious Circle*). But why does Klossowski characterize the eternal return as a 'vicious circle'? Nietzsche himself employs the phrase '*circulus vitiosus deus*' – meaning 'divine vicious circle' – in connection with the eternal return in *Beyond Good and Evil* 56. The term is taken from medieval scholastic philosophy, where it refers to a circular or question-begging argument. Klossowski emphasizes the character of Nietzsche's doctrine as a vicious circle because he interprets it as profoundly paradoxical, on at least three major levels:

1. It is an interpretation of reality which undermines the very notion of a stable and coherent reality.
2. It is a doctrine which undermines it's own status as intelligible and communicable knowledge.
3. It is a lived experience which undermines the identity of the experiencer, and thus the very coherence of 'experience'.

In what follows, we shall see how Klossowski interprets the eternal return as radically destructive of the three themes indicated here, which are central to both philosophy and to everyday experience: reality, knowledge, and the self.

Klossowski suggests that the eternal return may be understood as the willing of every *instant* of existence as *necessary*. In this sense, it may be understood as a response to the problem of *ressentiment*, and an attempt to overcome it. For Nietzsche, *ressentiment* involves a negative judgement against life which poisons the value of life itself. This negative judgement revolves around the view that things should be otherwise than they are, and that what has happened in the past should have happened otherwise than it did. But the fact that we are unable to change what has happened in the past produces in us a resentment against the world's temporal nature:

> The will projects its powerlessness on time, and in this way gives time its *irreversible* character: the will cannot reverse *the flow of time* – the non-willed that time establishes as an accomplished fact. This produces, in the will, the spirit of *revenge* against the unchangeable, and a belief in the *punitive* aspect of existence. (Klossowski, 2005, p. 52)

Nietzsche's response to this problem of resentment against temporality is to affirm everything that has happened and will happen as necessary, as if we had willed it as such (see Z 'Of Old and New Law Tables' 3). However, Klossowski adds a further dimension to this well-known aspect of Nietzsche's thought by suggesting that in the eternal return, the 'non-willed' (i.e. that which happens beyond our control) is willed and re-willed to happen again eternally in such a way that the *'once and for all'* character is removed from events (Klossowski, 2005, p. 52). In this way, the weight is removed from events, including one's own acts (ibid., p. 54), and they cease to be a burden and a cause for *ressentiment* and guilt.

Klossowski asserts that this affirmation of the necessary instant in fact reveals existence as meaningless. In the light of eternal return, existence appears as a series of instants with *no goal* except that of returning to themselves (Klossowski, 2007b, p. 100). This contention may be explained by further elaborating the relation between necessity and the will. Necessity implies the irreversibility of all the past moments of life (one can't change what has already happened). Now, Klossowski brings out the paradox here by pointing out that to will necessity as Zarathustra advocates is to will that which is, in fact, *beyond* will: as he phrases it, in the eternal return the non-willed is re-willed: that is, the affirmation of every instant as necessary includes the acknowledgement that what occurs is beyond our conscious control – what is, *just is*. As Ian James explains, this affirmation of necessity implies that existence is beyond any possibility of subjective determination: that is, existence exceeds human volition or consciousness (James, 2007, p. 210).

Western metaphysics has traditionally ascribed meaning to things by positing origins and ends, and in the affirmation of eternal return, there is no origin or end to existence. Nietzsche proposes that every instant be willed as such, and the significance of affirming *instants* lies in the fact that to impose a temporal structure is to create meaning, to set up a narrative. Thus, anything beyond the instant is subjectively determined as meaningful, and not an affirmation of the necessity of existence in itself, as non-willed. This interpretation of the eternal return – as willing the necessity of every instant – reveals existence as meaningless, as beyond those categories through which we impose meaning on existence, such as linear time, values, and the narrative of history which gives humanity a goal. Commenting on a passage in *The Gay Science* where Nietzsche compares the world to the endless cycle of crashing waves in an ocean, Klossowski writes:

> this glorification of motion for motion's sake destroys the notion of any sort of end of existence and exalts the useless presence of being in the

absence of every end . . . the anguish of an existence without purpose . . .
the *uselessness* of being. (Klossowski, 2007a, p. 11)

Like each breaking wave, every instant is singular and irreducibly different, and cannot be thought in terms of identity or sameness. According
to Klossowski, the effect of the thought of eternal return is the very dissolution of the 'World' and of the 'reality principle' (which determines
some subjective, willed constructs as conforming with objective, non-
willed reality, and others as not doing so). Moreover, in undermining the
notion of a stable and coherent reality we might have a knowledge *of*, the
eternal return undermines the possibility of knowledge itself. Existence
is revealed as a series of singular instants which are in fact ungraspable
by the categories of knowledge, and the eternal return itself becomes an
obscure doctrine insofar as it reveals existence to be obscure and meaningless. For this reason, Klossowski asserts that Nietzsche's attempt to
teach the doctrine of eternal return is an attempt to teach the
unteachable.

Klossowski further seeks to show how the eternal return dissolves *subjectivity* by disrupting the illusion of a stable self-identity. Here he focuses on
the lived experience of the thought of eternal return, which famously
struck Nietzsche like a thunderbolt at Sils-Maria on the shores of Lake
Silvaplana in 1881. Klossowski takes a key inspiration for this interpretation of the eternal return from a few lines from Nietzsche's unpublished
fragments:

*The incessant metamorphosis: in a brief interval of time you must pass through
several individual states* (quoted in Klossowski, 2005, p. 54).

In thinking that everything returns, we remember all the different selves
we have been in the past, and all the different future selves we might be.
Again, Klossowski emphasizes the return of the *different*: we must cycle
through innumerable different selves before we return to the 'same' self
who experiences the revelation of the eternal return. Klossowski writes
that '[t]he revelation of the Eternal Return brings about, as necessity, the
successive realisations of all possible identities' (Klossowski, 2005, p. 45).
The title of Klossowski's paper presented at the 1964 Royaumont colloquium on Nietzsche – 'Forgetting and Anamnesis in the Lived Experience of the Eternal Return' – highlights two significant points of his
interpretation. First, *forgetting* is crucial to establishing identity, because
our present sense of self depends on a select range of experiences and

memories with which we choose to identify. There are elements of our past selves (for example, from when we were 5 years old) which we need to forget in order to maintain a coherent sense of self. Thus, our current sense of identity depends on a forgetting of past selves. The eternal return, however, involves a remembering – an *anamnesis*[5] – of all past selves as 'fortuitous cases' (chance arrangements of impulses). This excessive remembering undoes the illusion of a coherent self-identity by 'overflowing' the self with the memories of multiple, inconsistent selves. Klossowski explains:

> Eternal Return is a necessity that must be willed: only he who I am now can will the necessity of my return and all the events that have led to what I am – insofar as the will here presupposes a subject. Now this subject is no longer able to will itself as it has been up to now, but wills *all* prior possibilities; for by embracing in a single glance the necessity of Return as a universal law, I deactualize my present self in order to will myself in *all the other selves whose entire series must be passed through* so that, in accordance with the circular movement, I once again become *what I am in the moment I discover* the law of the Eternal Return. (Klossowski, 2005, p. 45)

This experience undermines identity, since all selves, including the present one, are revealed as transitory, fortuitous cases: that is, the eternal return makes one aware that our identity changes over time, and that any particular 'self' is simply a fortuitous instance without any constant and unchanging self underlying them all. The sense of self-identity which is both an anchor-point for our everyday experience, and which forms the basis of 'the subject' as foundation for all knowledge in modern philosophy, is revealed as illusory.

A paradox emerges with this notion of eternal return: how can the dissolution of the self, asserted as an experience, *be experienced?* In the philosophical tradition, and in Kant's metaphysics of experience in particular, the self-identity and coherence of the subject is a necessary condition for the possibility of all experience (for Kant, the 'transcendental subject of apperception' is a formal unity which underlies all experiences, and which makes them *my* experiences). Thus, the eternal return appears to be an experience without an 'experiencer'. Klossowski will not resolve this paradox, and this is an important reason why he characterizes the eternal return as a vicious circle.

Culture and Conspiracy

A further major contribution that Klossowski makes to French Nietzscheanism concerns the interpretation of Nietzsche's political thought. Many French thinkers associated with poststructuralism moved away from mainstream political philosophy and party politics (Marxism and the Communist Party in particular) to develop new conceptions of the political. Such new conceptions are presaged in Klossowski's treatment of Nietzsche's politics. According to Klossowski, '[t]here can be no question, in Nietzsche's thinking [. . .] of instituting a political regime in any traditional sense' (Klossowski, 2009, p. 34). Instead, 'the political' in Nietzsche is to be understood through his critique of culture and his notion of 'conspiracy' (*complot*). These themes are developed primarily in Chapters 1 ('The Combat against Culture') and 6 ('The Vicious Circle as a Selective Doctrine') of *Vicious Circle*, and in the paper 'Circulus Vitiosus'.

For Klossowski, Nietzsche's political thought revolves around the opposition of two powers: 'the *leveling* power of gregarious thought and the *erectile* power of particular cases' (Klossowski, 2005, p. 5). In terminology more familiar to readers of Nietzsche, these two powers are the slave morality of the herd, and the noble or master morality of exceptional individuals. As is common in political philosophy, Nietzsche presents an image of an ideal society (however fragmentarily this image is sketched), an interpretation of contemporary society which criticizes it for radically deviating from ideal conditions, and a prescription for a kind of political action which will enable the ideal state of society to be attained. According to Klosssowski's interpretation, for Nietzsche the ideal state of society is one of inequality, elitism, and exploitation. Klossowski emphasizes that Nietzsche places little value on humanity itself *en masse*; the existence of humanity is only justified by the production of remarkable individuals who create and legislate values and the meaning of life for the herd. Ideally, the mass of humanity should play the role of raw material for experiments which will produce *Übermenschen*, and all their labouring power should be directed towards this goal, under the direction of noble masters.

According to Klossowski, there are two concepts of culture in Nietzsche. A *lived culture* can only be based on inequality and struggle, and never on a gregarious foundation. This form of culture is associated with Nietzsche's early conception of the Greek State and agonism or contest in Greek society, as well as the ideal of exploitation of the weak by the strong. On the other hand, the term 'culture' more often indicates the current social and ideological conditions Nietzsche pits himself against. In this negative sense, culture in general signifies the *ideological disavowal of the external constraints* a society necessarily exerts (Klossowski, 2005, p. 6). Specifically, however, culture in the contemporary world is the result of a complex alliance between Christianity and morality (which Nietzsche sometimes calls the 'Christian-moral interpretation' of life). Contemporary culture is the result of the 'slave revolt in morals', through which noble types are dominated by Christian morality (which of course for Nietzsche is a slave morality).

Nietzsche sees Christian morality perpetuated in social, political, and ideological forms which are not overtly Christian, including Darwinian science and industrial capitalism. Nietzsche criticizes the Darwinian theory of natural selection for failing to distinguish human beings from the rest of the animal kingdom. The distinctive feature of human beings which Darwin ignores is consciousness, which according to Nietzsche plays an important part in the process of selection. Consciousness and the culture to which it gives rise allow the selection of the *weak* over the strong in the case of human beings. By ignoring this, Darwin's theory serves the ends of Christian morality by covering over the fact that the weak dominate the strong, and present the current slave culture as though it were in fact the product of the 'survival of the fittest'.

Moreover, Nietzsche sees the general aims of science, and of industrialized economic planning in the capitalist system, as further contributing to the 'levelling' process instituted by Christian-moral culture. Both science and capitalist economics aim to preserve the human species as a whole at an *average* level. In a fragment which Klossowski sees as particularly prescient, Nietzsche identifies global economic planning as a kind of 'supergregariousness' which will have unprecedented levelling effects on humanity (Klossowski, 2005, p. 130). In addition to simply preserving the species as a whole, planetary economic management will reduce the meaning and value of human life, because then

> mankind will be able to find its best meaning as a machine in the service of this economy – as a tremendous clockwork, composed of ever smaller, ever more subtly 'adapted' gears; as an ever-growing superfluity of all dominating and commanding elements; as a whole of tremendous force, whose individual factors represent *minimal forces, minimal values.* (Klossowski, 2005, p. 123)

Klossowski identifies this complex of cultural factors which propagate the levelling effects of Christian morality as a kind of 'external conspiracy'.

Nietzsche's combat against culture then involves an alternative conspiracy, which Klossowski elaborates under the sign of the vicious circle. This counter-conspiracy will be composed of scholars, artists, and experimenters who will work in a clandestine fashion to harness the forces of the masses for the production of *Übermenschen*. Nietzsche proposes the eternal return as a principle of selection in opposition to the gregarious selection of the weak over the strong operating in the external conspiracy: the conspiracy of the vicious circle will be composed of those individuals who have been able to understand and incorporate the idea of the eternal return. The eternal return thus has a significant political meaning in so far as it acts as the primary differentiator between noble and slave types, between strong and weak. Moreover, the lived experience of the eternal return acts as an indicator for precisely what is singular and unexchangeable, and cannot be incorporated into the external conspiracy of gregarious levelling and absolute exchangeability in efficient economic regulation. Klossowski summarizes many of the above themes as follows:

> The selection expounded by Darwin coincides perfectly with bourgeois morality. This then is the external conspiracy – the conspiracy of the science and morality of institutions – against which Nietzsche projects the conspiracy of the Vicious Circle. This sign will henceforth inspire an experimental action – a kind of counter-selection that follows from the very nature of the interpretation of the Eternal Return, that is to say, from the *lived experience* of a singular and privileged case. The *unintelligible depth* of experience is thus in itself the challenge thrown up against the gregarious propensities, as they are expressed in everything that is communicable, comprehensible and exchangeable. (Klossowski, 2005, pp. 128–9)

Nietzsche seems to see the conspiracy of the vicious circle as a transitional stage, on the way to attaining the ideal state of society in which strong individuals will overtly take the reins of humanity and exploit the masses for their own ends. However, this idea of a conspiracy composed of singular individuals also offers an interesting conception of community which may be seen as an alternative to the traditional 'organic and homogenous' one. Gilles Deleuze draws out this possibility most clearly:

> What we call a society is a community of regularities, or more precisely, a certain selective process which retains select singularities and regularises

them. . . . But a *conspiracy* – this would be a community of singularities of
another type, which would not be regularised, but which would enter into
new connections, and in this sense, would be revolutionary. . . . the problem which we now inherit from [Klossowski] is to know if it is possible to
conceive of links between singularities which would have as their criteria
the eternal return, insofar as it implicates the loss of identity, not just for
individuals but also for societies and groups. (Deleuze in Klossowski,
2009, pp. 46–7)

While the French Nietzscheans influenced by Klossowski's interpretation
remained broadly Leftist in their political outlooks, and certainly never
would have endorsed Nietzsche's views on inequality and exploitation, we
can see them as influenced by the ideas of cultural critique and conspiracy we find here. The idea of conspiracy resonates with the 'micropolitics'
of specific struggles and interventions advocated by various poststructur-
alist thinkers in opposition to the 'macropolitics' of political parties and
government institutions. Moreover, as Joseph D. Kuzma notes (in
Klossowski, 2009, p. 32), the idea of conspiracy as Klossowski outlines it in
his Nietzsche interpretation anticipates the reworkings of the idea of community in later French works, such as Jean-Luc Nancy's *The Inoperable Community* (Nancy, 1991) and Maurice Blanchot's *The Unavowable Community*
(Blanchot, 1988).

Conclusion

What, then, are we to make of Klossowski's Nietzsche? In his introduction
to *Vicious Circle*, Klossowski himself writes that 'we have written a *false* study'
(Klossowski, 2005, p. xiii). There are at least two ways in which this admission might be understood, one which may tempt us to entirely dismiss
Klossowski's Nietzsche, and one which will enable us to appreciate it as
richly productive. First, Klosssowski's interpretation may well be questioned
as reliable Nietzsche scholarship, not only because of its bold creativity of
interpretation, but because he draws almost exclusively on Nietzsche's late
unpublished notebooks, which many Nietzsche scholars are unwilling to
admit into the class of texts truly representative of his thought. Second,
however, if we follow the trajectory of Klossowski's interpretation through
to the end, we may find ourselves with the possibility of attaching different
values to 'truth' and 'falsity', and with a different view of the value of pedan-
tic scholarly concerns.

For Klossowski, Nietzsche interrogates the *conditions* for thinking and philosophizing like no thinker before or since (Ansell Pearson, 2000, p. 250). He finds that the condition for intelligible and communicable thought is the unintelligible, incommunicable soul or body; the condition for identity is difference; the condition for reality is unreality; and the condition for truth is falsity. Thus, for Klossowski's Nietzsche the conditions for the most evident things do not at all resemble the things themselves: evident things are in fact *inverted products* of their conditions. Thus, from this perspective any study of Nietzsche's singular thought will be false because of the inescapable 'falseness' conditioning intelligibility itself. *Nietzsche and the Vicious Circle* is thus one more simulacrum of Nietzsche's phantasms. If we choose to follow Klossowski's interpretation of Nietzsche, a new criterion for assessing the text is presented to us, beyond truth and falsity: is it authentic, or inauthentic, with respect to the conditions of thought itself? But such choices remain for every reader to make for herself or himself.

Notes

Warm thanks are due to Daniel W. Smith, Ian James, and Sherah Bloor for their helpful comments on this chapter.

[1] Keith Ansell Pearson writes that *Nietzsche and the Vicious Circle* 'may well be the most extraordinary text on Nietzsche ever composed, as well as one of the most disconcerting and disquieting. . . . It is not a book that one can readily recommend as an essential text that anyone concerned with Nietzsche must read, simply because it is a quite terrifying reading of Nietzsche. At the end of it the reader, or should I say this reader, experiences utter vertigo' (Ansell Pearson, 2000, p. 248).

[2] Long accepted by most Nietzsche scholars to be syphilitic in origin, this view of Nietzsche's ill health has in recent years been convincingly refuted. See, for example, Sax (2003). Thanks to David Rathbone for bringing literature on this topic to my attention.

[3] In a letter to his mother, sent from Sils-Maria and dated mid-July 1881, Nietzsche writes: 'My nervous system is splendid in view of the immense work it has to do; it is quite sensitive but very strong, a source of astonishment to me' (quoted in Klossowski, 2005, p. 17).

[4] As Ian James notes, however, these signs must note be understood in the Saussurean sense as produced by structural, differential relations. Rather, signs for Klossowski are the translation of impulses; the generation of sense out of chaos (James, 2007, p. 214 note 15).

[5] In Plato's writings, the term 'anamnesis' designates the remembrance of knowledge gained in a previous existence.

Bibliography and Guide to Further Study

Klossowski's Nietzsche Interpretation

Klossowski, Pierre (1937), 'La création du monde'. *Acéphale* 2. An essay in a special issue – on the topic of 'Nietzsche and the Fascists' – of a journal edited by Georges Bataille. Untranslated.

— (1980), 'Deux interprétations récentes de Nietzsche', in *Acéphale: Religion, sociologie, philosophie, 1936–1939*. Paris: Jean-Michel Place. Contains Klossowski's 1939 review of Karl Löwith's book on Nietzsche. Untranslated.

— (1985), 'Nietzsche's Experience of the Eternal Return', trans. Allan Weiss, in David B. Allison (ed.), *The New Nietzsche*, 2nd edn. Cambridge, MA: MIT Press. Paper presented at the 1964 Royaumont Colloquium on Nietzsche and reworked as Chapter 3 of *Nietzsche and the Vicious Circle*.

— (2005), *Nietzsche and the Vicious Circle*, trans. Daniel W. Smith. London and New York: Continuum [1969]. Klossowski's major work on Nietzsche.

— (2007a), 'On Some Fundamental Themes of Nietzsche's *Gaya Scienza*', trans. Russell Ford, in Klossowski, *Such a Deathly Desire*. Albany: SUNY. An introduction to Klossowski's translation of Nietzsche's *The Gay Science*, 1954. Contains an early discussion of the paradoxical nature of the eternal return and its connection to the dissolution of subjectivity, linked with the problem of historicism in Nietzsche's second *Untimely Meditation*.

— (2007b), 'Nietzsche, Polytheism and Parody', trans. R. Ford, in id., *Such a Deathly Desire*. The seminal text of Klossowski's Nietzsche interpretation. Originally presented as a lecture to the Collège de Philosophie in 1957, and highly influential in renewing French Nietzsche interpretation.

— (2009), 'Circulus Vitiosus', trans. Joseph D. Kuzma. *The Agonist* 2, (1), 31–47. Full text available online: www.nietzschecircle.com/AGONIST/2009_03/translation-KlossowskiKuzma.html. Accessed 10/5/2011. Paper presented at the 1972 Cerisy-la-Salle Colloquium on Nietzsche. The English translation includes a brief but insightful preface by the translator, and a transcription of the following discussion.

Klossowski's Translations of, and on, Nietzsche

Heidegger, Martin (1971), *Nietzsche*, 2 vols. Paris: Gallimard.

Nietzsche, Friedrich (1954), *Le gai savoir et fragments posthumes, 1880–1882*. Paris: Club français du Livre.

— (1976), *Fragments posthumes, 1887–1888*. Paris: Gallimard.

Works on Klossowski's Nietzsche

Ansell Pearson, Keith (2000), 'A Superior Existentialism'. *Pli* 9, 248–56. Full text available online: http://www.warwick.ac.uk/philosophy/pli_journal/pdfs/

ansell_pearson_2_pli_9.pdf. Accessed 10/5/2011. A review of the English translation of *Nietzsche and the Vicious Circle*.

Faulkner, Joanne (2007), 'The Vision, the Riddle, and the Vicious Circle: Pierre Klossowski Reading Nietzsche's Sick Body through Sade's Perversion'. *Textual Practice*, 21, (1), 43–69.

Ford, Russell (2005), 'Tragedy, Comedy, Parody: From Hegel to Klossowski'. *Diacritics*, 35, (1), 22–46.

James, Ian (2000), *Pierre Klossowski: The Persistence of a Name*. Oxford: Legenda. Part II: 'Nietzsche'. The only book in English devoted solely to Klossowski. A clear, informative introduction.

— (2001), 'Klossowski, Nietzsche, and the Fortuitous Body'. *Romance Studies*, 19, (1), 59–70.

— (2007), 'Klossowski and Deleuze: Parody, Simulacrum and the Power of Return', in Barbara Bolt, Felicity Colman, Graham Jones, Ashley Woodward (eds), *Sensorium: Aesthetics, Art, Life*. Newcastle: Cambridge Scholars Publishing.

— (2009), 'Pierre Klossowski', in Graham Jones and Jon Roffe (eds), *Deleuze's Philosophical Lineage*. Edinburgh: Edinburgh University Press. This chapter charts Klossowski's influence on Deleuze, and includes significant discussion of Klossowski's Nietzsche interpretation.

James, Ian and Russell Ford (eds) (2005), *Whispers of the Flesh: Essays in Memory of Pierre Klossowski*. Baltimore: Johns Hopkins University Press. This is a book version of the journal *Diacritics* 35, (1), (2005), a special issue on Klossowski, containing several essays on Klossowski's Nietzsche listed separately in this bibliography.

Kaufman, Eleanor (2001), *The Delirium of Praise: Bataille, Blanchot, Deleuze, Foucault, Klossowski*. Baltimore: Johns Hopkins University Press. Chapter 5: 'Bodies, sickness, and disjunction : Deleuze, Klossowski, and the revocation of Nietzsche'.

Krell, David Farrell (1988), 'Consultations with the Paternal Shadow: Gasché, Derrida, and Klossowski on *Ecce Homo*', in David Farrell Krell and David Wood (eds), *Exceedingly Nietzsche: Aspects of Contemporary Nietzsche Interpretation*. London: Routledge.

Lingis, Alphonso (2005), 'Impulsive Forces In and Against Words'. *Diacritics*, 35, (1), 60–70.

Smith, Daniel W. (2005a), 'Translator's Preface', in Klossowski, 2005.

— (2005b), 'Klossowski's Reading of Nietzsche: Impulses, Phantasms, Simulacra, Stereotypes'. *Diacritics*, 35, (1), 8–21. A very useful guide to Klossowski's original philosophical concepts that inform his reading of Nietzsche.

Smith, Douglas (1996), *Transvaluations: Nietzsche in France 1872–1972*. Oxford: Clarendon Press. Chapter 5: 'Willful Acts, Diminishing Returns: Deleuze and Klossowski'.

Nietzsche Translations Cited

Nietzsche, Friedrich (1961), *Thus Spoke Zarathustra*, trans. R.J. Hollingdale. London: Penguin.

Nietzsche, Friedrich (2003), *Writings from the Late Notebooks*, ed. Rüdiger Bittner, trans. Kate Sturge (Cambridge: Cambridge University Press).

Other Works Cited

Blanchot, Maurice (1988), *The Unavowable Community*, trans. Pierre Joris. Barrytown, NY: Station Hill Press.

Foucault, Michel (1985), *Cachiers pour un temps*. Paris: Centre Georges Pompidou.

Nancy, Jean-Luc (1991), *The Inoperative Community*. Minneapolis: University of Minnesota Press.

Sax, Leonard (2003), 'What was the Cause of Nietzsche's Dementia?'. *Journal of Medical Biography* 11, 47–54.

Chapter 7

Müller-Lauter's Nietzsche

Ciano Aydin

Wolfgang Müller-Lauter, the author of probably one of the most important books on Nietzsche written in the last half-century – if not *the* most
important – died on 9 August 2001 from the effects of a brain tumor. His
book *Nietzsche: His Philosophy of Contradictions and the Contradictions of His
Philosophy* (1999a) and his many articles have been of crucial importance
for international Nietzsche research. These articles, which appeared over
the course of more than three decades, were compiled by him in three
impressive volumes two years before his death (1999c; 1999d; 1999e).
Before I elaborate on those books, I will give a short summary of his career,
mostly on the basis of the outline of his career that he himself gives in the
preface of his last book (1999e).

Müller-Lauter writes in that preface that he arrived quite late, via different detours, at Nietzsche's philosophy. That was partly due to the political
climate that prevailed in the years before and after World War II in East
Germany – Müller-Lauter was born in 1924 in Weimar. In that period
Nietzsche was considered to be the philosopher of fascism. Another reason
that he gives for his rather late intensive acquaintance with Nietzsche's philosophy was his need for conceptual clarity, which he found for a long time
mostly in Kant's writings. For Müller-Lauter, Nietzsche did not systematically elaborate his basic notions to a sufficient degree. (There are also in
our time, although their number is decreasing, academics who use these
two arguments against Nietzsche's philosophy and its worth.)

The reason that he ultimately embraced Nietzsche's philosophy had
partly to do with the fact that after World War II the intellectual life in
Germany slowly (in East Germany even more slowly) began to explore new
paths, partly under influence of Jean-Paul Sartre's 'philosophy of freedom'.
Via Sartre's *Being and Nothingness*, Müller-Lauter discovered in the fifties
Martin Heidegger's *Being and Time*. His investigation of that work resulted

in a 1960 dissertation entitled *Möglichkeit und Wirklichkeit bei Martin Heidegger* (*Possibility and Reality in Martin Heidegger*).

After his dissertation, Müller-Lauter intensively occupied himself with the late Heidegger (the Heidegger after the so-called '*Kehre*'), mostly in the context of the problem of historical relativism. In 1962 he published the article 'Konsequenzen des Historismus in der Philosophie der Gegenwart' ('Consequences of Historicism in Contemporary Philosophy').[1] At that point, he still did not take Nietzsche seriously enough to give him a voice within that framework. Müller-Lauter considered Nietzsche's philosophy important only as far as it provided a pathway to contemporary thinking. Nineteen-sixty-two is also the year that Müller-Lauter became full professor at the *Kirchliche Hochschule* in Berlin. Because he developed a special interest in the problem of nihilism, he announced for the winter semester of 1962/63 a course entitled: *Nietzsche und die Folgen. Zur Problematik des Nihilismus* (*Nietzsche and the Effects. Towards the Problem of Nihilism*). His objective was to penetrate into the nihilism of the twentieth century via Nietzsche.

The run-up to make the jump from Nietzsche's philosophy to the thinking of the post-modern era proved to be too short. Müller-Lauter got stuck in the elaboration of Nietzsche's position because he discovered for the first time the special character of the dimensions of multiplicity and struggle in Nietzsche's philosophy. I quote what Müller-Lauter says about this, also because this insight can be considered revolutionary within Nietzsche research: 'Foremost, one should not, I recognized, attach Nietzsche's thinking to the concepts that he uses. One should rather try to understand his ideas within their context – and in relation to other relevant contexts'. And in a footnote, he adds to this: 'The meaning of concepts in Nietzsche is subject to change dependent on certain circumstances. One should try to relate many texts to one another without trusting him on his word' (1999e, p. vii).[2] This recognition of the contextual dependency of the meaning of Nietzsche's concepts has, after a long and intensive investigation, lead to a more adequate approach to his basic notions, especially to his notion of the will to power. This recognition is represented in Müller-Lauter's earlier-mentioned Nietzsche book from 1971. The importance of this book for Nietzsche research cannot be stressed enough. In this light, it is very surprising that this book had to wait until 1999 for an English translation, especially if we also take into consideration that in the English-speaking part of the world few master the German language (it is even common to read Nietzsche's writings in translation).

Müller-Lauter's book is, in the first place, of such a great importance because it provides a convincing criticism of Heidegger's interpretation of

Nietzsche's thesis of the will to power. Heidegger understands the will to power as a metaphysical unity. This starting point determines his evaluation of Nietzsche's entire philosophy. Müller-Lauter shows that Nietzsche's notion of the will to power is not an *ens metaphysicum*, but rather refers to an irreducible multiplicity of partly struggling and partly cooperating 'wills to power'. These pluralities do not consist of indivisible atoms, monads, or other types of unities, but of ever more 'pluralities' (hence 'irreducible'). Every form of unity is being disclosed as a synthetic, fictionalized, or created unity, which presupposes multiplicity. Multiplicity and struggle constitute every form of reality. An unfortunate side effect of Müller-Lauter's criticism of Heidegger is that some readers not only take it as an important and fruitful *counter force* against Heidegger's interpretation but also understand it as a complete rejection or even obliteration of Heidegger's interpretation, despite the fact that Müller-Lauter always stressed the great value of Heidegger's Nietzsche books.

Besides the vital importance of its critique of Heidegger, there is also another reason why Müller-Lauter's book is of so much value: it made room for many other, diverse Nietzsche interpretations. His account of the meaning and worth of the multiplicity and struggle in Nietzsche's philosophy prompted many authors not only to come up with a different and better Nietzsche interpretation but also to elaborate further on themes that Nietzsche introduced. Furthermore, Müller-Lauter's insight that we should not take Nietzsche on his 'word' but should understand his views within the particular context in which they are used has greatly contributed to a more adequate reading of Nietzsche's texts. Many presumed irregularities in Nietzsche's philosophy often seem to be the result of the equation of concept with word.

After his book from 1971, Müller-Lauter published a great number of articles, mostly on Nietzsche and Heidegger's Nietzsche interpretation.[3]

Becoming and Will to Power

The central theme of the first volume of *Nietzsche-Interpretationen*, which consists of six articles, is Nietzsche's attack on all traditional metaphysical conceptions and his attempt, as a result, to do justice to the 'one and only world of becoming and decay'. The articles discuss, on the one hand, the different ways that becoming is spurred by the wills to power and, on the other hand, they try to explain why the explication (of Heidegger) of the will to power as a metaphysical principle is untenable. These two aspects (the recognition of the multiplicity and struggle in Nietzsche's philosophy and the criticism of Heidegger's Nietzsche interpretation, both of which relate to one another) form the *leitmotiv* in Müller-Lauter's entire work. A third important characteristic of his Nietzsche interpretation is, as we will see, his attention to Nietzsche's scientific reading and its influence on his (naturalistic) thinking.

The first article, 'Das Problem des Gegensatzes in der Philosophie Nietzsches' ('The Problem of Opposition in Nietzsche's Philosophy', 1999c, pp. 1–25), can be seen as a preparatory outline of the thesis that the will to power should not be conceived of as a metaphysical account of the essence of the world, and forms the onset for Müller-Lauter's Nietzsche book. This article tries to reveal the structure and nature of the oppositional line of thought in Nietzsche's work. Müller-Lauter shows that recognition of the different levels of oppositional imagery in Nietzsche's philosophy – on the level of logic and language, and on the level of power relations – and of the way concepts like 'unity', 'thing', 'subject', and 'will' are assessed in that context shed more light on the way Nietzsche tries to escape the metaphysical-dualist account of reality.

In the second article, 'Nietzsches Lehre vom Willen zur Macht' (1999c, pp. 25–97, translated as 'Nietzsche's Teaching of Will to Power', Müller-Lauter, 1992/3b), the special, a-metaphysical character of Nietzsche's ground principle is extensively elaborated. Müller-Lauter tries to show here that the will to power is not something that is the foundation of the world, that produces life, or that manifests itself as humanity. Rather world, life, and human beings *are* will to power (1999c, p. 44f.).[4] Müller-Lauter elaborates this view by showing that the will to power is not a real unity but rather is only a 'unity' as organization and ensemble of power quanta. What can be characterized as 'essence' or 'ground' is dependent on the relations between the different power quanta. A power quantum is only able to maintain its mastery over what it wants to dominate if it employs continuously different strategies. This is because not only what the power quantum wants to dominate changes continuously, but also because the power quantum's own organization, and with that its perspective, changes continuously. Qualifying something – for example, a subject, a thing, or an atom – as a 'unity', always involves simplification and fabrication, which presupposes an irreducible multiplicity. One never reaches a ground: an entity does not have an essence that permanently fixes its identity.

Müller-Lauter's view of the notion of the will to power was already outlined in his Nietzsche book. In this article he elaborates and sharpens the arguments that he had provided for his view by critically discussing different reactions to his interpretation of the will to power.[5]

Müller-Lauter also defends an interesting view regarding the problem of Nietzsche's unpublished notes and the related status of the book *The Will to Power*, which was published by Peter Gast and Elisabeth Förster-Nietzsche. This problem is still relevant today. He argues that there is much to say in favour of Heidegger's view that Nietzsche's published work is 'always foreground', and that his real philosophy has 'remained in the back as unpublished notes' (ibid., p. 30). Müller-Lauter's evaluation of Nietzsche's unpublished work, however, is more subtle than Heidegger's view. Which texts should receive more weight, the published or unpublished, depends, according to him, on the theme that is taken into consideration, and has to be judged, therefore, case by case. It is remarkable, though, that Müller-Lauter does not take notice of the discrepancies that often can be found between published and unpublished texts.

The third article, 'Der Organismus als innerer Kampf. Der Einfluß von Wilhelm Roux auf Friedrich Nietzsche' (ibid., pp. 97–141; translated as 'The Organism as Inner Struggle: Wilhelm Roux's Influence on Nietzsche' in Müller-Lauter, 1999a), has been (and still is) of great importance in Nietzsche research because it provides great insight into Nietzsche's naturalism in general, his concept of organism, and, in particular, the relation of his concept of organism to his notion of the will to power. Nietzsche elaborates the significance of the will to power within the organic through a critical integration of notions from the natural sciences of his time, such as 'self-regulation', life-drive', power discharge', and 'abundance'. Nietzsche criticizes, in the footsteps of the anatomist Wilhelm Roux,[6] Darwin's overestimation of the influence of external circumstances on the development of organs and organisms. He adopts Roux's thesis that an organism is above all determined by the internal struggle (for food, space, etc.) of its parts, and defends the primacy of active forces within natural processes (from a protoplasm to the complex organization of the human body). Characteristic for Nietzsche is that he immediately applies the newest scientific findings to aspects of human life (ibid., p. 109). He justifies this approach by rejecting the view that there is a categorical distinction between the human being and other 'lower' organisms.

Nietzsche does not, however, completely endorse Roux's mechanistic interpretation of the processes in nature. First of all, he considers all interpretations, including the mechanistic interpretation, to be metaphorical; all mechanistic laws are human constructions and do not refer to a certain intrinsic nature of things as such (ibid., p. 103–9, 117). This, however, does not mean that no differences can be made. Nietzsche prefers, as a hypothesis, a mechanistic interpretation over a teleological one because it presupposes fewer assumptions. Nevertheless, he considers the mechanistic interpretation to be 'stupid' because it does not take the realm of 'the mental' into account. In addition, he believes that Roux's mechanistic interpretation still contains various teleological presuppositions. He tries to get rid of both mechanistic and teleological presuppositions by understanding self-regulation from the perspective of domination and control (ibid., p. 118f.). Nietzsche interprets all processes of nature as a struggle between wills to power. He conceives every type of organization primarily in terms of the strength and persistence of internal power constellations. Even the laws of nature are for Nietzsche ultimately 'formulas' for power relations (ibid., p. 123). All reality, including the organic, is constituted by struggle. As a consequence, every possible metaphysical principle, including the idea of pre-given, eternal laws of nature, is problematized. This is a crucial aspect of Müller-Lauter's Nietzsche interpretation. In addition, Müller-Lauter shows how Nietzsche uses contemporary scientific findings to confirm his view that life is primarily characterized by internal struggle, which is another important feature of his Nietzsche interpretation.

The processes of the 'will to power' not only constitute natural but also cultural phenomena. In the fourth article, 'Über Stolz und Eitelkeit bei Kant, Schopenhauer und Nietzsche' ('On Pride and Vanity in Kant, Schopenhauer and Nietzsche', ibid., pp. 141–73), Müller-Lauter explains how, in a critique of Kant and Schopenhauer, Nietzsche's reinterpretation (*Umdeutenung*) of the phenomena of pride and vanity result in an alternative view of what is an 'ideal' person and a healthy community. The notions of power and struggle also play a crucial role in this context. Nietzsche characterizes modern individualism as a quest for equality. The vanity of the individualist cannot bear essential dissimilarity. According to Nietzsche, if the individual comes to recognize its true motive (will to power), it will realize that striving for equal rights cannot be a goal as such. Against modern individualism, Nietzsche postulates his idea of nobility (*Vornehmheit*), by virtue of which, according to him, the individual can become an authentic person. For Nietzsche, an authentic, genuine person is always somebody who thinks and lives outside the sphere of morality (*aussermoralisch*). *It is the human being that has detached himself or herself from the herd. Pride is always accompanied by seclusion* (ibid., p. 169). Only the great and solitary humans can build the foundation for 'aristocratic societies'.

Müller-Lauter is able to shed further light on the 'ideals' and 'moralities' that are presupposed in the different notions of what 'a (genuine) person' is by discussing Nietzsche's interpretation of vanity and pride in a confrontation with Kant's and Schopenhauer's views of these notions. Kant's desire for 'rest and certainty', which could be realized within a republic (ibid., p. 158), results in a different notion of personhood than that of Nietzsche, who endorses an aristocratic society of noble humans who try to excel in a permanent struggle with one another. In this instance, Müller-Lauter's Nietzsche interpretation is characterized not only by the perspective of struggle but also by his sophisticated elaboration of it. Müller-Lauter warns against a simplistic interpretation of the difference between, on the one hand, the noble, solitary type and, on the other hand, the herd type that is being produced in 'individualist' societies. This relation should, first of all, not be understood in terms of slaves and masters. Nietzsche emphasizes that the solitary type is vulnerable because it does not possess the defence instincts and 'certainties' of the herd. It ought to be protected against the brutal majority. Therefore, Nietzsche sometimes advocates that both types ought to live separately (ibid., p. 170f.).

There is also another, possibly more important reason for understanding the relation between the solitary type and the herd type in a more nuanced way: this opposition is not simply 'positive-negative'. Nietzsche, Müller-Lauter explains, does not interpret the herd type in exclusively negative terms. There are various passages in which Nietzsche argues that both the solitary type and the herd type are necessary because their antagonism is necessary. Nietzsche even says that the solitary type can, under certain conditions, evolve the easiest in a democratic society (ibid., p. 171).[7] In this context Müller-Lauter states: 'the person goes against the herd uniformity, although it is a product of it' (ibid., p. 172).

This explanation, however, does not imply that the question of how the solitary person could be realized is an easy question. In two footnotes (ibid., p. 171f.) Müller-Lauter indicates why this question poses great difficulties for Nietzsche. If we pick up Müller-Lauter's hints and try to elaborate his line of thought further, then it becomes clear that this problem is the result of the special character of Nietzsche's concept of *opposition (gegen)*. That notion indicates foremost a certain kind of detachment. The noble, solitary person is somebody who detaches himself from the morality of egalitarianism. Where that detachment will lead, what the goal of that detachment (the positive notion of detachment) is remains necessarily undetermined because otherwise it would acquire a teleological character, and, as a consequence, would be for Nietzsche a fictitious detachment. Recognizing this asymmetrical character of Nietzsche's notion of *gegen* could shed more light on the paradoxical character of the development of the solitary type out of the herd type.[8]

In the fifth article, 'Über das Werden, das Urteilen, das Ja-sagen' ('On Becoming, Judging, Yes-saying, ibid., pp. 173–329),[9] Müller-Lauter takes as a starting point for his interpretation Nietzsche's 'experience' of the decay of authorities and traditional values in the modern era. Nietzsche radicalizes the assumption of the 'liquefaction of all concepts, types, and kinds' (second *Untimely Meditation*), which are validated by the scientific views of the nineteenth century. Nietzsche goes so far as to declare this idea of liquefaction (*Verflüssigung*) a fundamental principle: 'everything is flowing' (ibid., p. 181f.). According to Nietzsche, becoming is primordial, but we cannot live without the fiction of being. Müller-Lauter elaborates this view in the first part of his article by investigating the status of our judgements and value assessments, which constitute the fiction of being. Nietzsche approaches the question of judgement from an evolutionary-historical perspective and traces it back to the pre-logical needs of the earliest living beings. Our judgements are being justified by a belief that is based on our (incorporated) value assessments. These value assessments in the end are generated by an 'initial' activity of striving for power (ibid., p. 199f.). This value assessment of the will to power is, in the second part of the article, characterized as a yes-saying. Müller-Lauter then unfolds the different stages of this yes-saying. The yes-saying process begins with a pre-conscious yes-saying, which gradually becomes manifest and leads to an all-encompassing yes-saying to life that stands against all forms of life denial. Nietzsche's philosophy of yes-saying finds its completion in the belief of the eternal recurrence of the same, which is expressed in its ultimate form as the Dionysian Yes (ibid., p. 248f.).

A great merit of Müller-Lauter in this context is that he shows that Nietzsche's genealogical deduction of our judgements and value assessments is not only much more stratified, but at the same time more coherent than Nietzsche's interpreters often recognize. The first part of Müller-Lauter's article contains microscopic analyses of the different stages of judgement in human development according to Nietzsche. These analyses provide solutions for many incoherencies that are often ascribed to Nietzsche. At the same time, Müller-Lauter knows how to place his meticulous findings in a greater framework, which greatly contributes to a better understanding of the different objectives (in Nietzsche's philosophy there is never only one objective) of Nietzsche's naturalist perspective (for example his critique of transcendent explanations of the human being by historicizing its nature). This results in a less fragmented Nietzsche.

The last article of this volume, 'Der Wille zur Macht als Buch der "Krisis" philosophischer Nietzsche-interpretation' ('The Will to Power as a Book of

"Crisis" of Philosophical Nietzsche Interpretation', ibid., pp. 329–75), discusses the impact of the book *The Will to Power* on the most influential German Nietzsche interpretations (Baeumler, Heidegger, Jaspers, Löwith, Schlechta, and Fink). Müller-Lauter shows how the orientation on Nietzsche's so-called *magnum opus* has continuously obstructed and frustrated an adequate investigation of Nietzsche's notion of the will to power. This is due especially to the fact that in the discussions of the book, philological and philosophical questions were often not adequately separated. Let me give an example: the fact that Nietzsche in the end cancelled his initial, temporary plan to write a book entitled *The Will to Power* does not imply that he had also given up the concept 'will to power' as a crucial concept for his notion of reality. This example indicates that Müller-Lauter's account in this article is valuable not only from a historical-philological perspective but also from a philosophical perspective. The different approaches to the inauthentic book *The Will to Power*, often assume an inexplicit interpretation of Nietzsche's notion of the will to power as well as an inexplicit answer to the related question of to what extent and in what sense Nietzsche's thinking could be systematized. Müller-Lauter's comparison and criticism of these different positions summon the reader to take a critical stand when confronted with these problems.

Freedom and Chaos

In the second volume of *Nietzsche-Interpretationen*, which consists of three articles (or better, of one article and two books), Müller-Lauter elaborates and deepens Nietzsche's conception of becoming as power processes in different directions. He investigates how Nietzsche diagnoses, on the basis of his notion of the will to power, aesthetic (Wagner's music), moral (freedom of will), and socio-economic (industrialization and modernization) phenomena as weak/sick and strong/healthy. Weakness is characterized as the incapacity to organize the internal multiplicity of struggling wills to power. A unity, such as the human being or a community, is strong or healthy if it consists of a maximum of internal struggle and succeeds in preventing that struggle from descending into chaos. In all the articles of this volume we can recognize Müller-Lauter's thesis that for Nietzsche unity can only exist as an irreducible multiplicity of struggling forces. He explicates Nietzsche's diagnosis that our modern culture lacks an adequate organization of this struggle. In the first and last articles we can again recognize Müller-Lauter's interest in the influences of the sciences on Nietzsche's thought.

In the first article, 'Artistische décadence als physiologische décadence. Zu Friedrich Nietzsches später Kritik an Richard Wagner' ('Artistic Decadence as Physiological Decadence. On Friedrich Nietzsche's Later Critique of Richard Wagner', 1999d, pp. 1–25), Müller-Lauter elaborates, as an example, why Richard Wagner's art is for Nietzsche an expression of physiological decadence. Wagner is used as an example because Müller-Lauter's goal is to shed light on Nietzsche's notion of decadence as such and because Wagner embodies Nietzsche's notion of decadence to a great extent. According to Nietzsche, Wagner's art is characterized by an 'incapability of organic construction', which manifests itself as a part becoming independent from the whole (ibid., p. 4). Nietzsche's attack on Wagner's personality indicates that he is not only interested in decadence as an aesthetic phenomenon. Wagner's art is an expression of physiological decadence, of physiological lack of organizational power. His physiological decay is not an isolated phenomenon but represents for Nietzsche the decay of life that can be observed in all regions. It can be especially used as an interpretative scheme in order to reveal the decadence in philosophy and religion (ibid., p. 9f.).

The most valuable aspect of this article is Müller-Lauter's detailed analysis of Nietzsche's concept of physiology. First of all, Müller-Lauter makes clear that Nietzsche's specific adaptation and application of this notion was prepared by Nietzsche's reading of Paul Bourget's *Essais de psychologie contemporaine* (*Essays in Contemporary Psychology*, 1883). Müller-Lauter's recognition of the influence of Bourget on Nietzsche sheds an interesting light on Nietzsche's view of decadence. Bourget explains decadence as a process in which parts of an organism (such as language and a community) become independent and ultimately lead to a state of anarchy (ibid., p. 2). Then, Müller-Lauter discusses three different meanings of the concept of 'physiology' in Nietzsche's work: 1) the meaning that it has in the natural sciences in Nietzsche's era (this meaning is not specified further); 2) the somatic, such as the organic functions and the affections or immediate bodily sensations; 3) the struggle between wills to power that are interpreting one another (ibid., p. 12f.). Müller-Lauter elaborates Nietzsche's critique of decadence in relation to the last meaning of 'physiology' – without denying the significance of the first and second meaning. In addition, he tries to give the cruel application of this notion that we often find in Nietzsche's later work more content. He does this, on the one hand, by explaining why Nietzsche constricts his physiological approach and, on the other hand, by correcting, as it were, the late Nietzsche from the perspective of the third meaning of physiology (ibid., p. 14).

Müller-Lauter's critical and creative approach reveals the inconsistencies that arise when Nietzsche narrows his conception of physiology. In his narrowed physiological approach, decadence is reduced to degeneration, which can only be fought by amputating and rejecting sick organs. Müller-Lauter strengthens his interpretation of Nietzsche's reductionism by referring to Nietzsche's reading of, among others, *Dégénérescence et criminalité* (*Degeneration and Criminality*) by the neurologist and internist Charles Féré. Nietzsche read this book in 1888 shortly after it was published (ibid., p. 17f.). Nietzsche contradicts himself when he, for example, on the one hand, understands the history of nihilism as an immanent consequence of the self-overcoming of morality, Christianity, and truth, and, on the other hand, explains this process of nihilism from a crude, narrow physiological point of view (ibid., p. 18).

The most interesting result of Müller-Lauter's analysis is that Nietzsche's reductionism leads to an inconsistent notion of what he conceives as a healthy life. Nietzsche's reduction of decadence to physiological degeneration, which can be fought by the elimination of sick organs, implies that health and sickness exclude one another. This implication is incompatible with Nietzsche's notion of healthy life as an all-encompassing yes-saying to an infinite multiplicity of *conflicting* experiences, as the total affirmation of all aspects of life, including the sick, decadent aspects.[10] We find this incompatibility also in his elaboration of the process of realizing the *Übermensch*. Müller-Lauter tries here to correct, as it were, Nietzsche's physiological reductionism by confronting it with Nietzsche's notion of struggle.

The second article, 'Freiheit und Wille bei Nietzsche' ('Freedom and Will in Nietzsche', ibid., pp. 25–131), discusses Nietzsche's deconstruction of the notion of freedom of will. Müller-Lauter focuses especially on Nietzsche's analysis of this concept from *Human, All Too Human* on. Nietzsche claims that, after extensive preparatory inquiry in earlier works, he is finally able to formulate his own perspective on the free will in *Human, All Too Human*. He elaborates his view in a critical confrontation with Schopenhauer and Kant. In order to disclose their presuppositions as metaphysical errors, Nietzsche applies his genealogical method: seemingly a-historical phenomena are traced back to *diesseitige* (pre-)historical processes. This way, Nietzsche repudiates all notions of free will that are grounded from a transcendent(al) point of view. Nietzsche, in opposition to metaphysical conceptions of free will, states his idea of the necessity of all that happens (ibid., p. 32f.). For Nietzsche the human being is ultimately nothing other than a temporary synthesis of wills to power, which, depending on certain power constellations, form a unity or fall apart in a process that proceeds in a necessary way. Whether a human being considers him or herself as free or un-free is ultimately an expression or symptom of the strength or weakness of the will to power that constitutes him or her (ibid., p. 86f.). Nevertheless, Nietzsche introduces what he calls an 'instinct of freedom', a *feeling* of being free that can be found among the strong. Although the human being cannot detach him or herself from the necessary process of becoming, he or she is a part of the forces that determine the direction of that development. From *Thus Spoke Zarathustra* on, Nietzsche tries to elaborate, in the context of the notion of the *innocence of becoming*, why the affirmation of this type of necessity is an important task for the strong human being. In addition, on the basis of the idea of 'instinct of freedom' as affirmation of oneself as will to power, Nietzsche introduces a new, a-metaphysical notion of responsibility (ibid., p. 96f.).

Müller-Lauter's reconstruction of Nietzsche's reinterpretation (*Umdeutung*) of the metaphysical concept of freedom is complex: different phases and different layers are differentiated and different relations between different aspects of these phases and layers are elaborated. I will confine myself to a short discussion of two 'new' notions of freedom that Nietzsche, according to Müller-Lauter, elaborates: a negative notion and a positive notion of freedom.

Müller-Lauter tries to show that from *Human, All Too Human* up to *The Gay Science* Nietzsche develops a negative concept of freedom. This negative notion of freedom is the direct result of Nietzsche's attempts to disclose the presuppositions of traditional concepts of freedom as errors. Nietzsche traces the inclination to view ourselves as free agents, and hence to ascribe to ourselves a certain intelligible causality, back to epistemological and psychological errors. As a consequence, our consciousness of guilt and responsibility is also disclosed as an error (ibid., p. 37f.). Müller-Lauter argues that, in the process of revealing guilt and responsibility as errors, Nietzsche discovers a 'new (negative) type of freedom'. Recognizing the necessary character of all that happens, and therefore of the un-freedom of our will, frees us from traditional morality (which is melded with metaphysics and religion). This 'new' freedom has a negative character because it is a *liberation from* moral responsibility and guilt (ibid., p. 45f.).

From *Thus Spoke Zarathustra* on, Müller-Lauter believes that he can find in Nietzsche a positive concept of freedom that goes beyond every moral, religious, and metaphysical account of this notion. This type of freedom involves a type of necessity as an involuntary process that merges with a feeling of power. This feeling of freedom is an expression of a feeling of power and can only be realized after the innocence of becoming has been recovered. The human being acquires a feeling and consciousness of total 'irresponsibility' if he goes through and detaches himself or herself from all the 'institutes of responsibility' in history, which were forced upon him or her externally: 'What remains is the whole world process, to which he is attached in a non-responsible manner, but still being a necessary part in its development' (ibid., p. 103f.). Müller-Lauter finds in the second essay of *On the Genealogy of Morality* the completion of this view of a 'new', recovered positive freedom (ibid., p. 105). In this essay, the will to power as an instinct of freedom is recognized as a positive, constitutive activity that is operative in all organic processes. The sovereign individual represents this new freedom and the new responsibility that goes with it.

Müller-Lauter gives several indications for how one could understand Nietzsche's positive notion of freedom, but an extensive clarification of its special and problematic character is lacking. What is clear is that he conceives the realization of this consciousness of freedom as a dialectical process. This characterization reveals even more clearly the problem that is not sufficiently elaborated by Müller-Lauter: how can a process be dialectical without being teleological (and, hence, metaphysical)? How can Nietzsche explain the possibility of redemption and recovery without positively determining a goal? Further reflection on Müller-Lauter's hints could be very fruitful here. The *principally indicative character* of Nietzsche's 'positive' depiction of freedom (which immediately implies that 'positive' should be put between quotation marks) ought to be taken into special consideration in this context.[11]

The third and last article of this volume, 'Über "das Ganze" und über "Ganzheiten" in Nietzsches Philosophie' ('On "the All" and "Wholes" in Nietzsche's Philosophy', ibid., pp. 131–413), deals with the different meanings of the concept of 'whole' in Nietzsche's works. For Nietzsche, the meaning of 'wholes' (*Ganzheiten*) is, first of all, 'organized "unities,"'[12] which can grow or decline in power'. The world consists of forms of organization (such as organs and people) that are or can become part of larger forms of organization (such as communities and states). A whole is always related to another whole: wholes constitute one another in a mutual struggle. Wholes are temporarily existing exponents of the will to power. A whole can, depending on its external or internal struggle, merge with another whole or fall apart in numerous wholes. These types of wholes must be strictly distinguished from another type of whole, which Müller-Lauter characterizes as 'the Whole' or 'the All' (*das Ganze*) (ibid., p. 139f.). The All is the total in which everything that emerges and perishes takes place. The All itself cannot be an organism or organization, and, therefore, cannot be a 'unity'. Nietzsche characterizes the All as chaos. The concept of 'chaos' expresses not only the ultimate external horizon of the All but is rather – and primarily – the 'ultimate internal', the final inner condition that we can find in the world. For Nietzsche, the human being is also chaos. In contrast to the All, it is organized but 'only as a temporary and highly unstable composition of a multiplicity of beings, which can grow and persist for a while' (ibid., p. 144). The human being is organized chaos (ibid., p. 144, 149). This internal chaos forms the breeding ground for the creation of future, more powerful 'species', of more powerful organizations. The notion 'chaos' expresses the unstable character of the struggle by virtue of which an organization (hence, all reality) exists. This notion confirms again Müller-Lauter's thesis of the primacy of struggle and multiplicity. Nietzsche applies this chaos–organization model to technological and economical developments in the nineteenth century and anticipates the future of humanity and the possibility of great individuals (ibid., p. 200f.).

Müller-Lauter's elaboration of the categorical distinction between wholes and the All indicates that it is impossible to determine the 'the totality of all that is (ibid., p. 142). The All is, in contrast to the wholes 'in' the world (such as the human being), not organized, which excludes the idea of an All as a (metaphysical) unity. The All is not an organized whole, not in the sense of an absolute space that forms the framework for all that happens, a great sensorium in which the plurality is regulated in one way or another, an inventory or power storage (referring to Leibniz and his adepts), a machine that has a particular goal, nor in the sense of an organism (ibid., p. 140). The idea that the All is not an organized unity confirms again the primacy of struggle and multiplicity. If all the wholes, the organizations 'in' the All, were organized, then a principle that organizes all those wholes would become necessary (e.g. a final creator). At this point it would be possible to reduce the multiplicity to unity. And this is precisely what is being rejected in Müller-Lauter's interpretation of the All.

Finally, I want to point to Müller-Lauter's elaboration of the influence of the economist Emanuel Herrmann on Nietzsche's economical interpretation of reality. Nietzsche never mentions Herrmann in his texts. It was Montinari who discovered Nietzsche's Herrmann reception, regrettably without recognizing its great influence and importance. Müller-Lauter shows that many of Nietzsche's late unpublished notes (especially the notes that he had collected for the temporarily planned book *The Will to Power*) would not only be difficult to grasp but even partly impossible to understand if Nietzsche's reading of Herrmann's book *Cultur und Natur* (*Culture and Nature*, 1887) were not taken into consideration. His findings correct interpretations like that of Pierre Klossowski, who believes that Nietzsche's 'economical fragments' are an application of John Stuart Mill's utilitarianism (see Klossowski, 2009). Müller-Lauter explains very impressively how Nietzsche adapts Herrmann's concept of an 'internal economical efficiency', which Nietzsche uses to characterize all processes in nature, the human, and society, in terms of his notion of the will to power.

Closing

I have tried to provide a detailed account of the content and significance of Müller-Lauter's Nietzsche interpretation. In my analysis I have also tried to show how Müller-Lauter works and what makes his way of doing things so special. Put differently, I have tried to elaborate his Nietzsche interpretation in a way that presents simultaneously his Nietzsche interpretation itself as well as his style of interpreting Nietzsche. The power of Müller-Lauter's approach to Nietzsche's work – and this could be characterized as a fourth feature of his Nietzsche interpretation – is that he, on the one hand, stays so close to Nietzsche's text that he is able to let us hear as much as possible what Nietzsche has to say, and, on the other hand, keeps enough distance from the text to be able to explain what Nietzsche says. The first aspect prevents Müller-Lauter from projecting ideas in Nietzsche's texts that are not there. The second aspect prevents his Nietzsche interpretation from becoming so immanent that it does not explain much, making a critique of Nietzsche impossible. It is this very special balance that has enabled Müller-Lauter to disclose the very special character of Nietzsche's thinking. This great prudence has enabled him to do justice to the multiplicity in Nietzsche's work without falling into arbitrariness. Müller-Lauter has complied with Nietzsche's appeal to learn to read him well.

Notes

[1] In a slightly revised version published in *Nietzsche-Interpretationen III*.

[2] All translations from Müller-Lauter's texts are my own.

[3] Furhermore, Müller-Lauter has published articles on, among others, Jacobi and Fichte, especially in relation to the problem of nihilism.

[4] See for example: *Nachlaß Frühjahr* 1888, 14[72].

[5] Especially the reactions of W. Weischedel (1973) and P. Köster (1973).

[6] Already the title of Roux's book rings a bell: *Der Kampf der Theile im Organismus. Ein Beitrag zur Vervollständigung der mechanischen Zweckmässigkeitslehre (The Struggle of the Parts in the Organism. A Contribution to the Completion of a Mechanical Theory of*

Teleology), 1881. The unpublished notes and summaries, which are published in KGW VII 1, indicate that Nietzsche has read this book very thoroughly and repeatedly (first in1881 and then more intensive in 1883 and 1884).

7 Nachlaß Herbst 1887, KSA 12: 10[59], p. 491v. and 10[61], p. 493v.

8 See *On the Genealogy of Morality* II, 2, which Müller-Lauter refers to earlier, and *Nachlaß* Frühjahr-Sommer 1883, 7[258], where the sovereign individual is characterized as a fruit of community.

9 Published for the first time in this volume. Another article, which was published in English, has laid out the framework for this article, namely: 'On Judging in a World of Becoming. A Reflection on the "Great Change" in Nietzsche's Philosophy' (Müller-Lauter, 1999b).

10 Müller-Lauter extensively elaborates this view on the healthy life in the fifth article of the first volume (1999c).

11 Müller-Lauter explicitly states in one place (p. 111) that the 'active advent of innocence is . . . *essentially* [my italics] oriented towards the future'.

12 Hence, these 'unities' are always only a unity as organization; they should not be understood as atomistic.

Bibliography and Guide to Further Study

Müller-Lauter's Nietzsche Interpretation

Müller-Lauter, Wolfgang (1992/3a), 'On Associating with Nietzsche', trans. R.J. Hollingdale. *The Journal of Nietzsche Studies* 4/5 (1992/3). This article appears in a special issue on 'The Work of Wolfgang Müller-Lauter'. The other articles in this issue follow.

— (1992/3b), 'Nietzsche's Teaching of Will to Power', trans. Drew E. Griffin.

— (1992/3c), '"A Continual Challenge": On Mazzino Montinari's Relationship with Nietzsche', trans. R. J. Hollingdale.

— (1992/3d), 'The Spirit of Revenge and the Eternal Recurrence: Heidegger's Later Interpretation of Nietzsche', trans. R. J. Hollingdale.

— (1999a), *Nietzsche: His Philosophy of Contradictions and the Contradictions of His Philosophy*, trans. David. J. Parent. Urbana and Chicago: University of Illinois Press [1971]. The major work of Müller-Lauter's Nietzsche interpretation. This translation also contains two later essays, 'Nietzsche's "Doctrine" of the Will to Power' and 'The Organism as Inner Struggle: Wilhelm Roux's Influence on Nietzsche'.

— (1999b), 'On Judging in a World of Becoming: A Reflection on the "Great Change" in Nietzsche's Philosophy', in Babette E. Babich and Robert S. Cohen (eds), *Nietzsche, Theories of Knowledge, and Critical Theory: Nietzsche and the Sciences I.* Boston: Klewer Academic Publishers.

— (1999c), *Über Werden und Wille zur Macht. Nietzsche-Interpretationen* I. Berlin and New York: De Gruyter. Volume 1 of Müller-Lauter's collected works on Nietzsche. Volumes 2 and 3 follow.

— (1999d), *Über Freiheit und Chaos. Nietzsche-Interpretationen* II. Berlin and New York: De Gruyter.

— (1999e), *Heidegger und Nietzsche. Nietzsche-Interpretationen* III. Berlin and New York: De Gruyter.

Works on Müller-Lauter's Nietzsche

Caygill, Howard (1992/3), 'Editor's Introduction', *The Journal of Nietzsche Studies* 4/5.
Köster, Peter (1973), 'Die Problematik wissenschaftlicher Nietzsche-Interpretation. Kritische Überlegungen zu Wolfgang Müller-Lauters Nietzschebuch', *Nietzsche-Studien*, 2, 31–60.
Schacht, Richard (1999), 'Foreword', in Müller-Lauter, 1999a.
Weischedel, Wilhelm (1973), 'Der Wille und die Willen. Zur Auseinandersetzung Wolfgang Müller-Lauters mit Martin Heidegger', *Zeitschrift für philosophische Forschung*, 27, 1, 71–76.

Other Works Cited

Klossowski, Pierre (2009), 'Circulus Vitiosus', trans. Joseph D. Kuzma. *The Agonist* 2, (1), 31–47.

Chapter 8

Kofman's Nietzsche

Duncan Large

Introduction: Kofman's Context

The French philosopher Sarah Kofman (1934–94) developed her ideas
over a remarkable range of areas as diverse as aesthetics, literary criticism,
the history of philosophy from the 'pre-Socratics' to Derrida, Freudian psychoanalysis, feminism, autobiographical writing, art and film criticism.
She is perhaps best known for her work on Freud, which was the first part
of her multifarious output to be made available extensively in English
translation – in particular her breakthrough book, a feminist interpretation of Freud, *The Enigma of Woman: Woman in Freud's Texts* (Kofman,
1985). Amid the wealth and diversity of her productivity, though, Kofman
also established herself as the most significant and authoritative female
interpreter of Nietzsche's work since the days of his sister Elisabeth and
Lou Andreas-Salomé. As Penelope Deutscher and Kelly Oliver point out,
'Kofman has been a consistently elusive figure, well known but hard to
classify within Nietzsche studies' (1999a, p. 2). This is largely on account of
her syncretistic style of interpretation, merging psychoanalytic, deconstructive and feminist perspectives (among others). The present essay
attempts, if not a definitive classification then at least a more adequate
appreciation of Kofman's substantial body of work in this area, which by
the time of her death amounted to five books and a number of other key
essays. Walter Kaufmann points out that another prolific Nietzsche commentator, Erich Podach, was able to publish six books about Nietzsche
even while maintaining that an intensive occupation with him 'is not one
of the pleasant things in life',[1] but in Kofman's case writing on Nietzsche
was an abiding fascination, a genuine labour of love, and she would return
to write on him throughout her career.

From the outset of her interest in Nietzsche, as a philosophy teacher at a
Parisian *lycée* in the mid-1960s, Kofman was reading him in tandem with

Freud, and this dual, mutually qualifying perspective marks perhaps the most distinctive aspect of her interpretative style more generally. She began a doctoral dissertation on 'The Concept of Culture in Nietzsche and Freud' at the Collège de France in 1966, under the Hegelian Jean Hyppolite; after Hyppolite's death in 1968 the dissertation supervision was taken over by his (signally more Nietzschean) former student Gilles Deleuze. Deleuze's *Nietzsche and Philosophy* (Deleuze, 1983 [1962]) played a crucial role in fuelling the intense interest in 'the new Nietzsche' that was shown in France in the 1960s and early 1970s – Kofman would later reveal that it was a course by Deleuze on the *Genealogy of Morals*, which she followed when she was studying for the *agrégation* examination, that first inspired her interest in Nietzsche. Based in Paris at this time, then, Kofman was well placed to profit from the 'linguistic turn' in Nietzsche interpretation, and she would emerge as one of its most important advocates.

While working towards her dissertation, Kofman published a first spin-off article on Nietzsche in 1968, discussing his analysis in *The Antichrist* of the historical transition from Judaism to Christianity in terms of will to power. Three further articles in 1970–1, on aspects of Nietzsche's use of figurative language, then prepare the way for the publication of her first book on Nietzsche, *Nietzsche and Metaphor*, in 1972 (Kofman, 1993c). Her debts to Deleuze here are evident, and go beyond the one explicit reference to *Nietzsche and Philosophy* (Kofman, 1993c, p. 163, note 31), but by now it is to Jacques Derrida that Kofman's work on Nietzsche owes the greatest debt of allegiance. In the late 1960s Kofman had begun attending Derrida's seminars at the École Normale Supérieure; she quickly came within Derrida's orbit and indeed gave a first version of *Nietzsche and Metaphor* to Derrida's seminar in the academic session 1969–70. Kofman first came to prominence in France as part of Derrida's circle, and she herself repeatedly acknowledged that her relation to Derrida was 'a real encounter' (Kofman, 1991c, p. 111; Kofman, 1993e, p. 11). Derrida's own principal text on metaphor, 'White Mythology: Metaphor in the Text of Philosophy', also precipitated out of the 1969–70 seminar, and was first published in 1971 in the same journal issue as the first version of Kofman's *Nietzsche and Metaphor* (Derrida, 1974).

Nietzsche and Metaphor (1972)

In 'White Mythology', Derrida sketches out a vast history of 'metaphor in the text of philosophy', from Plato and Aristotle to Lenin, Heidegger, and Lacan, marshalling Nietzsche along with all the rest in this 'mobile army' of proper names. Kofman's focus in *Nietzsche and Metaphor* is deliberately more concentrated, and yet it is not merely this restriction in the object of her analysis which constitutes the specificity of her study – it is also the nature of her method. In *Nietzsche and Metaphor*, Kofman pays attention deconstructively to what Derrida will later highlight as 'the question of style' in Nietzsche – to Nietzsche's language, and to Nietzsche's figurative language in particular. Coupled with her underlying Freudian interest, this technique develops into a powerful analytical method, a distinctively Derridean-Freudian approach, at once semiotic and symptomatic.

Her aim is to give a 'faithfully' Nietzschean reading of Nietzsche – an appropriate appropriation – and one of the main results is that, for all the 'penetration' of Kofman's treatment, her overriding interest in the textuality of Nietzsche's writing requires a strategic, deconstructive indulgence in the 'surface' at the expense, specifically, of addressing Nietzsche's 'grand doctrines'. Whereas the eternal return of the same, for example, had been one of the major preoccupations of the 1960s – in Deleuze's *Nietzsche and Philosophy*, and especially in the work of Pierre Klossowski – it impinges hardly at all on *Nietzsche and Metaphor*, and the same holds true for the overman or *amor fati*. Kofman uses *Thus Spoke Zarathustra* here very sparingly indeed, and the will to power, interpreted as an heuristic principle of interpretation, does not make an appearance until Section V.

In return for the return, Kofman gives us the concept of metaphor – and the concept *as* metaphor – in a series of micro-textual analyses. What is more, because her aim is 'to write conceptually in the knowledge that a concept has no greater value than a metaphor and is itself a condensate of metaphors' (Kofman, 1993c, p. 3), the polysemy of the concept and the original nature of metaphor inevitably surface periodically in her own writing in the form of puns. Such language-play exemplifies the speciousness of the very distinction between the literal and the metaphorical – with the concomitant denigration and subordination of the latter – which Nietzsche himself is out to deconstruct. Kofman's play with the 'literal', 'proper', 'clean', 'appropriate', and so forth meanings of the term '*propre*' (see Kofman, 1993c, pp. 149–50, note 5), for example, vitiates any use it might have within the binary oppositions of a rigid categorization.

On the other hand, pointing out the 'metaphorical' nature of the term 'metaphor' itself is such a rigorous *reductio* that the self-referential paradox which results is too unstable to be catered for by the establishment of 'the original nature of metaphor'. As Kofman points out, with such a generalization of metaphor and effacement of its binary opposite, the 'literal' – the strong claim in Nietzsche's 1873 essay 'On Truth and Lies in an Extra-Moral Sense' (couched in metaphorical language) that all language is ultimately metaphorical – a need arises for a new terminology. Hence aporia is avoided when the strategic use of metaphor which she discerns in Nietzsche's early texts, where his philological preoccupations are still uppermost, gives way to more general notions of 'text' and 'interpretation', and ultimately to 'will to power'. Once she has sketched out these moments on Nietzsche's 'conceptual' itinerary, then, from Section IV, which is largely based on a close reading of the 'On Truth and Lies' essay, Kofman fills out this developmental model and turns to a typology of the principal Nietzschean metaphors and their modulations. The argument culminates, typically, in the 'strategic' final footnote, where she stresses that Nietzsche is not so much concerned with inventing new metaphors as with revaluating and subverting some of the most traditional of philosophical tropes – the 'naked truth', knowledge as vision, the 'tree of knowledge', and so on.

Nietzsche and Metaphor would eventually prove to be the first of Kofman's books on Nietzsche to be translated into English complete (Kofman, 1993c), but a section from it was already available in 1977, as the first piece by Kofman of any kind to be translated into English, when it was included in *The New Nietzsche*, David B. Allison's ground-breaking collection of translated excerpts from post-war French and German Nietzsche interpretations (Kofman, 1977). It was in the wake of this partial translation (and especially its 1985 republication) that Kofman's Nietzsche began to be appreciated and commented on in the English-speaking world. Foremost among the first wave of reception were the favourable accounts by Alexander Nehamas, in his highly influential *Nietzsche: Life as Literature* (1985, pp. 15–17), and by Alan D. Schrift (1990, pp. 85–94, 166–8). Maudemarie Clark (1990, pp. 15–18) and Richard Weisberg (1990, pp. 112–20) were less positively inclined. More recently, Paul Patton (1999) gives a balanced evaluation which argues that 'the great merit of Kofman's study is to have analyzed Nietzsche's use of metaphor from the perspective of his views on the nature of thought and language' (1999, p. 97), but finds that 'her overall argument [. . .] retains the traditional concepts of both concept and metaphor' (1999, p. 105) which, for Patton, Derrida, and Deleuze/Guattari supersede.

'Baubô' (1975) and Nietzsche et la scène philosophique (1979)

Somewhat ironically, it was through her contact with Derrida that Kofman developed not only her deconstructive approach to Nietzsche but also the feminist perspective which would characterize her next key intervention. The most decisive early contribution to the 'Nietzsche was a feminist' debate, Derrida's *Éperons/Spurs*, began life as a lecture on 'the question of style', presented to the landmark conference on 'Nietzsche aujourd'hui?' held at Cerisy-la-Salle in July 1972. The conference proceedings contain a transcription of the ensuing discussion, which includes Kofman's rapturous reception: 'I wanted firstly to thank Jacques Derrida for having given such a fine paper. He spoke with really supreme authority, and there is nothing to say after him' (Gandillac and Pautrat, 1973, I, p. 288). Thankfully, Kofman proved herself wrong when she herself lectured on the figure of woman in Nietzsche at the Institut de Psychanalyse de Paris the following May and then published this work as the essay 'Baubô: Theological Perversion and Fetishism' in 1975 (Kofman, 1988).

'Baubô' passes under review the different figures of woman in Nietzsche's writings, from the infamous old woman who warns Zarathustra not to forget the whip when he goes among women, to the Homeric temptress Circe. Kofman demonstrates that these threatening women subvert and invert conceptual hierarchies, and the essay culminates in a discussion of the obscene title figure who in Greek mythology made the earth goddess Demeter laugh by immodestly lifting her skirts. Kofman takes Baubô (from a discussion by Nietzsche in the Preface to *The Gay Science*) to be the emblematic female double of Dionysus, and she mobilizes this figure not only to demonstrate Nietzsche's irreverence but especially to argue that Nietzsche should not be labelled a misogynist. The essay thus marks the first of several instances where Kofman is concerned to 'save' Nietzsche from condemnation – in this case as an anti-feminist (later, as we shall see, she seeks to rebut accusations that Nietzsche was anti-Semitic, or mad). In 'Baubô' Kofman's response to Nietzsche is more personal than in *Nietzsche and Metaphor*, for she reads Nietzsche here 'as a woman', paying attention to the sexual economy of his texts, yet the feminist strain in Kofman's Nietzsche will always be less pronounced than, for example, in Irigaray's. Nietzsche's figurations of woman are certainly highly symptomatic for Kofman, but the feminist perspective is hardly foundational to her approach, and ultimately she reads 'woman' in Nietzsche, rather, as just another deconstructive operator.

'Baubô' prefigures Kofman's later, more wide-ranging and influential discussions of the question of woman in the texts of philosophy, psychoanalysis, and literature, and she will leave Nietzsche behind to some extent in the 1980s, but not before publishing a second book-length study, *Nietzsche et la scène philosophique* (*Nietzsche and the Philosophical Scene*, Kofman, 1979). This collection (unfortunately only partially translated into English) incorporates the 'Baubô' essay but builds it into a surprising context. Here, in a succession of essays which arose out of her teaching, and which submit selected passages of Nietzsche to particularly close readings, Kofman reads

Nietzsche with and against earlier philosophers, situating him in relation to 'the philosophical tradition' with which he himself was engaging. Starting with his revaluation of the '"pre-Socratics"' (whom he prefers to call 'the ancient masters of Philosophy', as Kofman reminds us – 1979, p. 17), Kofman focuses on the ancient Greeks while ranging widely through Descartes, Spinoza, Pascal, Rousseau, Kant, Hegel, and Schopenhauer. Coincidentally published the same year as Lyotard's *The Postmodern Condition* (Lyotard, 1984), this collection of tactical hermeneutic interventions reinforces the suspicion with which Kofman greets the more strategic 'grand narratives' of Nietzsche interpretation.

In her preface to *Nietzsche et la scène philosophique*, Kofman modestly describes the book as 'a precise reading of a few texts' (1979, p. 7), but she also makes it clear that the book has a polemical intent. Just as Arthur C. Danto wrote his monograph *Nietzsche as Philosopher* (1965) in order to prove to the doubters that Nietzsche could be taken seriously as a philosopher at all, so in *Nietzsche et la scène philosophique* Kofman aims to cement Nietzsche's reputation as a philosopher and to rebut criticisms (stemming from the backlash against the 'new Nietzsche') that he should rather be considered as something else, such as a poet. Instead she argues that Nietzsche's account of the history of philosophy is compelling, and unavoidable for any reader seeking to engage with the philosophical 'classics' (Kofman, 1979, p. 7). Kofman's title also draws attention to what she calls the link between theory and theatre (later taken up in Sloterdijk, 1989), and her study emphasizes the comic talent Nietzsche displays in the course of his parodic critiques. Andrzej Warminski (1987, pp. xli–xliii) cites Kofman's discussion of an excerpt from *The Birth of Tragedy* in *Nietzsche et la scène philosophique* (Kofman, 1979, pp. 55–97) as a paradigm of deconstructive interpretation. In a more measured approach, Mary Beth Mader (1999) critically evaluates Kofman's discussion of Nietzsche's critique of the Aristotelian principle of contradiction in a *Nachlass* note (Kofman, 1979, pp. 137–63). More recently, the exemplary status of Kofman's approach to reading Nietzsche in this collection is also implicitly confirmed by Keith Ansell Pearson when he follows Kofman's lead in demonstrating *How to Read Nietzsche* (Ansell Pearson, 2005).

Nietzsche et la scène philosophique marks a temporary quietus with Nietzsche, as Kofman's attention then switches predominantly to Freud and to 'the question of woman', but from 1986 she began producing a further series of studies on Nietzsche's relationship to specific figures – Heraclitus, Socrates, Wagner (Kofman, 1987, 1991b/1998, 1994d). Even when not devoting a whole book to him, then, her interest in Nietzsche never entirely receded, and it would be triumphantly reasserted in the early 1990s with three books on Nietzsche in successive years (Kofman, 1992a, 1993a, 2007b/2008), which mark not so much a reorientation of Kofman's Nietzsche as a culmination of it.

Explosion (1992–3) and Scorning Jews (1994)

Explosion is a monumental two-part commentary on *Ecce Homo* in which Kofman devotes a separate chapter to each of its sections. The result is that her two books together amount to a work about eight times the length of Nietzsche's – she remarked in a radio interview that she set herself the task of explicating its every word (Kofman, 1993b). Her title derives from Nietzsche's celebrated claim in the text: 'I am not a man, I am dynamite' (EH 'Destiny' 1), but Kofman herself is out to explode the two most widely held assumptions concerning *Ecce Homo*, namely that it is 'simply' 'Nietzsche's autobiography' and, more perniciously, that it is the work of a madman, since it was written in the last few weeks before Nietzsche's collapse into indisputable insanity in Janaury 1889. Instead, Kofman takes this 'mad' text seriously, and in her analysis she follows Nietzsche himself in deconstructing the metaphysical opposition between 'reason' and 'unreason', building on some of her earlier work of the 1970s, especially her treatments of works by E. T. A. Hoffmann (see Large, 1999). Kofman severs the link between the pathological and the textual, generalizing on the basis of the originary, self-dramatizing self-doubling proper to any autobiographical writing so as to argue that the 'madness' of *Ecce Homo*, far from being a disqualification, is rather its very condition of possibility.

Until the *Explosion* books, Kofman herself passed over *Ecce Homo* – the specific problems raised by *Ecce Homo* – largely in silence; in both her previous books on Nietzsche she referred to it very sparingly indeed. The *Explosion* books are a 'first' for Kofman in several respects, then: not only do they mark her first extensive engagement with *Ecce Homo*, but it is the first time, indeed, that she devotes a work to a single book of Nietzsche's. For the first time, too, Kofman makes full use of biographical and genetic approaches to Nietzsche's work, drawing a good deal on his correspondence and on the notes and drafts for *Ecce Homo* which came to light only with the Colli-Montinari edition. In other ways, though, the *Explosion* books follow on closely from Kofman's previous studies, both of Nietzsche and of other writers. Methodologically, she applies here the same technique – a scrupulously attentive close reading of a series of shorter passages – as she developed in the 'case studies' of *Nietzsche et la scène philosophique*, she also continues her inquiry into Nietzschean metaphorics and textuality which she began in *Nietzsche and Metaphor*, with the same degree of sensitivity to his linguistic play (and Kofman herself was a phenomenal stylist). Above all, though, the *Explosion* books assert a methodological continuity with her earlier work in that, as she explains in the 'Rhapsodic Supplement' which concludes *Explosion II*, in order to prevent either Nietzsche or Freud gaining mastery over her, she plays off one against the other, reading Freud with a Nietzschean 'ear' and vice-versa (Kofman, 1993a, p. 372). In the *Explosion* books this interpretative strategy brings rich rewards, and her Freudian 'ear' picks up on a wealth of telling details, culminating in a lengthy speculation on Nietzsche's fascination with the number seven, where she extrapolates from its homonym, the verb '*sieben*', a screen for the childhood trauma associated with the untimely death of Nietzsche's younger brother Joseph (Kofman, 1993a, pp. 380–4).

Kofman's, then, is a highly celebratory reading of this most affirmative of texts. With the *Explosion* 'twins' (as she has called them), she herself doubles Nietzsche, and her thoroughgoing identification with him, which contrasts with her more critical position vis-à-vis Freud (in *The Enigma of Woman* and elsewhere), is explicitly acknowledged in the confessional conclusion. Here, Kofman allows herself to stand back from her achievement and speak with her own voice, declaring her love for her subject in the fullest sense ('All through this work, which followed him step by step, we will, in any case, have loved him') and expressing filial devotion ('Could I have written on Nietzsche and his children with accuracy, doing them justice, without myself becoming a child of Nietzsche's?'). She immediately follows her declaration of devotion to Nietzsche, though, by establishing a distance, characterizing herself in Nietzschean fashion as 'a child who [. . .] feels constrained, in the end, to cut the umbilical cord in order to become what he is' (Kofman, 1993a, p. 371). The 'autobiographical' 'Rhapsodic Supplement' is thus – inevitably, like any supplement – an element integral to Kofman's interpretative strategy, for not only is this moment of self-reflexion – the account of the genealogy of her own relation to Nietzsche (through Freud) – the moment at which her own interpretation acknowledges itself as such, but it is also the moment at which (*contra* Heidegger) 'life' emerges as the ultimate yardstick of the value of values. In turn, the 'Rhapsodic Supplement' has been the focus for the majority of the commentators on the *Explosion* books, drawn in by its personal tone of 'fantastic genealogy' and 'family romance'.[2]

Given Kofman's increasing preoccupation with 'life writing', it came as no surprise that soon afterwards she should publish an autobiographical account of her own childhood, *Rue Ordener, rue Labat* (Kofman, 1996 [1994]). At the same time, though, it turned out that Kofman was still not finished with Nietzsche (or he with her), for in spring 1994 she also published a final short book on him, *Scorning Jews: Nietzsche, the Jews, anti-Semitism* (Kofman, 2007b/2008). Again the book takes a very autobiographical approach, and Kofman adopts the last of her own subject positions in writing on Nietzsche, writing 'as a Jew'. It is also her last attempt to vindicate Nietzsche, 'saving' him from the accusations of anti-Semitism which arose from his association with the National Socialists in the minds of many – by dismissing his evident early anti-Semitism as a youthful aberration, citing anti-anti-Semitic passages in his later works, notes, and correspondence, and ultimately claiming that Nietzsche turns himself into a Jewish figure. The last move is a step too far for Alan D. Schrift, who is otherwise sympathetic to Kofman's account (1999, 2008), while Joanne Faulkner (2008) analyses such a claim as stemming from a problematization of Kofman's own Jewish identity.

Conclusion

Sarah Kofman committed suicide on the 150th anniversary of Nietzsche's birth, 15 October 1994 – even in death, she asserted her affinity with the great philosopher of the affirmation of life. How can we judge Kofman's Nietzsche in the round? One uncharitable, reductive way of looking at the matter is simply to label her a follower of Derrida – in the strict sense that *Nietzsche and Metaphor* follows Derrida's related essay 'White Mythology', 'Baubô' follows (the first version of) Derrida's *Spurs*, and even the *Explosion* project follows in the wake of Derrida's other book on Nietzsche, *Otobiographies* (Derrida, 1985), which thematizes and problematizes *Ecce Homo* as autobiography. Kofman always bristled when classified as a Derridean (1991c, p. 111), but even if she was closer to Derrida than she herself cared to admit, her interpretation of Nietzsche is not derivative, and one can truly talk of 'Kofman's Nietzsche' as having its own specific character.

Derrida himself gave Kofman scant acknowledgement while she was alive (their relationship was certainly highly asymmetric in this respect), but after her death he was more fulsome in eulogizing her as the twentieth century's best reader of Nietzsche and Freud.[3] This may seem like damning with faint praise, but it is an accolade Kofman herself would have welcomed. The emphasis this places on Kofman's twin reading of Nietzsche with Freud (and vice-versa) is hardly controversial, since the two thinkers were her twin preoccupations from the outset. Although she never completed her comparative doctoral dissertation as it was originally conceived (she was instead awarded a *thèse sur travaux* in 1976), and as a result never published a joint study of Nietzsche and Freud, the yoking of the two together is a deliberate feature of all of her work on the two in (supposed) isolation, so as to play one off against the other deconstructively.[4] Derrida's drawing attention to Kofman as a reader also accords with her own resistance (as a Nietzschean, and as a woman philosopher) to the grand conceptual structures of traditional patriarchal 'phallogocentrism'. Instead, Kofman was dedicated to the proposition that creative, innovative reading is not a contradiction in terms. As Pleshette DeArmitt comments, Kofman 'developed [. . .] a new form of textual analysis, one in which philosophy and psychoanalysis mingle together and the conceptual and the biographical cannot be separated' (2008, p. 2). Françoise Duroux describes how Kofman's technique of reading becomes a philosophical intervention in its own right, and numbers Kofman, with Hannah Arendt, among the women who have preferred to philosophize without pretending to construct a 'system', but who have been fundamentally innovative nonetheless (1999, p. 134).

For all the voluminousness of her writing, Kofman's Nietzsche is in some ways surprisingly selective. By the end of her career she had commented on most parts of Nietzsche's output, though in typically deconstructive fashion she preferred to draw attention to less trodden paths such as the *Untimely Meditations* and *Ecce Homo*, and was less partial to Nietzsche's 'middle period' writings or, notably, *Thus Spoke Zarathustra*.[5] Her preoccupation with reading Nietzsche through Freud was typical of much French Nietzsche interpretation in the 1960s and 1970s, although she distinguished herself as the most thoroughgoing practitioner of this approach. She was also highly atypical in resisting two of the main currents in contemporaneous Nietzsche interpretation, namely, the fashion to read Nietzsche – like Deleuze, Foucault and, especially, Lyotard – with Marx,[6] and to read him – like the other members of the 'Philosophie en effet' group, Lacoue-Labarthe, Nancy and, especially Derrida – through the prism of Heidegger's strong interpretation. The anti-Heideggerian nature of her approach to Nietzsche becomes apparent in several places, from her critical review of Jean Granier (Kofman, 1970) to the programmatic Introduction to *Explosion I* (Kofman, 1994b).[7] Unsurprisingly, given the level of her identification with this key philosophical precursor, what emerges from Kofman's interpretative readings is a Nietzsche in her own image, yes, with its emphasis on rhetorical features, the expressive textual symptom, the teasingly ludic and autobiographical; but also, at the same time (insofar as Nietzsche himself was a precursor of both psychoanalysis and deconstruction) a surprisingly faithful Nietzschean, against-the-grain reading of Nietzsche himself.

Notes

[1] Podach (1961), p. 431; cited in Kaufmann (1968), pp. v and 428.

[2] See Maurel (1997), pp. 57–8; Proust (1997), p. 6; McDonald (1998), p. 186; Duroux (1999), p. 139; Nancy (1999), pp. viii–ix; Oliver (1999), p. 183; Faulkner (2008); Naas (2008), p. 65.

[3] 'For she too was without pity, if not without mercy, in the end, for both Nietzsche and Freud, whom she knew and whose bodies of work she had read inside and out. Like no one else in this century, I dare say' (Derrida 2001, p. 173).

[4] See Kofman (1992b), p. 66; (1993e), p. 12; Deutscher (1999), p. 162.

[5] *Nietzsche and Metaphor* draws its examples mainly from Nietzsche's early period (especially the writings of 1871–3); *Nietzsche et la scène philosophique* focuses on passages from *Beyond Good and Evil* and Nietzsche's later (post-*Zarathustra*, 'Will to Power') notebooks; the *Explosion* books of course focus on *Ecce Homo*.

[6] With one exception: the chapter on Marx in *Camera obscura: de l'idéologie* (Paris: Galilée, 1973).

[7] See Large (1995); Proust (1997), p. 6.

Bibliography and Guide to Further Study

Kofman's Nietzsche Interpretation

Kofman, Sarah (1968), 'Métamorphose de la volonté de puissance du Judaïsme au Christianisme d'après "L'Antéchrist" de Nietzsche'. *Revue de l'enseignement philosophique*, 18/3 (February–March), 15–19. Reproduced in Kofman, *Le mépris des Juifs: Nietzsche, les Juifs, l'antisémitisme*. Paris: Galilée, 1994.

— (1970), 'Généalogie, interprétation, texte'. *Critique*, 26/275 (April), 359–81. Revised republication in Kofman, 1993c. Review article on Jean Granier, *Le problème de la vérité dans la philosophie de Nietzsche*. Paris: Seuil, 1966.

— (1971a), 'Nietzsche et la métaphore'. *Poétique*, 5 (Spring) (special number: 'Rhétorique et philosophie'), 77–98. Revised and extended republication in Kofman, 1993c.

— (1971b), 'L'oubli de la métaphore'. *Critique*, 27/291–92 (August–September), 783–804. Revised and extended republication in Kofman, 1993c. Review article on Friedrich Nietzsche, *Das Philosophenbuch/Le livre du philosophe: Études théoriques*, trans. Angèle Kremer–Marietti. Paris: Aubier–Flammarion, 1969; *La naissance de la tragédie*, trans. Geneviève Bianquis, 12th edn. Paris: Gallimard, 1949; *La naissance de la philosophie à l'époque de la tragédie grecque*, trans. Geneviève Bianquis, 7th edn. Paris: Gallimard, 1938.

— (1973), 'Le/les "concepts" de culture dans les "Intempestives" ou la double dissimulation', in Maurice de Gandillac and Bernard Pautrat (eds), *Nietzsche aujourd'hui*? (proceedings of the Colloque de Cerisy-la-Salle, July 1972), 2 vols. Paris: Union Générale d'Éditions ('10/18'), II ('Passion'), 119–46. Reproduced in Kofman, 1979.

— (1977), 'Metaphor, Symbol, Metamorphosis', trans. David B. Allison, in Allison (ed.), *The New Nietzsche: Contemporary Styles of Interpretation.* New York: Dell; 2nd edn., Cambridge, MA and London: MIT Press, 1985 [1972].

— (1979), *Nietzsche et la scène philosophique.* Paris: Union Générale d'Éditions ('10/18'). 2nd edn. Paris: Galilée ('Débats'), 1986. Partial English translations: Kofman, 1991a, 2007a.

— (1987), 'Nietzsche and the Obscurity of Heraclitus', trans. Françoise Lionnet–McCumber, *Diacritics,* 17/3 (Fall), 39–55 [1986].

— (1988), 'Baubô: Theological Perversion and Fetishism', trans. Tracy B. Strong, in Michael Allen Gillespie and Strong (eds), *Nietzsche's New Seas: Explorations in Philosophy, Aesthetics, and Politics.* Chicago and London: University of Chicago Press. Reprinted in Kelly Oliver and Marilyn Pearsall (eds), *Feminist Interpretations of Friedrich Nietzsche.* University Park: Pennsylvania State University Press, 1998 [1975].

— (1990), 'Metaphoric Architectures', trans. Peter T. Connor and Mira Kamdar, in Laurence A. Rickels (ed.), *Looking After Nietzsche.* Albany: SUNY Press [1972].

— (1991a), 'Descartes Entrapped', trans. Kathryn Aschheim, in Eduardo Cadava, Peter Connor and Jean–Luc Nancy (eds), *Who Comes After the Subject?* New York and London: Routledge [1979].

— (1991b), 'Nietzsche's Socrates: "Who" Is Socrates?' trans. Madeleine Dobie, *Graduate Faculty Philosophy Journal,* 15/2, 7–29 [1989].

— (1992a), *Explosion I: De l' "Ecce Homo" de Nietzsche.* Paris: Galilée ('La philosophie en effet'). Partial English translations: Kofman, 1994b, 1994c.

— (1993a), *Explosion II: Les enfants de Nietzsche.* Paris: Galilée ('La philosophie en effet'). Partial English translations: Kofman, 1995a, 1995b.

— (1993b), 'Explosion I' [interview with Alan Veinstein], *Du jour au lendemain,* France-Culture, 29 January; repeat broadcast 11 August 1993.

— (1993c), *Nietzsche and Metaphor,* trans. Duncan Large. London: Athlone Press; Stanford, CA: Stanford University Press [1972].

— (1993d), 'Nietzsche and the Painter's Chamber', trans. Will Straw, *Public,* 7 ('Sacred Technologies'), 153–70. Republished as 'Nietzsche: the Painter's Chamber', in Kofman, *Camera Obscura: On Ideology,* trans. Will Straw. London: Athlone Press; Ithaca, NY: Cornell University Press, 1997 [1973].

— (1994a), 'Et pourtant, elle tremble! (Nietzsche et Voltaire)', *Furor,* 26 (September) (special number: 'Voltaire'), 135–54. Reproduced in Kofman, *L'imposture de la beauté et autres textes.* Paris: Galilée, 1995.

— (1994b), 'Explosion I: of Nietzsche's *Ecce Homo*', trans. Duncan Large, *Diacritics,* 24/4 (Winter), 51–70. Reprinted in Daniel W. Conway with Peter S. Groff (eds), *Nietzsche: Critical Assessments,* 4 vols. London and New York: Routledge, 1998, I: 218–41. Translation of 'Introduction' to Kofman, 1992a.

— (1994c), 'A Fantastical Genealogy: Nietzsche's Family Romance', trans. Deborah Jenson, in Peter J. Burgard (ed.), *Nietzsche and the Feminine.* Charlottesville and London: University of Virginia Press [1992].

— (1994d), 'Wagner's Ascetic Ideal According to Nietzsche', trans. David Blacker and Jessica George, revised by Alban Urbanas and by Richard Schacht and Judith

Rowan, in Schacht (ed.), *Nietzsche, Genealogy, Morality: Essays on Nietzsche's* 'Gene-
    alogy of Morals'. Berkeley, Los Angeles, London: University of California Press
    [1992].
— (1995a), 'The Psychologist of the Eternal Feminine (Why I Write Such Good
    Books, 5)', trans. Madeleine Dobie. *Yale French Studies*, 87, 173–89 [1993].
— (1995b), 'Accessories (*Ecce Homo*, 'Why I Write Such Good Books', 'The Untime-
    lies', 3)', trans. Duncan Large, in Peter R. Sedgwick (ed.), *Nietzsche: A Critical
    Reader*. Oxford and Cambridge, MA: Blackwell [1993].
— (1998), 'Nietzsche's Socrates(es): "Who" Is Socrates?' in Kofman, *Socrates: Fictions
    of a Philosopher*, trans. Catherine Porter. London: Athlone Press; Baltimore: Johns
    Hopkins University Press [1989].
— (2007a), 'The Evil Eye', in Kofman, *Selected Writings*, ed. Thomas Albrecht with
    Georgia Albert and Elizabeth Rottenberg. Stanford, CA: Stanford University
    Press [1979].
— (2007b), 'Scorning Jews: Nietzsche, the Jews, anti-Semitism', trans. Ann Smock,
    in Kofman, *Selected Writings*, ed. Thomas Albrecht with Georgia Albert and
    Elizabeth Rottenberg. Stanford, CA: Stanford University Press [1994].
— (2008), 'Contempt of/for the Jews: Nietzsche, the Jews, anti-Semitism', trans.
    Tracy B. Strong, *New Nietzsche Studies*, 7/3–4 (Fall 2007 and Winter 2008) [1994].

Other Works by Kofman

Kofman, Sarah (1985), *The Enigma of Woman: Woman in Freud's Writings*, trans.
    Catherine Porter. Ithaca, NY and London: Cornell University Press [1980].
— (1991c), 'Sarah Kofman' [interview with Alice Jardine], trans. Janice Orion, in
    Jardine and Anne M. Menke (eds), *Shifting Scenes: Interviews on Women, Writing,
    and Politics in Post-68 France*. New York and Oxford: Columbia University Press.
— (1992b), 'La question des femmes: une impasse pour les philosophes' (interview
    with Joke Hermsen), *Les Cahiers du Grif*, 46 (Spring), 65–74.
— (1993e), 'Interview avec Sarah Kofman 22 mars 1991. Subvertir le philosophique
    ou Pour un supplément de jouissance' (interview with Evelyne Ender), *Compar(a)
    ison*, 1 (January), 9–26.
— (1996), *Rue Ordener, Rue Labat*, trans. Ann Smock. Lincoln, NE and London:
    University of Nebraska Press [1994].

Works on Kofman

Chanter, Tina, and Pleshette DeArmitt (eds) (2008), *Sarah Kofman's Corpus*. Albany:
    SUNY Press.
Clark, Maudemarie (1990), *Nietzsche on Truth and Philosophy*. Cambridge: Cambridge
    University Press. Discusses *Nietzsche and Metaphor* on pp. 15–18.
Collin, Françoise, and Françoise Proust (eds) (1997), *Sarah Kofman. Les Cahiers du
    Grif*, 3 (Spring).
DeArmitt, Pleshette (2008), 'The Lifework of Sarah Kofman', in Chanter and
    DeArmitt, 2008.

Derrida, Jacques (2001), '. . . . . ', trans. Pascale-Anne Brault and Michael Naas, in *The Work of Mourning*, ed. Brault and Naas. Chicago and London: University of Chicago Press [1997]. Derrida's response to Kofman's death.

Deutscher, Penelope (1999), 'Complicated Fidelity: Kofman's Freud (Reading *The Childhood of Art* with *The Enigma of Woman*)', in Deutscher and Oliver, 1999b.

Deutscher, Penelope, and Kelly Oliver (1999a), 'Sarah Kofman's Skirts', in Deutscher and Oliver, 1999b.

— (eds) (1999b), *Enigmas: Essays on Sarah Kofman*. Ithaca, NY and London: Cornell University Press.

Duroux, Françoise (1999), 'How a Woman Philosophizes', trans. Lisa Walsh, in Deutscher and Oliver, 1999b [1997].

Faulkner, Joanne (2008), '"Keeping It in the Family": Sarah Kofman Reading Nietzsche as a Jewish Woman', *Hypatia*, 23/1 (January–March), 41–64.

Large, Duncan (1993), 'Translator's Introduction', in Kofman, 1993c.

— (1995), 'Double "Whaam!": Sarah Kofman on *Ecce Homo*', *German Life and Letters*, 48/4 (October), 441–62.

— (1999), 'Kofman's Hoffmann', in Deutscher and Oliver, 1999b.

McDonald, Christie (1998), 'Sarah Kofman: Effecting Self Translation', *TTR: Traduction, terminologie, rédaction*, 11/2, 185–97.

Mader, Mary Beth (1999), 'Suffering Contradiction: Kofman on Nietzsche's Critique of Logic', in Deutscher and Oliver, 1999b. Critically evaluates Kofman's discussion of Nietzsche's critique of the Aristotelian principle of contradiction.

Maurel, Jean (1997), 'Enfances de Sarah', in Collin and Proust, 1997, 55–68.

Naas, Michael (2008), 'Fire Walls: Sarah Kofman's Pyrotechnics', in Chanter and DeArmitt, 2008.

Nancy, Jean-Luc (1999), 'Foreword: Run, Sarah!', trans. Paul Patton, in Deutscher and Oliver, 1999b [1997].

Nehamas, Alexander (1985), *Nietzsche: Life as Literature*. Cambridge, MA and London: Harvard University Press. Discusses *Nietzsche and Metaphor* on pp. 15–17.

Oliver, Kelly (1999), 'Sarah Kofman's Queasy Stomach and the Riddle of the Paternal Law', in Deutscher and Oliver, 1999b.

Patton, Paul (1999), 'Nietzsche and Metaphor', in Deutscher and Oliver, 1999b. Places *Nietzsche and Metaphor*'s discussion of 'originary metaphoricity' in the context of post-1968 rhetorical politics of difference.

Proust, Françoise (1997), 'Impasses et passes', in Collin and Proust, 1997, 5–10.

Schrift, Alan D. (1990), Nietzsche and the Question of Interpretation: Between Hermeneutics and Deconstruction. New York and London: Routledge. Discusses Nietzsche and Metaphor on pp. 85–94 and 166–8.

— (1999), 'Kofman, Nietzsche, and the Jews', in Deutscher and Oliver, 1999b.

— (2008), '*Le mépris des anti-sémites*: Kofman's Nietzsche and Nietzsche's Jews', in Chanter and DeArmitt, 2008.

Warminski, Andrzej (1987), *Readings in Interpretation: Hölderlin, Hegel, Heidegger*. Minneapolis: University of Minnesota Press.

Weisberg, Richard H. (1990), 'De Man Missing Nietzsche', in Clayton Koelb (ed.), *Nietzsche as Postmodernist: Essays Pro and Contra*. Albany: SUNY Press. Discusses *Nietzsche and Metaphor* on pp. 112–20.

Other Works Cited

Ansell Pearson, Keith (2005), *How to Read Nietzsche.* London: Granta.

Danto, Arthur C. (1965), *Nietzsche as Philosopher.* New York: Macmillan.

Deleuze, Gilles (1983), *Nietzsche and Philosophy,* trans. Hugh Tomlinson. London: Athlone Press; New York: Columbia University Press [1962].

Derrida, Jacques (1974), 'White Mythology: Metaphor in the Text of Philosophy', trans. F. C. T. Moore, *New Literary History,* 6/1 (Autumn), 5–74. Also trans. Alan Bass, in Derrida, *Margins of Philosophy.* Brighton: Harvester; Chicago: University of Chicago Press, 1982 [1971].

— (1979), *Spurs: Nietzsche's Styles/Éperons: Les Styles de Nietzsche,* trans. Barbara Harlow. Chicago and London: University of Chicago Press [1973; expanded version 1978].

— (1985), 'Otobiographies: the Teaching of Nietzsche and the Politics of the Proper Name', trans. Avital Ronell, in Derrida, *The Ear of the Other: Otobiography, Transference, Translation,* ed. Christie V. Macdonald. New York: Schocken [1984].

Gandillac, Maurice de, and Bernard Pautrat (eds) (1973), *Nietzsche aujourd'hui?* (proceedings of the Colloque de Cerisy-la-Salle, July 1972), 2 vols. Paris: Union Générale d'Éditions ('10/18').

Kaufmann, Walter (1968), *Nietzsche: Philosopher, Psychologist, Antichrist,* 3rd edn. New York: Vintage.

Lyotard, Jean-François (1984), *The Postmodern Condition: A Report on Knowledge,* trans. Geoffrey Bennington and Brian Massumi. Minneapolis: University of Minnesota Press [1979].

Podach, Erich F. (1961), *Friedrich Nietzsches Werke des Zusammenbruchs.* Heidelberg: Rothe.

Sloterdijk, Peter (1989), *The Thinker on Stage: Nietzsche's Materialism,* trans. Jamie Owen Daniel. Minneapolis: University of Minnesota Press [1986].

Chapter 9

Strauss's Nietzsche

Matthew Sharpe and Daniel Townsend

Introduction: the Strauss Controversy, Leo Strauss, and Nietzsche

Leo Strauss became nearly a household name in the first decade of the twenty-first century in the United States of America. This was due to the alleged role of Strauss's students and admirers in the neoconservative Bush government (2000–8), a regime which historians will associate with the 'war on terror', the invasions of Afghanistan and Iraq, and the United States' flouting of the United Nations. Liberal critics led by Shadia Drury, Peter Levine, and Nicolas Xenos, charged that Strauss and his students were a sect of secret or 'esoteric' Nietzscheans whose Machiavellian politics, and dreams of a renewed aristocratic rule of the strong, were cloaked behind a veil of noble-sounding calls for a return to national virtue, religious piety, and a defence of Western values.

These charges of Nietzscheanism were especially embittering to Strauss's students and followers, given that Strauss opposes the philosophical modernism represented by Nietzsche. In public lectures, Strauss claims that Nietzsche represents the 'third wave' of modern thought. This 'wave' is characterized by what Strauss denounces as radical 'historicism': the belief that all claims to excellence, virtue, or orienting normative value are entirely conditioned by the historical circumstances of their progenitors. For this reason, radical historicism means the end of philosophy as the search for transhistorical, transcultural Truth – the very type of classical philosophy Strauss writes of reviving. Notably, Strauss also damningly associates Nietzsche with the National Socialist disaster:

> . . . [Nietzsche] used much of his unsurpassable and inexhaustible power of passionate and fascinating speech for making his readers loathe, not

only socialism and communism, but conservatism, nationalism, and democracy as well. After having taken upon himself this great political responsibility he could not show his readers a way towards political responsibility . . . Nietzsche thus prepared a regime which, as long as it lasted, made discredited democracy again look like the golden age. (Strauss, 1988a, p. 57)

Yet Strauss's attitude towards Nietzsche is far more ambivalent, and much more philosophically interesting than what the above passage might suggest. Late in life, Strauss recalled how he had, in his early years, secretly admired Nietzsche. In an important 1936 essay, Strauss explicitly frames his return to premodern philosophy as the search for a middle ground between the 'master' and 'slave' moralities Nietzsche identifies in the *Genealogy of Morals* (Strauss, 1990, p. 14). Furthermore, in his later texts Strauss would recur in his own name to Nietzsche's strong dismissal of modern culture in *Thus Spoke Zarathrustra* as leading to a morass of conformist 'last men', understood as human beings unable to conceive of any higher goals than bourgeois comfort and base self-interest.[1] Most of all, when compiling his last published work, *Studies in Platonic Political Philosophy*, Strauss chose to place an extended essay on Nietzsche's work, 'A Note on the Plan of *Beyond Good and Evil*', as the numerically central eighth out of 15 chapters – a fact which Strauss's own, famous hermeneutics (see below) would point to as implying a central importance.

It is this 17-page essay, 'A Note on the Plan of *Beyond Good and Evil*', (Strauss, 1983) which we shall now scrutinize. It is difficult not to admire this extraordinary essay, even if we do not agree with Laurence Lampert's provocative assessment that it represents 'the best Nietzsche yet, the one nearest to the still almost secret Nietzsche of Nietzsche's great books' (Lampert, 1996, p. 1). In this essay, Strauss's earlier criticisms of Nietzsche's philosophy are qualified, if not overturned. The reader of 'A Note on the Plan' could be forgiven for forgetting Strauss's earlier dismissals of Nietzsche's work due to the powerful and coherent reconstruction Strauss provides of Nietzsche's elusive, most famous ideas: the will to power, the eternal recurrence, and the philosopher or overman as artist and legislator. She might also then recall that, although Strauss situates Nietzsche as the third wave of modern thought, in Plato's *Republic* – from whence, via Homer's *Odyssey*, Strauss's metaphor of three waves comes – the third wave is the saving wave that positions philosophers as law-making kings (*Republic* 472a, 484a–c, 487e,489b, 497c–d, 499b–d; see BGE 203, 211). Thus does Strauss, at the very centre of his last major work, quietly admit his secret proximity to Nietzsche? To assess these perplexities, and also to understand the peculiar nature of Strauss's writing style in 'A Note on the Plan', we must first explore some basic aspects of Strauss's thought.

Philosophy and Esotericism

Leo Strauss was born in 1899 in Germany to an orthodox Jewish family. As a young man, Strauss was passionately engaged by the debates concerning Zionism and the fate of his people. Strauss also became a dedicated student of philosophy. A member of the remarkable generation of Jewish intellectuals who would be exiled by the Nazis, Strauss studied with Max Weber, Hermann Cohen, and Martin Heidegger.

Strauss's research into medieval Jewish and Arabic philosophy in the 1930s led him to a controversial discovery that would shape his career. In certain medieval texts, such as Maimonides's *Guide for the Perplexed*, Strauss rediscovered an avowed practice of esoteric writing. The premise of esoteric writing is that the author writes multi-layered texts. On the surface of an esoteric text are edifying teachings available to all readers who stumble upon the book, teachings which accommodate the author's positions to the prejudices of their age. However, this exoteric layer serves to conceal the author's true, and often heterodox, views. Esoteric teachings are intimated by a variety of literary devices, such as using fables, allegories, metaphors, ambiguous words, characters, dramatic settings, and staged dialogues; assigning particular significance to certain numbers; writing behind the mask of a commentator, historian, or scholar; contradicting oneself on key issues; hiding more radical opinions in the central position in lists, paragraphs, sections, or within numbered chapters, books, or essays (see Strauss, 1988b, pp. 22–38).

While many contemporaries reacted sharply to Strauss's great study of esotericism, *Persecution and the Art of Writing* (Strauss, 1988b), there is overwhelming evidence attesting to the practice dating back as far as Plato. In the seventh *Letter*, for example, Plato frankly avows that he has never fully stated his true positions (341c–d; 342e–343a; see second *Letter*, 314c; *Phaedrus* 275c5–276; Strauss, 1964, pp. 52–5). Notably for us, Nietzsche too was aware of these unusual ancient writing practices; commenting on the 'noble lie' in *Twilight of the Idols*, Nietzsche asserts that 'Neither Manu nor Plato, neither Confucius nor the Jewish and Christian teachers, ever doubted their *right* to tell lies' (TI 'Improvers' 5).[2] *Beyond Good and Evil* 190 reflects on how Plato used Socrates 'in the manner of a popular tune from the streets', so his works are '*prosthe Platon epithen te Platon messe te chimaira* [Plato in front, Plato behind, in the middle a chimera]' (BGE 190; see BGE 28).[3] Most importantly for us – and as Strauss alerts us to in 'A Note on the Plan' – in *Beyond Good and Evil*, Nietzsche shows himself to be aware of, if not an advocate of, the practice of esoteric writing. Nietzsche tells of

> [t]he exoteric and the esoteric as philosophers formerly distinguished them, among the Indians as among the Greeks, Persians and Moslems, in short wherever one believed in an order of rank and *not* in equality and equal rights. (BGE 30. See BGE 40; also 7, 62, 198–203, 295; WS 71)

It is impossible to say whether Strauss's discovery of philosophic esotericism in the mid-1930s was a by-product of his youthful encounter with Nietzsche's texts. What is certain is that Nietzsche's 'deliberately enigmatic' (#7),[4] interrogative, tempting, even 'feminine' texts – not least *Beyond Good and Evil* – have many of the characteristics which Strauss uncovered in his readings of Plato, Xenophon, Farabi, Maimonides, and Machiavelli. But let us return to the surface. Strauss contends that Nietzsche was an esoteric writer and that esoteric writing begins with Plato. Does Strauss, then, consider Nietzsche an heir to Plato?

Nietzsche's Platonizing: on the Plan of Strauss's *Beyond Good and Evil*

Leo Strauss's orienting contention in 'A Note on the Plan of *Beyond Good and Evil*' is reflected in his central placement of the essay in *Studies in Platonic Political Philosophy*. It is to situate Nietzsche in the lineage of what Strauss terms 'Platonic political philosophy'. Strauss of course recognizes that Nietzsche opposed 'Platonism' understood as the invention of the 'pure mind' and the otherworldly ideas headed by 'the good in itself' (#4). Yet, citing Nietzsche's famous Preface of *Beyond Good and Evil*, Strauss argues that while Nietzsche explicitly 'presents himself as the antagonist of Plato' (#3), he *also* ranks Plato as 'the most beautiful growth of antiquity' (#22; see BGE 38, 190). What then are the dimensions of Nietzsche's Platonism?

There are three registers to the Straussian claim concerning Nietzsche's Platonism. The first six paragraphs of Strauss's 'Note on the Plan' allow us to see the first register. These paragraphs concern what Strauss terms Nietzsche's 'platonizing' regarding the 'form' or literary character of Nietzsche's *Beyond Good and Evil* (#3). Strauss means that Nietzsche has written BGE with all the subtlety with which Plato constructed his 35 dialogues. Strauss's essay opens with the remarkable claim that *Beyond Good and Evil*, far from being an aleatory collection of aphorisms and apercus, is characterized by a 'graceful subtlety as regards form, as regards intention, as regards the arts of silence' (#2).

Strauss draws our particular attention to *Beyond Good and Evil's* subtitle, 'A Prelude to a Philosophy of the Future' as indicating a key to its meaning, its hidden form, and its relation to *Thus Spoke Zarathrustra*, which Nietzsche called his 'most profound' book. Strauss says:

> The book is meant to prepare, not indeed the philosophy of the future, the true philosophy, but a new kind of philosophy by liberating the mind from the 'prejudices of the philosophers,' i.e. of the philosophers of the past (and the present). At the same time, or by this very fact, the book is meant to be a specimen of the philosophy of the future. (#4)

This is why *Beyond Good and Evil* must open by identifying and attacking, as it duly does, 'the prejudices of the philosophers' and be followed by a second chapter on 'the free mind' or 'free spirits'. These free spirits, Strauss suggests, are the privileged *addressees* of Nietzsche's book, since they are the hoped-for 'heralds and precursors' of the philosophers of the future that Nietzsche's *task* looks towards (#5; see BGE 44, 203).

These considerations about Nietzsche's addressees lead to the second, substantive register to Strauss's claim concerning Nietzsche's platonizing. This is that Nietzsche's *Beyond Good and Evil*, like Plato's *Republic*, is first of all a book *about* philosophy (#5). One register of what the mature Strauss understood by 'Platonic political philosophy' is a reflection on philosophy as an activity or way of life, in relation to religion, morality, art or poetry, and other political phenomena. With this in mind, Strauss's sixth paragraph gives a significant summary of the plan he perceives as structuring *Beyond Good and Evil*. The first three chapters, particularly Chapter III, Strauss claims, concern the relation of philosophy with (the) religion(s). The fourth chapter of BGE, 'Sayings and Interludes', divides this half of the book from the last five chapters (V–IX), which are devoted to philosophy in its relations to morals and politics. Philosophy alone occupies all of *Beyond Good and Evil*, albeit in different ways.

Thirdly, Strauss is aware in 'Note on the Plan' of the strange proximity between the elevated understanding of the rightful, governing political role of philosophy Nietzsche develops in BGE (38, 203, 211), and Plato's politics in books like the *Republic* (see Strauss, 1989a, pp. 41–2; 1989b,

p. 97). In Nietzsche's thought, Strauss suggests, the will to power combines the roles Plato assigned to *Eros* (philosophical desire) and the pure mind. For Nietzsche, philosophy is the highest or 'most spiritual' manifestation of the will to power, as it was the highest species of *Eros* in Plato; this means that it consists in *prescribing to nature what or how it ought to be* (BGE 9) (#7; see Strauss, 1989b, p. 96). Above all else, like Plato's philosopher-kings, Nietzsche's philosopher of the future is, in Strauss's reading, willing to take on political leadership:

> The leaders who can counteract the degradation of man which has led to the autonomy of the herd can however not be merely men born to rule like Napoleon, Alcibiades or Caesar. They must be philosophers and commanders, the philosophers of the future. Mere Caesars, however great, will not suffice; for the new philosophers must teach man the future of man as his will. (#25)

Strauss's Nietzsche's Anti-Liberalism

For readers raised in a period of left-liberal and post-structuralist readings of Nietzsche, Strauss's 'Note on the Plan of *Beyond Good and Evil*' can appear shocking, not only in its form, but also in Strauss's substantive claims. Certainly, Strauss places greater emphasis on those parts of the Nietzschean *oeuvre* some are tempted to quarantine or pass over (for example: BGE 203, 211; see #25–7, 29–31). Unlike the 'weakened' Nietzsches that emerge in many post-modern readings, Strauss's Nietzsche is very much the writer who once claimed that he was 'dynamite'. Strauss's Nietzsche is outspokenly hostile to modern liberalism, egalitarianism, democracy, and feminism:

> The official high priests of democracy with their amiable reasonableness were not reasonable enough to prepare us for our present situation: the decline of Europe, the danger to the West, to the whole Western heritage, which is at least as great and even greater than that which threatened Mediterranean civilization around 300 of the Christian era. Nietzsche once described the change which has been effected in the second half of the nineteenth century in continental Europe . . . every day something new with no reminder of duty and exalted destiny . . . the specialisation compensated by sham universality, by the stimulation of all kinds of

interests and curiosities without true passion; the danger of universal phil-
istinism and creeping conformism. (Strauss, 1989a, p. 31)

Three of Strauss's central paragraphs in 'Note on the Plan' (#23–5) address
Beyond Good and Evil aphorisms 197–202, in which Nietzsche rails against
the modern 'morality stemming from timidity', a 'herd' morality the very
opposite of the new values Nietzsche would propound (#25). This 'morality
of the human herd' (#23) was once the outgrowth of a 'healthy' instinct of
the weak, to elevate what is of 'utility to the herd' as the standard of the
Good (#24). However, unlike in earlier hierarchical societies, Strauss's
Nietzsche laments that this morality 'has become simply predominant in
contemporary Europe', even in its greatest philosophers (#22, 24). The
result is that, whereas in the past this herd morality still allowed for vital
aggression towards external and internal enemies, the new herd morality of
contemporary Europe

> takes the side of the very criminals and becomes afraid of inflicting pun-
> ishment: it is satisfied with making the criminals harmless; by abolishing
> the only remaining ground of fear, the morality of timidity would reach
> its completion and thus make itself superfluous. (#24; see BGE 73)

Strauss's 'Note on the Plan' also pointedly raises – in a single, intriguing
paragraph at the end of the seventh subsection (#36) – the subject of
women and feminism which occupies the end of BGE's own, seventh chapter. In these paragraphs, introduced by Nietzsche's ungainly emphasis that
they are '*my* truths' (BGE 231), Nietzsche lambasts women (e.g. 'Stupidity
in the kitchen; woman as cook . . . '; 'Young: a cavern decked about. Old: a
dragon sallies out' (BGE 234; 237)). Strauss takes these paragraphs seriously enough to interrupt the apparent flow of his own exegesis. Moreover,
he makes this interruption to highlight that when Nietzsche pillories feminism, he does so above all on grounds that it is hostile to what he calls 'the
natural hierarchy' that exists between men and women (#36).

Nietzsche and Nature

The red thread that in fact runs through Strauss's 'Note on the Plan of
Beyond Good and Evil' is the claim that at the heart of Nietzsche's thought is
a new conception of nature. In contrast to Strauss's earlier essays, Nietzsche
is no longer presented as a moral and epistemological relativist who believes

that there is, in the absence of Truth, only a multiplicity of perspectives on the world. Rather, Nietzsche seems a harbinger of a new, modern or post-modern doctrine of natural right. Strauss's eighteenth paragraph in 'Note on the Plan' turns to Nietzsche's central (fifth) chapter in *Beyond Good and Evil*, noting in typical Straussian fashion that this numerically central chapter in Nietzsche's book bears the only chapter heading which refers to 'nature'. Strauss's Nietzsche is aware that while one can try to push nature away as with a hayfork – for instance by promoting 'unnatural' modern, democratic, and feminist ideas (see #18) – she always returns (see #22; BGE 264; 83; Strauss, 1953, pp. 201–2).

At the heart of Strauss's Nietzsche's concept of nature are the fundamental teachings of will to power and eternal recurrence. Together, they form what Strauss calls a new kind of 'transmoral' anthropocentrism (#7) whose nature is what the second half of 'Note on the Plan' is devoted to showing.

Invoking Nietzsche's second *Untimely Meditation*, Strauss claims that for Nietzsche, *contra* figures like Jean-Jacques Rousseau,

> the truth is not attractive, lovable, life-giving, but deadly, as is shown by the true doctrines of the sovereignty of Becoming, and the fluidity of all concepts, types and species, and of the lack of any cardinal difference between man and beast . . . It is shown most simply by the true doctrine that God is dead. (#7)

Yet for all that, and despite Nietzsche's avowed perspectivism, Strauss claims that Nietzsche in no way denies that there *is* a fundamental, if deadly, truth. Rather than the relativization of all truths, we might say, Strauss's Nietzsche elevates *the unrelativizable Truth of relativism*. Strauss makes two parries at clarifying this inconsistency. First, he distinguishes between truths and a meta-Truth, 'the truth regarding all truths': 'in other words, by suggesting *that* the truth is human creation, [Nietzsche] suggests that *this truth* at any rate is not a human creation' (#7; italics ours).

Second, Strauss enigmatically comments that Nietzsche considered the error of all previous philosophers was that they sought to 'discover' the truth, rather than to 'invent' it (loc cit.; see #11). If 'some of his readers' (#9) wish to know what Nietzsche means when he accepts that the will to power is one more interpretation or invention, Strauss contends, they ought to pay particular heed to *Beyond Good and Evil* 34, a central aphorism in that work's second chapter. Here, the distinction is raised between the world as it appears to us (as fictions and interpretations), and the world as it is in itself (the text), which Nietzsche says is of no concern to us. Strauss argues that

> what [Nietzsche] seems to aim at is the abolition of the fundamental distinction: the world as will to power is both the world of any concern to us and the world in itself. Precisely if all views of the world are interpretations, i.e. acts of the will to power, the doctrine of the will to power is at the same time an interpretation and the most fundamental fact, for, in contradistinction to all other interpretations, it is the necessary and sufficient condition for the possibility of any 'categories'. (#8)

A sceptical reader of 'Note on the Plan' might be tempted to assert that 'the problematic, tentative, tempting, hypothetical character' of Strauss's comments on the will to power here are fundamentally incoherent (#8). On the one hand, and as in previous philosophies, there is an invocation of some non- or supra-human Nature or Truth which would precede and make possible all interpretations, and their critical assessment: 'the highest culture of the future must be in accordance with the natural order of rank among men which Nietzsche, in principle, understands along Platonic lines' (Strauss, 1989b, p. 97).

On the other hand, the Truth seems to belong to a certain *way* of interpreting the world, even of actively *prescribing* to nature what it ought to be, if only that of the six or seven overmen at whom nature aims (#17; see #7, 25; BGE 126). This thought implies that at least *some* privileged human beings can *recreate* nature according to their will. The circle can be squared only by maintaining that this very act of willing, and the complementary men or philosophers of the future who undertake it, will themselves *embody* the Truth of will to power, as living syntheses of is and ought, nature and human creation. This is Strauss's interpretation:

> [T]he new philosophers must teach man the future of man as his will, as dependent upon human will . . . The subjugation of nature depends then decisively on men who possess a certain nature. Philosophy, we have heard, is the most spiritual will to power (aph. 9): the philosophers of the future must possess that will to a degree which was not even dreamed of by the philosophy of the past: they must possess that will in absolute form. The new philosophers *are or act*, we are tempted to say, to the highest degree according to nature. (#25; italics ours)

Eternal Recurrence: Nietzsche's Religiosity

We can attempt to make Strauss's elusive ideas concerning Nietzsche clearer by addressing another key, unusual element of his reading: on Nietzsche's attitudes towards religion. In 'A Note on the Plan', Strauss singles out two key aphorisms (BGE 36 and 37) on Nietzsche and religion in *Beyond Good and Evil*, Chapter III (#8). Strauss is taken particularly by Nietzsche's highly gnomic aphorism 37:

> 'What? Does that, to speak vulgarly, not mean: God is refuted but the devil is not – ?' On the contrary! On the contrary, my friends! And who the devil compels you to speak vulgarly!

As this playful jibe comes straight after a decisive aphorism (BGE 36) on the hypothesis of the will to power (#8), Strauss claims that 'the doctrine of the will to power–the whole doctrine of *Beyond Good and Evil*–is in a manner a vindication of God (see 150 and 295, as well as *Genealogy of Morals*, Preface 7)' (#8). The nature of this vindication is discovered by Strauss in BGE Chapter III (46–8; 52). Herein the Torah and pagan religions are admired for their 'great style' not because of the greatness of the holy God of which the former speaks, Strauss contests, but for the power of the human *will* such visions attest to (#10). Strauss's Nietzsche's 'vindication of God' is hence atheistic, in line with most other readings of Nietzsche (#11). Since the advent of Christianity and the triumph of slave morality, Nietzsche teaches elsewhere, God has died as a powerful or life-giving creation in the minds of the moderns (see BGE 53).

Yet Strauss notes that Nietzsche is careful to distinguish between this senescent, post-*Christian* God (see BGE 49–51) and what he terms 'religiosity' or the 'god-forming instinct' in human beings. The latter instinct Nietzsche sees as alive and well in the moderns. Only the old, life-denying God of what Nietzsche elsewhere calls 'monotonotheism' is refuted by the will to power. This leaves open the possibility of some new form of more life-affirming religiosity:

> Could atheism belong to the free mind as Nietzsche conceives of it while a certain kind of non-atheism belongs to the philosopher of the future who will again worship the god Dionysus or will again be, as an Epicurean might say, a *dionysokolax* [actor/ worshipper or flatterer of Dionysus] (see 7)? (#11)

For Strauss, Nietzsche's other great teaching, the eternal recurrence, is the heart of his alleged, new religious philosophizing. In a central subsection of *Beyond Good and Evil*, Chapter III (#55–56) – surrounded by the earlier fragments on older religions (47–54), and on religion per se (56–62) – Strauss notes that Nietzsche's reflections ascend through three rungs of what he terms the 'great ladder of religious cruelty' (BGE 55). First, human beings were sacrificed to the Gods; then, ascetics would sacrifice their own instincts or nature to their God. In aphorism 56, Nietzsche looks forward now to a third stage: ' . . . the sacrificing from cruelty, i.e. from the will to power turning against itself, of God which prepares the worshipping of the stone, stupidity, heaviness (gravity), fate, the Nothing . . . ' (#12). This sacrifice does not represent a world-denial or end in itself, for Nietzsche or his privileged addressees. Rather, Strauss's Nietzsche's 'enigmatic desire'[5] is that *by* plumbing the most extreme pessimism and world-denial, the way towards a new religiosity, one of the eternal recurrence, is opened:

> The adoration of the Nothing proves to be the indispensable transition from every kind of world-denial to the most unbounded Yes: the eternal Yes-saying to everything that was and is. (#13)[6]

'We' Scholars

We are becoming clearer concerning Strauss's Nietzsche's remarkable views concerning the philosophers of the future. These extraordinary men will recognize the truth of all truths, concerning the will to power. This recognition, which looks like the most far-reaching pessimism about higher values, will lead them to a hitherto unheard-of religiosity, through the affirmation of the eternal recurrence of what was and is. It is not clear, to say the least, whether all men are capable of this elevated spirituality. More clear is that these philosophers of the future will also be *dionysokolax*, lovers of Dionysus, and perhaps 'invisible spiritual rulers' (#30; see BGE 61).

One obvious objection to such a vision runs like this: can even those who feel drawn to affirming that modernity is 'a form assumed by man in decay', possibly look towards *new philosophers* as the means of their redemption (BGE 207)? As Nietzsche's Preface in *Beyond Good and Evil* sets out, are not philosophers the most incompetent of dogmatic blunderers when it comes to the ways of women and the world of power? Here we return to the question, mooted above, of Nietzsche's addressees. For Strauss's Nietzsche, we above all must not confuse the 'sorry lot' of men and women who pass for philosophers today for the type of philosopher Nietzsche means to elevate (#28). The academics who 'do philosophy' today, Strauss writes, are only 'in rare cases scholars or scientists, i.e. competent and honest specialists who of right ought to be subservient to philosophy or handmaidens to philosophy' (loc cit.).

Strauss's Nietzschean philosopher (see #26), in contrast to such academics, is a decidedly untimely man. *Contra* Hegel, he knows the philosopher is not the son of his time. He is its step-son: 'the philosopher as philosopher belongs to the future and was therefore at all times in contradiction to his Today: the philosophers were always the bad conscience of their time' (#30). So elevated is Nietzsche's conception of such philosophers that in their shadow thinkers of the rank of Hegel and Kant are only 'philosophic labourers' (loc cit.; BGE 211–12). True Nietzschean philosophers create values, rather than patiently mirroring what is; far from being disengaged from the ways of the world, they are going to affirm it in all its misery and its splendour, ' "to endure the weight of the responsibility for the future of man . . . " (*Gay Science* 34)' (#27).

Notably, it is in the paragraphs on 'We Scholars' from Strauss's 'Note on the Plan' that Strauss seems to align himself most closely with the Nietzschean philosophy he is expounding. 'Note on the Plan', paragraph 28, highlights the fact that Nietzsche's *Beyond Good and Evil* Chapter VI has the only chapter heading containing the first person of the personal pronoun 'we'. Provocatively, Strauss ends his paragraph devoted to this part of Nietzsche's book with his own personal observation: 'The things which *we* have observed in the twentieth century regarding the sciences of man confirm Nietzsche's diagnosis' (#28; italics ours; see #26).

Our Virtues: Retranslating History Back into Nature

As we have said, Strauss's manifest appreciation for Nietzsche's rival Platonism is a key charge in the controversy surrounding his philosophic or political legacy. One thing Strauss says of Nietzsche can also be said of Strauss: that his philosophic work is untimely, at least in the sense that Strauss very rarely commented in print on the events of the day. In Strauss's 'Note on the Plan of *Beyond Good and Evil*', an article central to any left-liberal critique of Strauss, only a single paragraph, the thirty-seventh, raises Nietzsche's political reflections in BGE, Chapter VIII, concerning a united confederacy of states of Europe (#37).[7]

Whatever sympathies Strauss may intimate between his views and Nietzsche's in this essay, it has to be strongly stated that Strauss maintains Nietzsche's association with nineteenth-century historicism in 'Note on the Plan': ' . . . the alleged realisation that truth is a function of time (historical epoch) or that every philosophy belongs to a definite time and place (country) . . . ' (#29). Strauss seems to be underlining this proximity between Nietzsche and historicism by, strangely, citing Marx and Engels some *three times* in the 'Note on the Plan' (#12; #25; #32) – which is hardly a flattering gesture under Strauss's pen. When Strauss turns to *Beyond Good and Evil*, Chapter VII, 'Our Virtues', in the seventh part of his own essay, he spends most time discussing Nietzsche's embrace of the 'historical sense' of the nineteenth-century scholars, in order to overturn the nineteenth century's drift towards democratic mediocrity. For Strauss's Nietzsche, the free spirit must develop his historical sense or 'probity' to see the multiple different moralities human history exemplifies, up to the master morality of men like Caesar or Alcibiades (see #25; #31; BGE 186; 226–7). How though can this backward-looking probity be coupled with Nietzsche's forward-looking to the philosopher of the future (#13)? As Strauss queries: 'How indeed can the demand for something absolutely new, this intransigent farewell to the whole past, to all "history" be reconciled with the unbounded Yes to everything that was and is?' (#27).

Strauss's answer is that Nietzsche, however much his historicism might seem to push nature out with a hayfork (see #29), aspires to what BGE terms the 'retranslation' of 'the terrible basic text *homo natura*' – which would include human history – back into nature. Strauss's interpretation of Nietzsche here is that the conscious willing of new values by the philosophers of the future represents the culmination of human history, as the classless society was supposed to be for Marx and Engels (see Strauss, 1989b, pp. 97–8). However, Strauss now adds to his earlier claims concerning the philosophers of the future the claim that for Nietzsche all human history was *the necessary precondition* for this new species of philosophy:

That is to say, the *Vernaturlichung* [naturalization] of man presupposes and brings to its conclusion the whole historical process–a completion which is by no means necessary but requires a free, creative act. Still, in this way history can be said to be integrated into nature. (#34; see also #35)

This is the most philosophic content that can be given to Strauss's repetition of the Nietzschean claim that the complementary man or philosopher of the future is he 'in whom not only man but the rest of existence is justified (see BGE 207)' (#30; see #31). In the closing paragraphs to 'Note on the Plan', Strauss enumerates the untimely political aspects of this position. The complementary man knows, on the ground of his own individual nature, that 'there is an order of rank of the natures; at the summit of the hierarchy is the complementary man' (#35). Far from striving to eliminate suffering and inequality, Strauss's Nietzsche realizes that these are 'the prerequisites of human greatness (BGE 239 and 257)' (#35).

However, whereas hitherto such suffering and inequality have been taken for granted as 'given' or imposed on man by nature, '[h]enceforth, they must be willed' (loc cit.):

> While paving the way for the complementary man, one must at the same time say an unbounded Yes to the fragments and cripples. Nature, the eternity of nature, owes its being to a postulation, to an act of will to power on the part of the highest nature. (#35)

Strauss's Legacy: Stanley Rosen's Nietzsche

It is interesting, and telling, in light of the charges that Strauss above all corrupted his youthful students, to examine how at least one of Strauss's most renowned and brilliant students, Stanley Rosen, confirms that there *are* similarities between Strauss and Nietzsche. Strauss is 'almost a Nietzschean, but not quite', as Rosen says (Rosen, 1987, pp. 125–7, 180). Rosen's own reading of Nietzsche, moreover, bears significant marks of Strauss's influence, as we will now consider in closing. Stanley Rosen's fascinating, at times confronting, contention concerning Nietzsche is that Nietzsche's publication of the 'deadly truths' of will to power, nihilism, and perspectivism was rhetorical, as much as philosophical – a first, decisive sign of Strauss' influence upon him. Far from a neutral or simply 'scholarly' author, Rosen's Nietzsche was both anticipating and advocating for the philosophy of the future he preached: first of all by trying to 'accelerate' the destruction of Western society and modern values premised upon the dead, post-Christian God. This Nietzsche's aim was indeed to actively overcome modernity through his books, in two ways, corresponding to the two levels of what Rosen calls his 'double-rhetoric' (Rosen, 1989a, p. 190).

On a first, exoteric level, Rosen's Nietzsche thought to persuade 'the mediocre, the foolish, and the mad' to believe that *they* are the complementary men. This would encourage these lesser types to embrace a life-denying and destructive relativism, clearing the cultural state for the addresses of the second, esoteric level of his message. The second, other side of Nietzsche's philosophical rhetoric, according to Rosen, involved the more elevated attempt to midwife the true 'artist-warriors', the 'highest, most gifted human types', who will actively shape the future by creating the new values necessary for human existence (Rosen, 1989a, pp. 189–191).

It is then easy to see in Rosen's Nietzsche a reflection of Strauss's earlier reclaiming of Nietzsche as a profoundly aristocratic thinker – yet one who was not for all that in any way 'conservative', due to the radical nature of his program (Rosen, 1989a, p. 19; see Strauss, 1989a, p. 40). Again, when we consider what type of society Rosen understands Nietzsche to envision as his goal, it is clear how Rosen, like Strauss (#25), points to those passages where Nietzsche speaks highly of *conquering* men and races such as the Romans, Arabians, the Renaissance city states and *poleis* of Homeric Greece (Rosen, 1989a, pp. 192–3, 196). Rosen's Nietzsche's use of historical paradigms is meant to indicate to the few, superior readers of the future the possibility of 'fulfilment of human existence at its best' (loc. cit.) and that such possibilities – again as in Strauss's interpretation of Nietzsche – are from here on to be consciously willed. The values, or art, willed by the highest human types on this view will be of greater value than any previous 'truth' (WP 853 (IV)) on the basis that art 'not merely enhances but produces life: art is the illusion by which we are inured, or rather charmed, into living a noble lie' (Rosen, 1989a, p. 198; see Strauss, 1953, p. 26). However much this position reflects Strauss' influence, it is fair to say that Strauss was never anything like so bold in the expression of his teachings (see Strauss, 1953, p. 26).

Notes

[1] In a lecture on Heideggerian existentialism, the mature Strauss intimated to his audience that he believed no one had written more nobly on what a philosopher is than Friedrich Nietzsche (Strauss, 1989a).

[2] Translations of TI here are from *Twilight of the Idols / The Anti-Christ*, trans. R.J. Hollingdale. London: Penguin, 1990.

[3] Except when quoting from Strauss's text, translations of BGE here are from *Beyond Good and Evil*, trans. R.J. Hollingdale. London: Penguin, 1990.

[4] Following Lampert (1996), we will reference 'A Note on the Plan of *Beyond Good and Evil*' from here on via numbered paragraphs (#-).

[5] For, as Strauss notes, Nietzsche is far from categorical in his presentation of the eternal recurrence and its significance in *Beyond Good and Evil*. Like aphorism 37, aphorism 56 ends with a playful, theological question which entices readers without providing any clear answer: 'And this [the eternal recurrence of what

was and is] would not be *circulus vitiosis deus* [the vicious circle made God]?"'
(BGE 56; #13).

[6] One further point concerning Strauss's Nietzsche's religiosity is concealed in
Strauss's passing, cited reference in paragraph 11 to how the new, religious philosophers of the eternal recurrence will again be '*dionysokolax*' (#11). Following
Strauss's reference to BGE 7, we see that this term, which means 'actors', was used
by the Epicureans to attack the Platonists for being 'tyrants' hangers on and lick-
spittles'–after Plato himself who famously tried to install himself as the invisible
advisor-teacher of the Syracusan tyrant Dionysos (BGE 9). Strauss's recurrence to
this 'venomous' Epicurean criticism of Platonic political philosophy seems
unusual in the context of his evocation of the experimental religiosity of the philosophers of the future. What it perhaps points us towards is the final section of
BGE chapter III, which Strauss passes over, where Nietzsche remarkably states a
variant of the old Platonic teaching concerning the political value of theology as
a noble fiction or lie, *viz*: 'For the strong and independent prepared and predes-
tined for command in whom the art and reason of a ruling race is incarnated,
religion is one more means of overcoming resistance so as to be able to rule; a
bond that unites together ruler and ruled, that hands over to the former the conscience of the latter, all that is hidden and would like to exclude itself from
obedience . . . (BGE 61)'.

[7] To this, we could add only one, earlier comment of Strauss' own, on the concern
of Nietzsche's philosophers of the future to preserve the united states of the new
Europe from the threat posed by Russia (#30).

Bibliography and Guide to Further Study

Strauss's Nietzsche Interpretation

Strauss, Leo (1983), 'Note on the Plan of *Beyond Good and Evil*', in id., *Studies in
Platonic Political Philosophy*. Chicago: University of Chicago Press. Strauss's only
dedicated mature piece on Nietzsche, and the indispensable statement of
Strauss's considered position on Nietzsche's *oeuvre*.

— (1988a), 'What Is Political Philosophy?' in id., *What Is Political Philosophy? and
Other Studies*. Chicago: University of Chicago Press. This extended essay, written
as a public lecture on the history of Western political philosophy, culminates in
an account of Nietzsche.

— (1989a), 'Introduction to Heideggerian Existentialism', in Thomas L. Pangle
(ed.), *Rebirth of Classical Political Rationalism*. Chicago: University of Chicago
Press. Fascinating, sweeping reading of Heidegger, including an intriguing central engagement with Nietzsche and Nietzsche's critique of modernity.

— (1989b), 'Three Waves of Modernity', in Hilail Gildin (ed.), *An Introduction to
Political Philosophy: Ten Essays by Leo Strauss*. Detroit: Wayne State University Press.
Famous, accessible essay on the evolution of modern thought from Machiavelli,
Hobbes, and Locke, via Rousseau, which culminates in Nietzsche as the ambigu-
ous third wave of modernity.

Other Works by Strauss

— (1953), *Natural Right and History.* Chicago: University of Chicago Press.

— (1964) *The City and Man.* University of Chicago Press: Chicago.

— (1988b), *Persecution and the Art of Writing.* Chicago: University of Chicago Press [1952].

— (1990), 'Some Remarks on the Political Science of Maimonides and Farabi', trans. Robert Bartlett, *Interpretation*, 18, (1), 3–30.

Works on Strauss's Nietzsche

Lampert, Laurence (1996), *Leo Strauss and Nietzsche.* Chicago: University of Chicago Press. Indispensable text on Strauss's text on Nietzsche, centring around a paragraph-by-paragraph reading of 'A Note on the Plan of *Beyond Good and Evil*'.

Drury, Shadia (1988), *The Political Ideas of Leo Strauss.* New York: St. Martin's Press. Chapter 8: 'Post-modernity–Plato or Nietzsche?' Drury's book is a *success de scandal* in Strauss scholarship, universally reviled by his students, it includes a culminating chapter which argues that Strauss's Platonism is a concealed Nietzschean political philosophy.

Levine, Peter (1995), 'A "Right" Nietzschean: Leo Strauss and his Followers', in id., *Nietzsche and the Modern Crisis of the Humanities.* Albany: SUNY Press. Controversial paper which tries to prosecute a case similar to that of Drury, 1988: that Strauss is an esoteric Nietzschean.

Waite, Geoffrey (1996), *Nietzsche's Corps/e: Aesthetics, Politics, Prophecy, or the Spectacular Technoculture of Everyday Life.* Durham, NC: Duke University Press. Contains sustained engagement with Strauss and his students' 'Right Nietzsche', in particular the work of Stanley Rosen.

Works on Nietzsche by Students of Strauss

Lampert, Laurence (1986), *Nietzsche's Teaching: An Interpretation of* Thus Spoke Zarathustra. New Haven: Yale University Press. Extended commentary on *Thus Spoke Zarathrustra* as Nietzsche's 'most profound' work.

— (1993), *Nietzsche and Modern Times: A Study of Bacon, Descartes, and Nietzsche.* New Haven: Yale University Press. Intriguing study of early modern thought in the light of the Straussian esotericist hypothesis, which culminates in an engagement with Nietzsche as a distinctly modern thinker.

— (2001), *Nietzsche's Task: An Interpretation of* Beyond Good and Evil. New Haven: Yale University Press. Detailed, section-by-section study of *Beyond Good and Evil*, in extended discussion with Strauss's 'A Note on the Plan of *Beyond Good and Evil*'.

Rosen, Stanley (1987), *Hermeneutics as Politics.* Oxford: Oxford University Press.

— (1989a), *The Ancients and the Moderns: Rethinking Modernity.* Newhaven, CT: Yale University Press. Contains the important essay 'Nietzsche's Revolution' in which Rosen announces many of the ideas concerning Nietzsche's 'double rhetoric' and strategy to overcome modern nihilism he would develop in *The Mask of Enlightenment* (2004).

— (1989b), 'Remarks on Nietzsche's Platonism', in Tom Darby, Béla Egyed, and Ben Jones (eds), *Nietzsche and the Rhetoric of Nihilism: Essays on Interpretation, Language and Politics*. Canada: Carleton University Press.

— (2002), 'Wittgenstein, Strauss, and the possibility of Philosophy', in id., *The Elusiveness of the Ordinary*. New Haven: Yale University Press.

— (2004), *The Mask of Enlightenment: Nietzsche's Zarathustra*, 2nd edn. New Haven: Yale University Press. Definitive statement of Rosen's radical, post-Straussian reading of Nietzsche's philosophy and politics.

— (2009), 'Nietzsche's Double Rhetoric: Which Nihilism?', in Jeffrey A. Metzger (ed.), *Nietzsche, Nihilism, and the Philosophy of the Future*. London and New York: Continuum. Shorter public statement of many of the positions in Rosen's *The Mask of Enlightenment*.

Zuckert, Catherine (1996), *Postmodern Platos*. Chicago: University of Chicago Press. Especially Chapter 1 (on Nietzsche) and Chapters 4–6 (on Strauss). Extended, clearly written engagement with Nietzsche as a respondent to Plato, and Strauss as a respondent to both Plato and Nietzsche.

Chapter 10

Vattimo's Nietzsche

Robert T. Valgenti

. . . Nietzsche is well aware that the violence that gives birth to metaphysics and that it represents is not completely gone, and in fact demands a 'violent' decision that eliminates it from everything by positing the real conditions of a world and of a thinking that are no longer metaphysical. Thinking that is no longer metaphysical not only demands that the conditions of life in nature are no longer precarious and insecure as they were with primitive humanity; it also demands from these new, mature conditions a truly different humanity, one equal to the new situation.

Vattimo, 1974[1]

Gianni Vattimo, the Italian philosopher, cultural critic and politician, interprets the legacy of Western metaphysics as one burdened by a fundamental violence. But Vattimo also suggests that this inheritance, if interpreted carefully and with a sense of the times in the manner suggested by Nietzsche, could support a philosophical project of human liberation. Nietzsche's nihilism, so often misunderstood as a form of radical scepticism, is in Vattimo's estimation the key to interpreting metaphysics in terms of its continual weakening rather than its final overcoming. Such a position is more reliant than others on a cohesive, if not systematic reading of Nietzsche; yet, Vattimo truly breaks stride with other interpreters through his consideration of Nietzsche as a pre-eminently hermeneutic philosopher whose thoughts have profound, and ultimately positive, political consequences.

In the broadest sense, a positive reading of Nietzsche and his particular emphasis on the idea of an 'accomplished nihilism' is what most profoundly distinguishes Vattimo from his French (and even American) counterparts. The Italian interpreters of Nietzsche from the 1960s through the 1980s proposed in general a more 'constructive' reading that tried to move beyond the merely 'critical' Nietzsche of French interpreters such as

Klossowski, Foucault, Derrida, and others. Yet, even among Italian interpreters, Vattimo's emphasis on liberation underscores the uniqueness of
his reading: Nietzsche as the herald of post-metaphysical thinking, which is
grounded in nihilism, the dissolution of Being, and the possibility of its
being 'accomplished' in the fullest sense that one can give to the term. This
move differs greatly from the 'vitalistic' readings of Nietzsche that rely on
an essentialization of life and its creative powers (Klossowski, Bataille and
Deleuze), but also from the more 'aesthetic' readings of Nietzsche (Derrida
and Nehemas), which see radical critique and revolution as matters of style
(Vattimo, 2006, pp. 200–1). The pervasiveness of the 'aesthetic' reading is
in Vattimo's estimation symptomatic of our age, due to the general loss of
hope that a revolutionary change of the capitalist system is possible and
imminent.[2] Thus, these readings are 'a characteristic facet of a nihilism that
has no hope of constructing anything historically and no prospect of becoming a "state"' (2006, p. 201).

  This orientation toward the political outcomes of nihilism is present
throughout Vattimo's readings of Nietzsche, from his earliest studies in the
1960s to the formulation of his emblematic 'weak thought', and most
recently, in his notions of an 'ontology of actuality' and of 'hermeneutic
communism'. And while Vattimo's reading of Nietzsche borrows some of its
transformative force from Wilhelm Dilthey's characterization of Nietzsche
as a 'life' philosopher, it is more importantly Heidegger's understanding of
Nietzsche as a traditional philosopher concerned with the question of Being
(Vattimo, 2001, pp. 1–7) that underscores the epochal nature of Vattimo's
recovery of and from nihilism. Vattimo therefore reads Nietzsche through
the problems of Being and truth as they unfold within history and within
the ever-changing world of life and existence. What he discovers is not vital-
ism, but instead, the beginning of hermeneutic ontology: the inception of
a form of philosophy that begins with the premise that 'there are no facts,
only interpretations', and then interprets Being and truth from within the
very history of their decline and weakening. Vattimo's Nietzsche unfolds as
part of a broader attempt – one that he argues is central to hermeneutic
ontology – to recover the positive features of nihilism and to establish a
philosophy of liberation and non-violence.

The Problem of History: Nihilism

The opening chapter of Vattimo's 1963 book on Heidegger[3] presents a positive interpretation of Heidegger's thesis that 'Nietzsche is the completion

of the history of metaphysics and thus the prophet of the modern world'
(p. 15). Nietzsche transforms the thinking of metaphysics and prophesizes
its overcoming by diagnosing nihilism as the fundamental condition of
modern society: it is symptomatic of the crisis regarding the meaning of
Being and truth, a crisis which includes the alienating forces of industrialized capitalist production and modern techno-science. At this very
early stage of his career Vattimo articulates the full arc of his thinking of
liberation by linking Nietzsche's philosophical program with Heidegger
and Marx: 'What for Marx is alienation, and what for Heidegger is the
forgetting of Being, Nietzsche calls nihilism' (Vattimo, 1963, p. 49). In
the very *summa* of the errors of metaphysics, Vattimo discovers the possibility for an active nihilism and a recovery from the fundamental violence of metaphysics.

With Heidegger's thesis in mind, Vattimo interprets Nietzsche as the
prophet of the *decline*, and not the culmination, of Western metaphysics. In
his earliest works on Nietzsche,[4] Vattimo presents the integral connection
between history, metaphysics, and the destiny of Being as a challenge to
resist the tendency to read Nietzsche as either the completion and most
extreme form of metaphysics – the mark of Heidegger's reading, as well as
the politicized interpretation of 'will to power' embraced by National Socialism – or the reduction of all value to the endless play of historical forms. One
could say that Vattimo interprets the broad range of Nietzsche's terminology
– nihilism, the doctrine of eternal recurrence, the *Übermensch*, and the will to
power – as the end of thinking value in terms of absolutes, and ultimately,
the end of the violence of metaphysics. This does not mean, however, that
the belief in absolutes gives way to an unending conflict of interpretations or
a complete aestheticization of experience. Central to Vattimo's reading of
Nietzsche is the philosopher's awareness of her own historical context and
the way it reorients the questions of Being and truth.

In his interpretation of *The Birth of Tragedy*, where the tragic age of Greek
society transforms into the ideal of Socratic *ratio*,[5] Vattimo isolates a central
problem: how would an exit from the age of metaphysics and the dominance of Socratic *ratio* ever be possible for human beings? Vattimo's reading of the second of the *Untimely Meditations* pushes this question even
further, as its anti-historicism and 'critique of modernity as "mass society"'
sustain his interpretation of Nietzsche as a socially and politically relevant
thinker (Vattimo et al., 2009, pp. 316–17). The key discovery of this meditation is that the rational study of history is by its very nature historical, and
thus is itself a historical innovation rather than a set of claims that corres-
pond to past events. The society and individuals who suffer from the

historical malady bear the mark of historicism: the acceptance of a providential order to history and the absolute relativization of human activity to the epoch in which it occurs; they exhibit a 'homelessness' and are unaware that human life is 'an imperfect tense that can never become a perfect one' (HL 1). Lacking any deep connection to the origin (and thus plastic, creative forces) of culture and its forms, they can at best copy, catalogue, and codify the experiences of life and history.

As mentioned, Vattimo's concern reaches beyond the vitalistic and existential implications of Nietzsche's diagnosis and interprets Nietzsche as a critic of modern, capitalistic consumption (Vattimo, 2006, pp. 6–7). For a society that has lost its creative capacity, even historical knowledge becomes an object of manipulation in the name of scientific objectivity, a commodity that can be reproduced, repeated and perfected according to the desires of those who claim to control it. In response to these symptoms of Socratic *ratio*, the work of the philosopher and philologist – the recognition of and resignation to the irrationality of history – is still only the precondition for taking a stance toward it, and not yet a choice and a decision. Nonetheless, such a stance allows history to be grasped as a living and always-transforming fact, and this, rather than the sheer creative force of human will, is how Vattimo understands the 'highest strength of the present' from which the past can be interpreted and, in a sense, made anew.

Nihilism, as this acute historical awareness *and* the historical inheritance that constitutes its possibility, is not enough to overcome the yoke of metaphysics because this possibility presents itself as a universal and permanent condition constitutive of humanity. While such a claim seems to contradict Vattimo's reading of Nietzsche as anti-essentialist through and through, nihilism nonetheless and unavoidably *appears* as a 'natural' trait as long as society exists in the epoch of nihilism; as cause and symptom, it will remain as long as its diagnosis is taken as the truth – in an objective sense – of society's shared history. From Vattimo's perspective, the spirit of Nietzsche's early works does not aim to critique a form of life that could simply be replaced, but to offer a diagnosis of a historical condition that *seems* unavoidable from within the throes of nihilism.

Vattimo nonetheless finds in the 'plastic power' of the doctrine of eternal recurrence[6] the possibility of an active, transformative form of nihilism. He suggests that 'the whole significance of Nietzsche's philosophical stance – whether his thought is merely a *symptom* of European decadence (as many of his interpreters, including perhaps not just Lukács but even Heidegger, to some degree, have thought) or also a practicable way of escaping from decadence – depends on the possibility of drawing a clear distinction between the two meanings of nihilism' (Vattimo, 2001, p. 134). Passive nihilism, the symptom of a decadent age, is reactive, refuses to acknowledge the dissolution of all values, and is marked by its 'yes' saying – to truth, to objectivity, to eternal values – through the symbolic forms of art, religion and morality. Active nihilism, on the other hand, is marked by its ability to say 'no' to the eternal and unchanging values of decadent society; through the dissolution of values, it strives to create new values.

There is, however, a logical catch for Vattimo, since the absolute promotion of newly minted values would merely fall back into the 'yes' saying of passive nihilism. While active nihilism is most often understood in two ways – a hermeneutic self-awareness and sense of ironic detachment whereby one lives as if one were continuing to dream (GS 54), or an extra-hermeneutic power driven by the vital force to create ever-newer interpretations in perpetual conflict with each other – Vattimo's strategy is to show that neither reading taken exclusively is adequate to Nietzsche's intention, since even the vitalistic position, so favoured by French interpreters, rests upon an essentialized notion of 'life' which is just as symptomatic of decadence and nihilism as is a detached self-awareness. Vattimo's interpretation suggests that the critical spirit and necessity of being 'untimely' is retained only by attempting to transform the violent thinking that defines the history of Western metaphysics. In this way, the problem of nihilism is tied to the broader problem of the forgetting of Being, when rational history (or more properly, positive techno-science) becomes the foundation and characteristic expression of modern society.

The Problem of Liberation: Masking and Unmasking

Vattimo, on the heels of the social and political turmoil of 1968, intensifies his political reading of Nietzsche as a philosopher of liberation, an intellectual companion to the real proletariat. This spirit coalesces in *Il soggetto e la maschera* (*The Subject and Its Mask*, 1974), a work that reflects the political spirit of the time and that Vattimo himself hoped would make him 'the ideologist for the radical libertarian Left' (Vattimo et al., 2009, p. 322). The central thesis of *Il soggetto e la maschera* argues that the liberation *from* the symbolic or Dionysian realm, characteristic of Socratic *ratio*, can be undermined through a liberation *of* the symbolic or Dionysian realm, and thus, a liberation of all forms of knowing from the foundational thinking of metaphysics. While the motif of the mask is not common in Nietzsche, Vattimo utilizes it to discuss the relation between humans and the practice

of 'masking' characteristic of metaphysics – an inevitable, human consequence born from insecurity about the flux of history and the inevitability
of death. In light of this tendency, the task of the philosopher, or even the
philologist, is not to describe reality 'truthfully', but to embrace that flux
and interpret reality as a project of liberation for humanity that must be
constructed.

The itinerary of *Il soggetto e la maschera* ranges across Nietzsche's entire
corpus in order to illustrate how the 'unmasking of metaphysics' transforms
into a thoroughgoing 'unmasking of unmasking' in response to the dominion of scientific reason. Vattimo isolates three essential discoveries: in the
early works, the Dionysian and thus non-decadent character of art is presented as a positive alternative to the dominance of Socratic *ratio*; in the
'middle period', the shared moral-metaphysical nature of all symbolic
forms, including art, is exposed, preparing a reading of 'eternal recurrence'
that separates art's positive quality from its negative; and in the works following *Zarathustra*, as imagined in the figure of the *Übermensch*, the freedom
of symbolic forms is no longer considered the domain of the artist and art,
but constitutive of the historical and concrete existence of all humanity
(Vattimo, 1974, pp. 305–6).

Vattimo begins this work by reconsidering the thesis that the tragic is a
more originary alternative to the decadent masking of the Apollonian spirit
and Socratic *ratio* – the tragic is now understood as a 'peculiar form of
mask' (ibid., p. 20). However, there is a distinction to be made: there is the
particular mask of decadence, and there is also masking in general that
delimits a horizon, or in Heideggerian terms, 'opens a world'. By Vattimo's
account, Nietzsche's early works theorize decadence and its overcoming in
a manner that is still decadent and thus problematic; yet, these works nonetheless expose the guiding thread Vattimo wants to follow: the frustration of
the individual's power in the face of Socratic *ratio*, or in its more modern
form, the scientific-technological organization of the world. In terms of the
work's thesis – the liberation of the Dionysian, the liberation of the symbolic – the creative, plastic, life-empowering force must be understood as a
'freely political' possibility that lives within the world of forms, a liberation
of the Dionysian and the symbolic from the foundational thinking of
metaphysics.

The second part of *Il soggetto e la maschera* centres upon Vattimo's developing attempt to read Nietzsche as a critic of the history of metaphysics
and a philosopher who is relevant for the political Left. Through *Human
All Too Human*, *Daybreak*, and *The Gay Science*, Vattimo identifies Nietzsche's
central concern as the problem of 'decadence and possibility', namely,

the solidification of various fictions into truth and the subsequent inability of anything new to ever truly be created. Even modern technology and the promise for a new world offered by scientific reasoning cannot break the spell of metaphysics, which permeates every form of social life from religion and morality to history and science. What Nietzsche proposes as a solution is not simply an unmasking of the masking characteristic of all symbolic forms – this would only be *critique* as yet another form of masking – but an *appropriation* of the history of decadent society in order to complete 'the unmasking in order to unmask the unmasking itself' (ibid., p. 83) and to show how reason and science participate in the *Dionysian* or *symbolic* generation of masks (see WS 43).

Vattimo's interpretation of science as a continuation of the process of masking uncovers the deep connection between metaphysics and violence, which he sees primarily in Nietzsche's aphorisms dedicated to the question of human struggle and survival (see WS 61). The most powerful 'fable' or ruse that the history of metaphysics has perpetrated is the belief in a fundamental essence – God, nature, and so forth – and the institution of a system, born of human insecurity, which in the name of that essence perpetuates and institutes that very same violence and insecurity. This reduction of all things to the basic principles of substance and freedom are what Nietzsche calls the 'fundamental errors' put forward as fundamental truths (see HAH 18). If a way out of this logic of absolutes is possible, it begins with an awareness of human finitude and historicity, such that even the most basic and elemental struggles of primitive humanity – the birth of morality as a salve for the displeasures of scarcity, violence, and a need for security – are understood as symbolic forms or constructions that shape the humanity of that time, but not in an essential or absolute way. So even though metaphysics is 'born in a threatening and violent situation' (Vattimo, 1974, p. 114), such an origin is not taken as unchanging and absolute, and thus resistant to anything new; rather, the origin points to changing conditions, and thus the demand for a changing notion of humanity (see KGW XVI, 52; IV, 3). The new is possible *because* there is no absolute origin, no ultimate ground or essence to which all things must return or remain true, but only the play of appearances as the liberation *of* the symbolic.

Vattimo is not convinced that Nietzsche's solution in the middle works is up to the task of grasping truly new possibilities by embracing the 'truth' of error. Yet in art, the privileged metaphysical form for Nietzsche, Vattimo finds a possibility because it momentarily suspends the laws of reality by presenting a world different from that of everyday insecurity, a perfection of its representative products that neither theorizes nor promises in the ways characteristic of metaphysics and religion (ibid., p. 135). Its *emphemerality*, the root of its decline, is also the source of its ability to revel in its multiform nature. Art is therefore especially threatened because the scientific reasoning of metaphysics reduces everything, including art, to its utility and its narcotic function. Given this critique, 'error' (HAH 19–34) cannot be evaluated according to how it *functions* for humans (which would be to still interpret it in terms of *ratio*), but as evidence of the very multitude of forms of life. The 'free spirit' (introduced in HAH 30) as the one who tolerates error, who lives with the 'good mask' and resists the reactive tendency to be driven by survival, vengeance, and struggle, represents a positive possibility in the face of a metaphysics of decline.

The method of genealogy also exposes the self-negation of metaphysics, which occurs when the symbolic order turns back on itself and reveals the violence at the root of metaphysical reasoning: 'The history of the genesis of thought, not as the history of its *origin*, but of its *becoming*, is thus the true liquidation of the notion of the thing in itself, and implies the birth of a new thinking no longer oriented by the metaphysical impulse of foundation in any of its forms' (Vattimo, 1974, p. 146). Vattimo distinguishes his position from the still-metaphysical readings of genealogy given by Gilles Deleuze and Jean Granier, emphasizing above all that genealogy is not the critique and refutation of morality; rather, it is the history of its origin as the process of becoming. The 'death of God' is in a sense the birth of 'becoming' and true liberation *of* the symbolic, with 'the unmasking of morals' and 'the unmasking of unmasking' catalyzing this event: 'In this activity, the thinker is the one who, on the one hand, contributes to the preparation of the new world (together with which other forces?); on the other hand, in his way of being and thinking, already anticipates the characteristics of the existence of the new human, as though the "historical" consciousness recovers for himself the freedom of the symbolic, as the comic actor and the artist' (ibid., p. 164). The exact form of this new human, one who could lift herself above metaphysics and out of the climate of violence, is the focus of the final part of *Il soggetto e la maschera*, illustrating the centrality of *Thus Spoke Zarathustra* and the concept of the *Übermensch* to Vattimo's interpretation. The challenge, however, is both a theoretical and practical framing of the problem of the new: how to define such a human, and how to bring such a human into existence?

At this point, Vattimo returns to the doctrine of eternal recurrence presented in 'On the Vision and the Riddle' (Z 3) to suggest its role as a transformative catalyst of the world and humanity: 'to bring about the eternal recurrence therefore means, and here is its point of contact with the doctrine of the overman, to produce a humanity capable of willing repetition, capable of living without the anxiety of time as the tendency towards a completion that is always beyond, always yet to come' (Vattimo, 1974, p. 207). The *Übermensch* is the one who can will eternal recurrence, the one who is joyful and wills the transformative power of decision. This human cannot break entirely free from the structures of violence (as the 'break' entails its own violence), but can release itself from any dependence on external values, criteria, foundations, and origins by embracing the moment of decision. The doctrine of the eternal recurrence is therefore not an ecstatic theory of time, but a critique of the subject as consciousness and the internalization of the structures of domination – it is, ultimately, a critique and negation of transcendence, whereby the shepherd who bites off the head of the snake enacts 'a reduction *to* decision and a reduction *of* decision' (ibid., p. 210) so that the unity of Being and meaning can finally be lived.

Such liberation is possible when the love of error and the creative force of the will coalesce in the *Übermensch* as a rejection of domination and the fragmentary character of human existence. For Vattimo, this is once again evident in Nietzsche's critique of industrial society and the division of labour under capitalism. This reading must be taken, as Vattimo himself attests, with some caution given Nietzsche's general stance against socialism. Nonetheless, the capitalist organization of labour displays in an exemplary fashion the structure of domination and the logic of the herd mentality, where the subject(ed) does not will herself, is reduced to a set of functions and becomes alienated from the very objects of her labour. Being is grossly separated from meaning when 'the market' serves as the criterion for the reduction of the human to her function: 'The man engaged in commerce understands how to appraise everything without having made it, and to appraise it *according to the needs of the consumer*, not according to his own needs' (D 175, p. 106). In response to these conditions, the *Übermensch* can reject domination and bring about the unity of meaning and Being–the reduction of time to decision–through a '*hermeneutic* superiority: his capacity to construct meaningful unities where the prior human saw and experienced nothing but happenstance' (Vattimo, 1974, p. 274). Vattimo's reading is not ultimately a reduction to aestheticism, but rather a conception of existence that requires no transcendent or external basis for meaning, and thus, no logic of domination.

The Problem of Violence: Weakening Nietzsche

In the years after *Il soggetto e la maschera*, a series of political and personal encounters[7] leads Vattimo to reconsider the unification of Being and meaning, in both its individual and socio-political contexts, as a real possibility for humanity. In these same years, Vattimo also develops his famous conception of 'weak thought' (see Vattimo 1984), which proposes a form of philosophical hermeneutics, still largely informed by Nietzsche and Heidegger, whose political orientation shifts away from transformative liberation and more toward the reduction of violence. There is a modicum of resignation in this re-orientation, but one that nonetheless retains the hope that nihilism can be read positively, and in some way, accomplished. In this period (roughly 1975–85), Vattimo's prolific writing on Nietzsche nuances his earlier stance such that the violent thinking of metaphysics is not presented as a hurdle to overcome, but rather as a historical condition from which we must recover – in Heideggerian terms, a *Verwindung* rather than an *Überwindung* (overcoming) of metaphysics.[8] Given the centrality of the 'historical malady' in Vattimo's earlier writings on Nietzsche as a description of what ails modern society, it is useful to think that the 'recovery' from metaphysics is more likely a resignation to the fact that we cannot defeat this illness entirely (which would recreate the violent thinking of metaphysics), but must live with it and control it so that it does not overtake us completely. This 'weakened' stance, and its effects on Vattimo's interpretation of Nietzsche, are perhaps best understood through two ideas controversial in Nietzsche scholarship: the will to power and the *Übermensch*.

Vattimo's stance against violence brings his reading of Nietzsche's work into direct conflict with those who either paint Nietzsche as a total irrationalist, or those who (following Heidegger) see Nietzsche as the culmination of Western rationality, and thus the dangers of the will to power best exemplified in the 'total technocratic organization of the world' (Vattimo, 1993, p. 88). As we saw in *Il soggetto e la maschera*, art remains central to the conceptualization of a recovery from metaphysics – in particular, the 'destructuring aspect' of the will to power as art. But art is not to be understood in terms of its will to a particular order or form, but as Dionysian chaos, genius, and the formless dance of Zarathustra – a world that creates itself without relying on any external criteria or forming ground. After the world has been revealed as a 'fable' with 'no facts, only interpretations', the model of the artist is properly de-centred and dis-located through 'a radical disorganizing of the subject' so that 'the invigorating function of art is not exercised in the (artist's) domination of materials and tools or in the (spectator's) domination of passions, but rather in the potentation of the passions as a means by which humans can assert themselves over against the apparent negativity of existence' (Vattimo, 1993, p. 99).[9]

This weakened, no longer fully metaphysical subject is the centrepiece of a collection of essays entitled *Al di là del soggetto* (*Beyond the Subject*, 1981), which develops the theses of *The Adventure of Difference* toward an 'ontology of decline'. Here we also encounter Vattimo's more explicit rendering of the prefix *über-* ('beyond' in German) as a weakened revision of the notions of *Übermensch* and *Überwindung*. Vattimo attempts to revise what might, given the Marxist trajectory of *Il soggetto e la maschera*, be an overly 'dialectic' and thus metaphysical understanding of the subject identified with the unity of meaning and Being, or in other terms, the 'sublated' Hegelian subject.[10] The subject, one of the 'errors' of metaphysics, is merely a *Bezeichnung*, a sign or play on words – and this is the most originary relation, an effect of language as the subject itself. Understanding the *über-* in *Übermensch* is the key to understanding the theoretical importance of Nietzsche's overcoming of metaphysics: 'the idea that the revelation of the nihilistic essence of historical becoming is an event that derives from the very same logic of the development of metaphysics; and that taking note of it constitutes a true transformation of the history of metaphysics itself' (Vattimo, 1981, pp. 35–6). The attitude of this subject is a *hubris* in the face of nature and history, in the face of humans themselves: 'The path to the ultra-human condition, like the path from passive nihilism to active nihilism, does not maintain itself in a healthy condition of the soul, of clarity, of the reconciliation and end of all conflicts; but as a liberation of the game of forces, an intensification of all the vital activity that consists, as he says in *Beyond Good and Evil*, in "the violating, the preferring, the being unjust, wanting to be different"' (ibid., pp. 36–7; see also GM III, 9 and BGE 9). The *Übermensch* is thus the 'man of the beyond', so that the 'going-beyond or over' is the act of *hubris*. There is, however, no final unity of meaning and Being, but only the event of Being. In political terms, there is no Gramscian hegemony since interpretation is constitutively injustice, suppression, and violence; and yet, as a check on such violence, the *Übermensch* exercises this power self-reflectively (ibid., pp. 38–9).

The Nietzschean subject is now *solely* appearance. What was 'Being' or 'Truth' is now only interpretation or becoming, the 'unmasking of the unmasking', Zarathustra as the solver *and* creator of enigmas. There is no longer a subject to be emancipated in this activity, and the activities of interpretation, of falsification and violation, are considered 'experiments'. The experimental quality of the *Übermensch* is its heroism, which 'means nothing

other than to take notice of the hermeneutic nature of being and experience' (ibid., p. 44). There is a play of forces, as forces are never absolute
and defined only in relation to other forces, but there is no doctrine of
pure will to power, since that would suppose a war between subjects who
were fixed and final metaphysical entities. In the end, Vattimo argues that
Nietzsche sketches out a hermeneutic ontology in two senses of the term: 'a
knowledge of Being that comes from an unmasking reconstruction of the
"human all too human" origins of values and supreme objects of traditional
metaphysics; and a theory of the conditions of the possibility of a Being that
is given explicitly as the result of interpretative processes' (ibid., p. 47).

And yet for Vattimo, even this interpretation of Nietzsche is intensely
epochal, as the guiding thread to such a reading comes once again from
Heidegger's understanding of the destiny of Being. Vattimo's attempt has
been to offer an interpretation that resists the metaphysical pitfalls of the
overtly political readings (pure will to power) while fortifying the politically
languid 'aesthetic' readings with something more than change based on a
random 'roll of the dice' (Vattimo, 2006, p. 204). The 'logic' capable of
bridging this gap is 'the history of nihilism, which arrives at recognition of
the absence of foundation only at the conclusion of a process that demands
to be recognized, interpreted, assumed as a destiny . . . ' (ibid., p. 207).

Vattimo often points to the notes on 'European Nihilism' collected in *The
Will to Power* where the moderate individual is the one who can survive the
crisis of nihilism. Here the artist is once again emblematic:

> These terms define the artist in relation to his capacity to grasp, accept,
> even augment the problematic and terrible aspects of life in a sort of
> experimental hubris that allies him to the technicians and engineers of
> whom *The Genealogy of Morals* (3.9) speaks. From this perspective, the
> moderation . . . is an acceptance of extreme risk, which can be called
> moderation only insofar as–and this is its essential aspect–it transcends
> the interests that drive the struggle for life. (Vattimo, 2001, p. 139)

The attempt to overcome self-preservation and seek out a moderate way of
life ultimately places the active nihilism of Vattimo's interpretation rather
close to passive nihilism, for it takes place as a reading and response to the
weakening of Being. Active nihilism entails the passive resignation to a destiny we have inherited, along with its more active recovery through our
interpretation of it – an interpretation that cannot be avoided, as it is the
constitutive character of *any* historical, and thus human, engagement within
the ever-weakening and distorting wake of metaphysics.

Notes

1 For the purposes of this essay, I have freshly translated all quotations from Vattimo's original work.

2 Vattimo identifies the end of real socialism – marked by the term '*riflusso*' (reflux) or 'the big chill' – as an 'epochal' event (with the end of metaphysics) that characterizes our late modern society and the challenges it faces. See Vattimo (2004), p. 81.

3 The opening chapter of *Essere, storia e linguaggio in Heidegger* is entitled 'Who is Heidegger's Nietzsche' and includes one of Vattimo's most developed analyses of metaphysics.

4 Four early essays on Nietzsche, dating from 1961–1967, were collected in *Ipotesi su Nietzsche* (Turin: Giapichelli, 1967), and now appear in English as the first four chapters of *Dialogue with Nietzsche* (Vattimo, 2006).

5 This is the term that Vattimo initially uses to discuss Nietzsche's critique of Socrates's 'theoretical optimism' (BT 12–13), but that quickly represents the entire way of thinking characteristic of the history of Western philosophy up to Nietzsche, its scientific-technical reasoning and the instrumentality of its many forms (modern technology, political economy, etc.), and ultimately, what he identifies as 'the instinct of revenge' and the violence of metaphysics.

6 In his earliest study of Nietzsche, entitled 'Nihilism and the Problem of Temporality' (this essay is the first chapter in *Dialogue with Nietzsche* (Vattimo, 2006)), Vattimo suggests that Nietzsche's eternal recurrence undermines the notion of time as a sequence of ordered, linear events and instead construes time in the moment of decision, an event in which time itself unfolds. What 'eternally recurs' is not the content of a decision (a moral decision reducible to its epoch), but the plastic and life-giving force of the will already diagnosed as absent within the modern age.

7 These events, centred primarily around the climate of terror produced by the Red Brigades, are documented in the interview 'Gianni Vattimo: Philosophy as Ontology of Actuality' (Vattimo *et al.*, 2009) and, more fully, in *Not Being God* (Vattimo, 2009).

8 The term *Verwindung*, which Vattimo takes from Heidegger, carries the various connotations of recovery, remission, convalescence, (dis)torsion, twisting, recuperation, etc. as the character of our relation with metaphysics. This term is central to Vattimo's work from this period until the present day. Jon R. Snyder provides an excellent analysis of the concept in his introduction to *The End of Modernity* (Vattimo, 1988).

9 It would be correct to associate this general aestheticization of experience with Vattimo's similar affirmation regarding the linguistic, and thus fluid, destructuring and decentering character of Being (Vattimo, 1993, p. 93). See also WP 800 and 821, quoted at length in the essay.

10 Vattimo's self-critique on this matter is most evident in the preface he writes for the Italian publication of *The Gay Science* (Einaudi, 1979), now Chapter 10 of *Dialogue with Nietzsche* (Vattimo, 2006). Here Vattimo connects the term 'convalescence' from the 1887 preface to *The Gay Science* with Heidegger's understanding of *Verwindung*, which hints at a kind of knowing that, like the 'continuing to dream' scenario of aphorism 54, distinguishes Nietzschean 'convalescence', if any distinction were needed, from any sort of Hegelian, dialectical process of *Aufhebung* (Vattimo, 2006, p. 151).

Bibliography and Guide to Further Study

Vattimo's Nietzsche Interpretation

Vattimo, Gianni (1974), *Il Soggetto e la maschera: Nietzsche e il problema della liberazione* (*The Subject and Its Mask: Nietzsche and the Problem of Liberation*). Milan: Bompiani. No complete translation of this work exists in English; however, 'a condensation and extensive revision' of the book's third section by the editors of *Common Knowledge* has been translated by Dannah Edwards and published in two parts: 'Beyond Despair and Conflict: A Reading of Nietzsche's Positive Nihilism, Part One', in *Common Knowledge*, 7(1), 1998, 15–59; and 'Beyond Despair and Conflict: A Reading of Nietzsche's Positive Nihilism, Part Two: The Spirit of Revenge', in *Common Knowledge*, 7(2), 1998, 27–56.

— (1977), 'The Crisis of the Notion of Value from Nietzsche until Today', in AA.VV., *The Search for Absolute Values: Harmony Among the Sciences*, vol. I. New York: The International Cultural Foundation Press.

— (1981), *Al di là del soggetto: Nietzsche, Heidegger, e l'ermeneutica.* (*Beyond the Subject: Nietzsche, Heidegger, and Hermeneutics*). Milan: Feltrinelli Editore. This work, yet to be translated into English, continues the trend of a 'weakened' reading of Nietzsche.

— (1982), 'Bottle, Net, Truth, Revolution, Terrorism, Philosophy', trans. Thomas Harrison. *Denver Quarterly*, 16, 24–34. This work was originally the preface of *Al di là del soggetto*.

— (1986a), 'Nietzsche and Heidegger', trans. T. Harrison. *Stanford Italian Review*, 6, 19–29. Re-translated as Chapter 13 of *Dialogue with Nietzsche*.

— 1986b), 'The Crisis of Subjectivity from Nietzsche to Heidegger', trans. Peter Carravetta. *Differentia. Review of Italian Thought*, 1, 5–21.

— (1993), *The Adventure of Difference: Philosophy after Nietzsche and Heidegger*, trans. Cyprian Blamires. Baltimore: The Johns Hopkins University Press [1980]. Chapters 1–4 in particular demonstrate Vattimo's slightly less utopian view of Nietzsche's potential as a political thinker, a trend that can also be found in his prefaces to Italian translations of Nietzsche's books included in *Dialogue with Nietzsche*.

— (2001), *Nietzsche: An Introduction*, trans. Nicholas Martin. Stanford: Stanford University Press [1985]. This is Vattimo's clearest and most systematic presentation of his interpretation of Nietzsche, which as he states in the first chapter, is conducted in light of Heidegger's question of Being and a reassessment of his thesis that Nietzsche is the ultimate thinker of metaphysics. The book also includes a very helpful history of Nietzsche reception, a bibliography, and a list of secondary sources on Nietzsche.

— (2006), *Dialogue with Nietzsche*, trans. William McCuaig. New York: Columbia University Press [2000]. This collection of essays, ranging from 1961 to 2000, presents the full arc of Vatimo's thinking on Nietzsche. In particular, the volume includes four early essays that comprised *Ipotesi su Nietzsche* (1967), as well as his prefaces to the Italian translations of *The Gay Science* (1979), *Daybreak* (1979), and *Thus Spoke Zarathustra* (1979). A full list of the original sources for these essays can be found on pages x–xi of the preface to *Dialogue with Nietzsche*.

Other Works by Vattimo

Vattimo, Gianni (1963), *Essere, storia e linguaggio in Heidegger.* Genova: Marietti. The first chapter of this work ('Chi è il Nietzsche di Heidegger?') is particularly relevant.
— (1984), 'Dialectics, Difference, and Weak Thought', trans. T. Harrison. *Graduate Faculty Philosophy Journal*, 10, 151–63. Vattimo's contribution to, *Il Pensiero Debole* (*Weak Thought*), ed. G. Vattimo and Pier Aldo Rovatti. Milano: Feltrinelli Editore, 1983.
— (1988), *The End of Modernity*, trans. Jon R. Snyder. Baltimore: The Johns Hopkins University Press.
— (1992a), 'Optimistic Nihilism'. *Common Knowledge*, 1, 37–44.
— (1992b), *The Transparent Society*, trans. David Webb. Cambridge: Polity Press.
— (1997), *Beyond Interpretation: The Meaning of Hermeneutics for Philosophy*, trans. D. Webb. Cambridge: Polity Press.
— (1998), *Belief*, trans. Luca D'Isanto and D. Webb. Cambridge: Polity Press.
— (2002), *After Christianity*, trans. L. D'Isanto. New York: Columbia University Press.
— (2004), *Nihilism and Emancipation*, trans. W. McCuaig. New York: Columbia University Press.
— (2009), *Not Being God*. New York: Columbia University Press.
Vattimo, G., Luca Savarino, and Federico Vercellone, (2009), 'Gianni Vattimo: Philosophy as Ontology of Actuality'. *Iris*, 1(2), 311–50.

Chapter 11

Derrida's Nietzsche

Carolyn D'Cruz

From the late 1960s until his death in 2004, Jacques Derrida's work made him almost as controversial a philosopher as Nietzsche before him. Both thinkers have been subject to divergent, and sometimes nihilistic, interpretations of their work. Derrida's own interest in Nietzsche therefore provides a particularly striking point of departure for asking how one takes responsibility for the political appropriations – both progressive and conservative – of an author's thought when their work becomes the object of competing interpretations. To complicate matters further, both thinkers put into question the very status of interpretation as decidable and singular. While Nietzsche constantly draws attention in his works to the multiplicity and duplicity of meaning that exposes the 'untruth of Truth', Derrida emphasizes the *structural necessity* of meaning *not* being able to (finally) arrive at its intended destination as a condition of possibility for anything to be rendered legible at all. The confrontations with language and logic that such thought advances are difficult to untangle, and one function of this chapter is to note the similarities and differences between Nietzsche and Derrida on this matter.

This chapter will highlight the importance of 'style' in both thinkers' works, and begin by exploring the connections between what will be described as Nietzsche's critique of antithetical values and Derrida's critique of the metaphysics of presence. The chapter will then examine how Derrida puts Nietzsche's styles to work regarding the subject of Woman – both in relation to Truth and to politics. The chapter then turns to Derrida's consideration of the question of how authors might take responsibility for textual interpretations and appropriations of their works, as he asks what level of complicity (if any) might be attributed to Nietzsche regarding Nazi appropriations of his writings. Finally, the chapter reflects on the implications Derrida's readings of Nietzsche might have for further negotiating relations between philosophy, politics, and ethics.

Reading Derrida Reading Nietzsche

Philosophers remain divided when assessing Nietzsche and Derrida's 'playfulness' with style; for both, the question of style is inextricably bound up with content. Under the heading, 'Why I am So Clever', in *Ecce Homo*, Nietzsche states: 'I do not know any other way of associating with great tasks than *play*: as a sign of greatness, this is an essential precondition' (1989a, p. 258). This play with style requires the reader to become as attentive to rhythm and tone in writing as to content. It is little wonder then that Nietzsche constantly alerts readers to pay attention to his mode of address as a summons to *hear with the correct ear*. But adjusting one's ears to read Nietzsche is possibly one of the most challenging tasks when entering his discursive regime (how often are we asked to *read* with our *ears?*). For, as one of his principal translators Walter Kaufmann notes, Nietzsche's books are 'easier to read but harder to understand than those of almost any other thinker' (1968, p. 72). His tenor can shift from a yell to a whisper within a single aphorism, while the aphoristic form itself disrupts conventional philosophical standards that demand particular forms of presenting reasoned and cogent arguments. Furthermore, what is said in the context of one aphorism or text is often seemingly contradicted in another. In a later reflection on *Thus Spoke Zarathustra*, Nietzsche warns, 'above all one must *hear* aright the tone that comes from this mouth, the halcyon tone, lest one should do wretched injustice to the meaning of its wisdom' (1989a, p. 219). When placed alongside Nietzsche's instructive alternate/subtitle to *Twilight of the Idols* – '*or How to Philosophise with a Hammer*' (1990b) – it seems that one has to reach a certain depth of despondency before being able to embrace Zarathustra's cheerful and life-affirming disposition. As Derrida (1982b, p. xiii) reads it, philosophizing with a hammer finds Nietzsche 'asking himself if he will have to puncture them, batter their ears . . . with the sound of cymbals or tympani . . . [i]n order to teach them to "hear with their eyes" too'. Evidently this question of tone has certainly not eluded Derrida. For like Nietzsche, Derrida realizes there is a limit to philosophy; such a limit needs to find a way of gesturing toward its other side, as an exterior that it can never quite reach. Derrida constantly reminds readers that to speak of this limit, while trying to avoid returning this limit back to what he calls the metaphysics of presence, one must engage with several styles and registers at once. Understanding Derrida's critique of the 'metaphysics of presence' is therefore crucial for coming to terms with deconstructive strategies of reading and writing more specifically.

Conventionally, following Aristotle, metaphysics is concerned with accounting for the persistence of essential qualities within each thing that exists in a constantly changing world. Metaphysics concerns those first principles that form the structures and foundations necessary for any thought or experience to take place at all. Derrida argues that all Western thought and experience is structured by the inheritance of the historical-conceptual apparatus of metaphysics in such a way that it presupposes and prioritizes the value of 'presence'. Put simply, the temporal and spatial dimensions of the here and now are privileged, presupposed, and deemed accessible in grounding 'what is'. Derrida argues that in the very asking of the question of 'what is', we become bound to presuming that something 'is' and has an essence to begin with. So the problem for Derrida emerges when attempts to reach such essences expose their impossibility. Derrida thus exposes the paradox of inescapably relying on the language of the metaphysics of presence in the very moment that we speak of its impossibility. Nietzsche's works constantly express the need to escape metaphysics, as do those of Heidegger after him. Derrida joins his predecessors in chasing the same questions, but underscores the point that there is no escaping metaphysics. Since there is no escape from the language of presence, one has to learn how to put such language to work otherwise through style and register.

Now while Nietzsche's styles are not usually chastised for being overly complex, Derrida's work is widely renowned for its extreme difficulty in both readability and think-ability. In recounting Derrida's reckoning with Nietzsche, we can see how such difficulty in comprehension becomes the necessary consequence of writing in a way that remains faithful to philosophy's passion to seek the truth – as Plato had put it – at the same time that a certain form of philosophy is called into question. Contrary to popular belief, neither Derrida nor Nietzsche relinquishes the desire to seek the truth; their philosophical journeys merely track the impossibility of ever arriving at a singular, transparent picture of Truth in 'reality' or actuality. So for both writers, the question of style is not at all bound to a simple philosophical taste for obscurity. Rather, style becomes a means by which to expose the faulty foundations of what Nietzsche calls the metaphysical 'faith in antithetical values'.

Metaphysics and the Faith in Antithetical Values

The alliance between Nietzsche's critique of antithetical values and Derrida's critique of the metaphysics of presence is most economically captured in the latter's paper, '*Différance*' (1982a). *Différance* expresses how the acquisition of meaning takes place in a non-totalizable space and time, and draws out implications from this fact. This is to say, there is no fixed reference point or centre (such as God, Humanity, or Reason) that enables either finality or *presence* to definitively ground meaning. In Nietzsche's terms, there is no outside to the transitory world that could ground the origin of meaning and value, and he condemns philosophers for supposing that there is. Nietzsche is not at all reticent (he writes as if he is shouting and banging his fists on the table) in expressing his animosity to those who make the metaphysical blunder that presumes

> the things of the highest value must have another origin *of their own*—they cannot be derivable from this transitory, seductive, deceptive, mean little world, from this confusion of desire and illusion! In the womb of being, rather in the intransitory, in the hidden god, in the 'thing in itself'—*that* is where their cause must lie and nowhere else!—This mode of judgement constitutes the typical prejudice by which metaphysicians of all ages can be recognized; this mode of evaluation stands in the background of all logical procedures; it is on account of this their 'faith' that they concern themselves with their 'knowledge,' with something that is at last solemnly baptized 'the truth.' The fundamental faith of metaphysicians is the *faith in antithetical values*. (1990a, pp. 33–4)

Derrida claims that Nietzsche's attack on antithetical values is negotiated through style; it is only through the *play* of opposing forces that oppositional thinking and values can be challenged. For Nietzsche there is nothing but opposing forces in life, and he calls the internal mechanism of such forces, which act upon and transform the world, *the will to power* (see Nietzsche, 1968). We will return to this when discussing the place of degenerative and regenerative values. For now, let's look at how Derrida understands the will to power as a play of opposing forces in the concept of *différance*.

Nietzsche's will to power is listed among other 'indices' that help situate *différance* as the general economy in Derrida's critique of presence. Following Nietzsche, Derrida argues that the force inhering in the will to power is a play of differences, which can never settle into a unity. This non-synthesizable play of differences suggests we can never render anything known 'in or of itself' in the way in which the metaphysicians criticized by Nietzsche would have us believe. Rather, this play of forces marks an irreducible *absence* that can never be present. Without the metaphysical grounds (in God, Being, etc.) with which to mark this play of forces with an origin, the will to power helps to situate *différance* as the 'groundless ground' that makes at one and the same time the *presumption* of presence possible *and* the *capturing* of presence impossible.

From the General Economy of *Différance* to the Particular Ruse of Woman

A particular instance in which Derrida follows Nietzsche's undoing of anti-thetical values is his best-known text on Nietzsche, first presented at the famous colloquium held at Cerisy-la-Salle in July 1972, and subsequently published in book form as *Spurs: Nietzsche's Styles* (1978b). In part, this text considers the figure of 'Woman'. While *différance* situates the *general* econ-omy that produces the effect of presence, yet reveals presence to be impos-sible, Derrida marks the subject/object of *Woman* as performing a structurally similar, yet singular, function in the opposition between truth and untruth in Nietzsche's texts. It is not quite accurate to say that *différance* holds the master key for connected terms such as 'pharmakon', 'supple-ment', and 'hauntology', to name a few, in a deconstructive chain to which Woman belongs. However, it is fair to say that Derrida's readings of other thinkers' texts often identify particular philosophical battles with the meta-physics of presence, in which these connected terms disrupt the hierarchy and presumed independence between the two sides of an oppositional pair. Each of the aforementioned terms in the deconstructive chain act as an 'infrastructure' (see Gasché, 1986) within the text in question, such that oppositional pairs such as poison or cure, inside and outside, life and death, are disrupted and cannot be settled into a final presence; they therefore function as *undecidable*. To speak of Woman in this deconstructive chain is therefore *not* to arrive at a final word on Woman. Rather, it is to disrupt and reveal as undecidable, what might be uncritically taken as Truth with regard to Woman or Woman with regard to Truth. Like Nietzsche before him, Derrida favours active interpretation, where philosophy plays a dynamic role in *creating* values as well as affirming and transforming life. Focusing on Woman in *Spurs*, Derrida not only speaks of the ruse of Woman as a symp-tom of metaphysical closure,[1] but takes the opportunity to discuss the figure of Woman as she was played out at that time in the arena of political liber-ation movements.

Derrida tracks how Woman occupies Nietzsche's texts in a way that 'sus-pends the decidable opposition of the true and non-true' (1978b, p. 107). He writes:

All the emblems, all the shafts and allurements that Nietzsche found in woman, her seductive distance, her captivating inaccessibility, the ever-veiled promise of her provocative transcendence, the *Entfernung*, these all belong properly to a history of truth by way of the history of error. (Derrida, 1978b, p. 89)

In *Beyond Good and Evil*, before claiming truth might perhaps originate in error, and before proposing that the two terms are better thought as being crocheted together rather than opposed through mutual exclusion, Nietzsche opens his preface with the line: 'Supposing Truth to be a Woman—*What?*' (1990a, p. 31). He continues playfully. If philosophers – dogmatic philosophers – approach Woman with the same 'gruesome earnestness' and 'clumsy importunity' with which they approach truth, it is little wonder that they have not been able to win her over! Nietzsche concludes that such philosophers approach truth as deceptively and clumsily as they approach women. But what is to be made of this association? To my knowledge, prior to Derrida's *Spurs* there were no Nietzschean scholars who seized upon this seemingly peculiar juxtaposition of the multifarious references to Woman's entanglements with truth within the Nietzschean corpus.[2] Derrida very publicly focused on truth, error, and politics through the figure of Woman by re-reading – during the height of second-wave feminism in the late sixties and early seventies – the works of a thinker who had been traditionally cast as a misogynist.

Derrida identifies at least three conflicting 'positions' of Woman in Nietzsche's texts.[3] The first is where Woman can be likened to a man who believes in truth. If an anti-feminist tone can be detected in Nietzsche's writings, it comes through passages where Woman aspires, like dogmatic philosophers seeking truth, to be equal with men. This woman believes in these philosophers' truth insofar as she erroneously believes she can present herself 'as she is' – as if Woman, like the dogmatist's objective truth, is a 'thing in itself'. This egalitarian woman is treated with the same kind of contempt Nietzsche wages against advocates of democratic ideals; such equalizing belongs to a herd mentality rather than the creation of values fit for leaders. Nietzsche's second figure of Woman is likened to an actor who adopts the point of view of man by feigning truth. She plays the role of a dissimulating woman because this gets her what she wants. Nietzsche muses over Woman's dissimulatory power: 'they "put on something" even when they take off everything' (1974, p. 317). She might not believe in the truth she has been assigned, but she nevertheless plays with this version of herself through simulation. Even with her clothes off, she can be putting something (you, for example) on! The dissimulating woman might be so invested in playing the illusion for her own benefit that she dangerously forecloses any possibility of occupying the multiplicity of positions that Woman might otherwise take.

The foreclosure of multiplicity binds the first two positions of Woman in Nietzsche's texts as mirror opposites. Both can produce what Nietzsche would term degenerative effects on life-affirming principles. This does not mean that such positions are always aligned to the degenerative; there are instances where each of these positions of Woman might be put to the regeneration of values (See Oliver, 1998). The third position for Woman operating within Nietzsche's works breaks with the closed circuit of truth, where the affirming woman neither equalizes herself to truth, nor feigns the illusion of truth; instead, she exposes the 'untruth of truth'. Derrida writes:

> There is no such thing as the essence of woman because woman averts, she is averted to herself. Out of the depths, endless and unfathomable, she engulfs and distorts all vestige of essentiality, of identity, of property. And the philosophical discourse, blinded, founders on the shoals and is hurled down these depths to its ruin. There is no such thing as the truth of woman, but it is because of that abyssal divergence of the truth, because that untruth is 'truth.' Woman is but one name for the untruth of truth. (1978b, p. 51)

While practical politics might sometimes call for Woman to occupy the two aforementioned positions, Woman as one name for the untruth of truth explicitly resonates with Derrida's critique of presence.

Feminism, Slave Morality, and *Ressentiment*

Unsurprisingly, Derrida's recasting of one of philosophy's most notorious alleged misogynists as constructive for feminist thought prompted much debate regarding the *place* of Woman in both feminist theory and practice (see Gallop, 1995; Spivak, 1984; Grosz, 1995). When Christie McDonald asked where he might locate the place of Woman, a decade after *Spurs* was published, Derrida suggests – in a tone not antithetical to the feminist slogan that claims 'woman's place is everywhere' – that there is no *one* place for Woman (Derrida, 1985a, p. 168). Still, Derrida is not uncritical of certain feminist positions in which Woman might serve what Nietzsche calls degenerative values.

For while feminist movements might focus on 'contesting the institutionalising of inequalities for women', Derrida warns that such organized struggles are sometimes propelled through *reactive* principles that Nietzsche situates as hostile to, rather than affirmative of, life (1985a, p. 166). In Nietzschean terms, a reactive feminism is based on a 'slave morality' rather than a 'master morality'.

For Nietzsche, master morality involves an active creation of values while slave morality is fundamentally reactive. Mistrustful and suspicious of the powerful, slave morality has its roots in *ressentiment*:

> While every noble morality develops from a triumphant affirmation of itself, slave morality from the outset says No to what is 'outside,' what is 'different,' what is 'not itself'; and this No is its creative deed. This inversion of the value positing eye—this need to direct one's view outward instead of back at oneself—is the essence of *ressentiment*: in order to exist, slave morality always first needs a hostile external world. (Nietzsche, 1989b, pp. 36–7)

In feminist terms, the hostile external world is traditionally described as patriarchy. A feminist *ressentiment* situates women as powerless victims to an all-pervasive patriarchal structure on the one hand, while maintaining moral superiority on the very basis of such powerlessness on the other hand (see Tapper, 1993). When Derrida broaches the topic of a reactive feminism he distinguishes between the everyday *practical* struggles of this liberation movement from the *necessary*–yet faulty–metaphysical presuppositions that propel that movement. Of course, Derrida acknowledges, feminist struggles often require the 'preservation of metaphysical presuppositions' in order to challenge structures of phallogocentrism (put crudely, the complicity between a certain (phallic) masculinism and reason). But he insists that 'the specular reversal of masculine "subjectivity," even in its most self-critical form – that is, where it is nervously jealous of itself and its "proper" objects – probably represents only one necessary phase' of deconstruction (Derrida, 1985a, p. 166). Speaking elsewhere on the question of Woman, Derrida states that reversing the binary opposition between woman and man is not enough; a second stage would involve displacing the opposition itself (1987, pp. 194–5).

Woman as a name for the un-truth of truth, or the undecidable opposition between the true and untrue, as indicated earlier, is not to be taken as a position in itself. The second level of deconstruction is invested with *transforming* an oppositional structure rather than merely subverting the

hierarchy contained within it. It is only through a transformative move –
one that for Nietzsche involves the creation of new values – that a liberation movement can turn against its own reactive impulses and activate
affirmative values.

Contrary to appearances, this does not necessarily suggest an uncritical
acceptance of the division between slave and master moralities. Derrida
reminds us *not* to treat each side of the opposition between reactive and
active forces, regenerative and degenerative values, and master and slave
moralities as if they corresponded a priori to progressive and conservative
positions, or to two antithetical political contents. For it is not at all the case
that the advocacy of the creation of new values, supposedly realized through
the propagation of a master morality, will necessarily lead to a more progressive and liberatory politics. The Nazi appropriation of Nietzsche's works
glaringly stands as testimony to *an interpretation* of a master morality creating the worst kind of degenerative principles against life. Interpretive decisions therefore require *an accounting* for *how the same Nietzschean texts* can be
so readily appropriated for opposing purposes. Derrida sets himself this
task when dealing with Nietzsche's complicity with Nazi appropriations of
the latter's works.

Derrida Reading Nazi Appropriations of Nietzsche

Derrida offers no easy positioning to absolve Nietzsche from all responsibility for fascistic interpretations of his works, or, conversely, to render
Nietzsche wholly culpable for such interpretations. Anti-Nietzscheans, like
Geroge Lukács (1980), point to passages *within* Nietzsche's texts to prove a
lineage between Nietzsche and Nazism, while Nietzscheans like Walter
Kaufmann (1968) claim to prove the opposite. For Derrida, the question
cannot be settled. He does not attempt to clear Nietzsche's name; he does
not hold Nietzsche wholly culpable for being interpreted as a proto-Nazi;
nor does he deem the matter no longer pertinent to philosophical and
political discussion. Instead, Derrida wonders

> [h]ow and why what is so naively called a falsification was possible (one
> can't falsify just anything), how and why the 'same' words and the 'same'
> statements—if they are indeed the same—might several times be made to
> serve certain meanings and certain contexts that are said to be different,
> even incompatible. One may wonder why the only teaching institution or
> the only beginning of a teaching institution that ever succeeded in taking

as its model the teaching of Nietzsche on teaching will have been a Nazi one. (1985b, p. 24)

Derrida focuses on two seemingly marginal texts to account for Nietzsche's relationship to Nazism. In 'The Teaching of Nietzsche and the Politics of the Proper Name' (1985b), Derrida cites from Nietzsche's unconventional 'autobiographical' work, *Ecce Homo* (1989a), alongside a reading of a lecture (published posthumously against Nietzsche's wishes) from a series that Nietzsche had delivered as an academic titled, 'On the Future of Our Educational Institutions' (Nietzsche, 1964).

In choosing these texts, Derrida forces a confrontation with the 'problems of the borderline', which arise when trying to maintain the rigour of conceptual oppositions governing disputes over interpretation (Derrida, 1985b, p. 13). For Derrida, there is no absolute criterion for separating an author's life from his or her works; no absolute criterion for demarcating what constitutes the inside, and what is the outside, of philosophy; and no absolute criterion for determining the proper context by which the intentions of an author can delimit his or her corpus. Recalling *Spurs* momentarily, Derrida infamously refers to disputes over the propriety of the Nietzschean corpus regarding the inclusion of the phrase, 'I have forgotten my umbrella' in the margins of one of Nietzsche's published notebooks. The decision to leave the marginal note complete with quotation marks for publication cannot disclose to readers the significance, relevance, or meaning the phrase has within the Nietzschean corpus; it remains undecidable. For Derrida, this phrase draws attention to the bleeding of borders between one's life and one's philosophical works. With this in mind, let us move on to Derrida's deliberate textual choices for working through questions of authorial responsibility for appropriations of their works. As a text that can be marked neither within a determinable border of the author's life, nor within a closed delimitation of that author's philosophical system, *Ecce Homo* guides Derrida's approach to 'The Future of Our Educational Institutions' as a way of 'moving between the issue of the pedagogical institution on the one hand, and, on the other, those concerning life-death, the dead-the-living, the language contract, the signature of credit, the biological and biographical' (Derrida, 1985b, p. 22).

Turning to the fifth and last of Nietzsche's lectures, Derrida focuses on the theme of degeneration and regeneration of values in the German University. Specifically, Derrida underscores Nietzsche's claim that the regeneration of cultural values begins not with academic freedom but with constraint, obedience, and discipline; students purportedly need a '*grosse Führer*' for spiritual and intellectual guidance. While Derrida acknowledges that it would be 'naive and crude simply to extract the word '*Führer*' from this passage and to let it resonate all by itself in its Hitlerian consonance . . . it would be just as peremptory to deny that something is going on here that belongs to the same' (1985b, p. 28). The resonance between Nietzsche's thematic of degenerative and regenerative values (which, Derrida notes, is further elaborated in the *Genealogy of Morals*) and Nazi ideology is more than disquieting.

Even though Derrida emphasizes the fact that 'one can't falsify just anything' (1985b, p. 24), he also demonstrates how each and every mark of meaning or text is inscribed by the *structurally essential condition* of breaking with a specific context of signification and grafting on to other interpretive chains. In other words, the possibility of misinterpretation, or other forms of textual appropriation, is something that is *structurally constitutive of meaning*; without the capacity for a mark to be repeated and cut off from its 'original' context, there would be no possibility of meaning at all (Derrida, 1988, p. 8). As such, interpretive disputes cannot simply be *settled* by drawing a line between an author's intentions and the contingent forces, procedures, and investments conditioning the 'context' within which certain motifs of a text have been appropriated. This does not mean that a writer is therefore absolved from taking responsibility for what they write, or that a text can mean anything that we want it to. As Derrida emphasizes, it is not just a question of decipherment, but also of 'transformation' (1985b, p. 30). A transformative reading is interested in 'recognis[ing] and respect[ing] all the instruments of traditional criticism' (Derrida, 1976, p. 158) as essential for deciphering what might be 'in the Nietzschean corpus that could help us to comprehend the double interpretation and the so-called perversion' (Derrida, 1985b, pp. 32–3). It is the doubling commentary, which also involves the *re-writing* and *opening* of a reading to future destinations. Importantly, an 'interpretative decision does not have to draw a line between two intents or two political contents' (Derrida, 1985b, p. 32). For the destinational structure – the potential destinations in which the meaning of a text may or may not arrive – inhering in all so-called post Hegelian texts can always produce both 'left' and 'right' readings.

There is no escaping this destinational structure; for Derrida, this *heightens* rather than dissolves one's responsibility for textual interpretation; the non-unity and multiplicity of interpretation is *divided and doubled, not meaningless and endless*. More importantly, and in contrast to Nietzsche, Derrida attempts to mark the destinational structure of his texts with a responsibility and obligation *for* the Other, where the self's relation to the Other is what defines Emmanuel Levinas's ethical relation (see Levinas, 1969). It is over the status of this kind of Other that Derrida departs most widely from Nietzsche.

Countersigning the Singularity of the Event for the Other

Before considering these differences regarding the status of the Other, it is necessary first to acknowledge that for all Nietzsche's emphasis on self-creation in the process of questioning the value of values, the self is nonetheless divided from itself as well as from others. From the beginning of 'The Teaching of Nietzsche', Derrida acknowledges that the distance inhering within the self and in relation to others informs Nietzsche's employment of his proper name as his *signature* to write 'philosophy and life, the science and the philosophy of life *with his name and in his name*' (1985b, p. 6). As such Nietzsche writes with awareness that his name is pluralized and left open to a future that remains open to countersignatures – to those who attach their own signatures to, and interpretive stamps on, his works. This awareness extends to the fact that 'putting one's name on the line' involves a 'line of credit' to a future in which the *bearer* of the name cannot receive what returns to, or what becomes entangled with, the legacy of that name. As Derrida elaborates:

> Only the name can inherit, and this is why the name, to be distinguished from the bearer, is always and a priori a dead man's name, a name of death. What returns to the name never returns to the living. (1985b, p. 7)

We have already seen that Derrida does not absolve Nietzsche from complicity with Nazi appropriations, but such complicity does not lend itself to the view that nothing *remains* to be read of Nietzsche's texts. The credit Nietzsche extends to himself – recounting how he has become who he is, within a context where his contemporaries do not have the ears to hear him – is a credit that 'implicate[s] all of us in this transaction through what, on the force of a signature, remains of his text' (Derrida, 1985b, p. 8). Thus the 'I' that Nietzsche addresses in *Ecce Homo* is also destined, 'through the credit of the eternal return' (p. 13) to 'nameless parties to the contract' (p. 19) – you and me, for example.

The eternal return is perhaps the most complicated doctrine encountered within Nietzsche's works. For Derrida the eternal return joins the will to power as a formative influence in situating the general economy of *différance*. An affirmative reading of the eternal return suggests that 'it cannot let itself be heard or understood in the present; it is untimely, differant, anachronistic' (Derrida 1985b, p. 19). Yet, Derrida notes, the affirmation in the eternal return is repeated such that the logic that 'affirms the return . . . and a certain kind of reproduction that preserves whatever comes back . . . must give rise to a magisterial institution' (Nietzsche cited in Derrida, 1985b, p. 20). Recalling that Nietzsche believed his contemporaries did not have ears to hear him, he writes of a future when new teaching institutions 'will be needed in which men live and teach as I conceive of living and teaching'. Here, Nietzsche explicitly projects the interpretation of the master, Zarathustra, to the future of a magisterial teaching institution. We must remind ourselves of the monstrous form such an institution might take. Consequently we must accept negotiating chance and necessity as a *differing-deferring play of forces* in whatever politics we promise for future destinations. Politics is not exempt from the play of *différance*; the necessary presumption of presence that 'grounds' our political projects is unavoidably bound to the 'contingent foundations' in which such projects acquire their meaning. An emancipatory politics can therefore never be 'present-ed' as such.

The stakes perhaps could not be higher. Nietzsche predicted his name might one day be associated with something 'monstrous'. We have lived and live in times where Nietzsche's name has been caught up with the most monstrous and worst kinds of politics – fascism and totalitarianism, for example. If there is one thing that remains in Derrida's texts that warns us to be mindful of how the promise for an affirmative life can too readily turn into a reactive and degenerate form of politics it is to safeguard such a promise from being given over to the presumption of presence. We therefore cannot name a promise for a progressive politics in terms that claim to know the actuality of its contents, whether that is in the name of a republic, a master morality, feminism, communism, or democracy, to name a few contenders. The imperative is to keep the promise open to our calls for justice, which by its very nature cannot be anticipated, predicted – *presented*. In a certain sense, Derrida's call to keep the promise open shares with Nietzsche's will to power the openness to surprise and unpredictability. But whereas for Nietzsche the life-affirming creation of new values through the play of differential forces strives for and celebrates rank and order between 'higher' and 'lower' beings, Derrida's play of differences concerns the alterity (otherness) of the Other. For Derrida, following Levinas, the Other falls below recognition in rank and order – perhaps the biblical widow, the orphan, or the child with AIDS, John Caputo suggests (1993, p. 85). This openness to the Other is thus quite different from Nietzsche's envisaged empowering of the forces for a higher rank of 'becoming' (Caputo, 1993, p. 49).

In sum, we can say that Derrida's reading of Nietzsche is both parasitic and transformative. No doubt, Derrida's elaboration of *différance* is indebted to Nietzsche's critique of antithetical values and the latter's dedication to taking philosophy beyond metaphysics. Yet, for Derrida there is no outside to metaphysics. While Derrida appreciates the aphoristic form and focus on style as a means to deal with the 'untruth of Truth', his overt attention to *giving an account* for how thought is bound to *both* the possibility and impossibility of the metaphysics of presence distinguishes him from Nietzsche. Derrida is more concerned than his predecessor ever appeared to be with the question of how one takes *responsibility* for what might become appropriated from one's writings while overtly addressing questions of politics. As neither dismissive nor defensive of Nietzsche's legacy, Derrida maintains a certain spirit of the former's 'master morality', which affirms life and seeks the creation of values. But while Nietzsche's self may move toward the Other through a 'superfluity of power' (1990a, p.196), Derrida's self is *disrupted* and *seized* by the Other's call for justice.

Notes

[1] On metaphysical closure in Derrida's works see Critchley (1992).

[2] Derrida distinguishes his own from Heidegger's commentary of Nietzsche's 'How the 'Real world' at last Became a Myth' in *The Twilight of the Idols* around the question of Woman. Derrida notes how 'Heidegger analyses all the elements in Nietzsche's text with the sole exception of the idea's becoming female'. Derrida claims that Heidegger '*skirts* the woman, he abandons her there'. In doing so, Heidegger loses the opportunity to follow the entanglement between the history of truth and the history of Woman, where 'truth has not always been woman nor is the woman always the truth' (Derrida, 1978b, pp. 85, 86, emphasis added). See Heidegger (1979).

[3] This commentary of Derrida's reading of Woman in Nietzsche's texts is indebted to Spivak (1984) and Oliver (1998).

Bibliography and Guide to Further Study

Derrida's Nietzsche Interpretation

Derrida, Jacques (1976), *Of Grammatology*, trans. Gayatri Chakravorty Spivak. Baltimore: Johns Hopkins University Press [1967]. References to Nietzsche are littered throughout the book.

— (1978a), 'Structure, Sign and Play', trans. Alan Bass, in id., *Writing and Difference*. Chicago: Chicago University Press [1966]. Marking Derrida's entry into the USA, this paper ends with a nod to Nietzsche's emphasis on play.

— (1978b), *Spurs: Nietzsche's Styles*, trans. Barbara Harlow. Chicago and London: The University of Chicago Press [1972]. Embracing Nietzsche's styles to confront the 'untruth of truth' through the figure of Woman, Derrida offers a convincing counterpoint to Heidegger's attempt to 'arrest' a reading of Nietzsche. See interview below with Rottenberg.

— (1982a), 'Différance', in *Margins of Philosophy*, trans. A. Bass. Chicago and London: University of Chicago Press [1968]. Derrida names Nietzsche alongside Freud, Heidegger, Hegel, Levinas and de Saussure as part of the indices that form the general economy of *différance*.

— (1982b), 'Tympan', in *Margins of Philosophy* [1972]. While Nietzsche is not the object of analysis, his call for reading with one's ears and to hear with one's eyes sets the tone for Derrida's approach for thinking philosophy's other.

— (1985a), 'Choreographies', trans. Christine McDonald, in C. McDonald (ed.), *The Ear of the Other: Otobiography, Transference, Translation*. Lincoln and London: University of Nebraska Press [1982]. This interview/correspondence reflects on Woman as a trope in *Spurs* in relation to feminism as a political movement. It also revisits Derrida's differences with Heidegger regarding sexual difference and ontology.

— (1985b), 'Otobiographies: "The Teaching of Nietzsche and the Politics of the Proper Name"', trans. Avital Ronell, in *The Ear of the Other* [1984]. Derrida's most overt engagement with Nietzsche's relationship to Nazism.

— (1988), *Limited Inc*. Evanston: Northwestern University Press [1977]. Discusses context and intentionality, which are crucial for reading Derrida's treatment of Nietzsche's relations to Nazism discussed in *The Ear of the Other*.

— (1997), *The Politics of Friendship*, trans. George Collins. London and New York: Verso. Nietzsche is overtly discussed in three chapters in this book to calculate with the incalculable promise for a democracy to come.

— (2002), 'Nietzsche and the Machine', trans. Richard Beardsworth, in Elizabeth Rottenberg (ed.), *Negotiations: Interventions and Interviews, 1971–2201*. Stanford: Stanford University Press. This interview would be the best place to start for those new to Derrida.

Derrida, Nietzsche, and Feminism

Derrida, Jacques (1987), 'Women in the Beehive: A Seminar with Jacques Derrida', trans. James Adner, in Alice Jardine and Paul Smith (eds), *Men in Feminism*. New York: Methuen.

Gallop, Jane (1995), 'Women in *Spurs* and Nineties Feminism'. *Diacritics*, 25(2), 125–34.

Grosz, Elizabeth (1995), 'Ontology and Equivocation: Derrida's Politics of Sexual Difference'. *Diacritics*, 25(2), 114–24.

Oliver, Kelly (1998), 'Woman as Truth in Nietzsche's Writings', in Kelly Oliver and Marilyn Pearsall (eds), *Feminist Interpretations of Friedrich Nietzsche*. University Park, PA: Pennsylvania State University Press.

Patton, Paul (ed.) (1993), *Nietzsche, Feminism and Political Theory*. St. Leonards: Allen and Unwin.

Spivak, Gayatri (1984), 'Love Me, Love My Ombre'. *Diacritics*, 14(4), 19–36.
Tapper, Marion (1993), '*Ressentiment* and Power: Some Reflections on Feminist Practices', in Patton, 1993.

Nietzsche Translations Cited

Nietzsche, Friedrich (1961) *Thus Spoke Zarathustra: A Book for Everyone and No One*, trans. R. J. Hollingdale. Harmondsworth: Penguin.
— (1968), *The Will to Power*, trans. W. Kaufmann and R. J. Hollingdale, ed. W. Kaufman. New York: Vintage Books.
— 1974), *The Gay Science*, trans. Walter Kaufmann. New York: Vintage Books.
— (1989a), *Ecce Homo: How One Becomes What One Is*, trans. W. Kaufmann. New York: Vintage Books.
— 1989b), *On the Genealogy of Morals*, trans. W. Kaufman. New York: Vintage Books.
— (1990a), *Beyond Good and Evil*, trans. R. J. Hollingdale. Harmondsworth: Penguin.
— (1990b), *Twilight of the Idols / The Anti-Christ*, trans. R. J. Hollingdale. Harmondsworth: Penguin.

Other Works Cited

Caputo, John D. (1993), *Against Ethics: Contributions to a Poetics of Obligations with Constant Reference to Deconstruction*. Bloomington and Indianapolis: Indiana University Press.
Critchley, Simon (1992), *The Ethics of Deconstruction: Derrida and Levinas*. Oxford and Cambridge: Blackwell.
Gasché, Rodolphe (1986), *The Tain of the Mirror: Derrida and the Philosophy of Reflection*. Cambridge, MA: Harvard University Press.
Heidegger, Martin (1979), 'Nietzsche's Overturning of Platonism', in *Nietzsche*, 2 vols., trans. David Farrell Krell. San Francisco: Harper Collins.
Kaufman, Walter (1968), *Nietzsche: Philosopher, Psychologist, Antichrist*, 3rd edn. Princeton: Princeton University Press.
— (1989), 'Editor's Introduction', in F. Nietzsche, *The Genealogy of Morals*. New York: Vintage Books.
Levinas, Emmanuel (1969), *Totality and Infinity*, trans. Alphonso Lingis. Pittsburgh, PA: Duequesne University Press.
Lukács, Georg (1980), *The Destruction of Reason*, trans. Peter R. Palmer. London: Merlin Press.
Spivak, Gayatri (1976), 'Translator's Preface', in Derrida, 1976.
Tanner, Michael (1990), 'Introduction', in Nietzsche, 1990.

Chapter 12

Irigaray's Nietzsche

Joanne Faulkner

Luce Irigaray is a Belgian philosopher, linguist, psychoanalyst, and feminist, best known in the Anglophone academy for her books *Speculum of the Other Woman* (1974) and *This Sex Which Is Not One* (1977). Irigaray is a pioneer of 'difference feminism'. Critical of second-wave feminism inspired by Simone de Beauvoir's *The Second Sex* (1949, translated 1953), Irigaray contends that this model of gender equality assumes the priority of traditionally 'masculine' values (i.e. it is an 'equality of sameness'). Irigaray's philosophical analysis takes sexual difference as its primary focus. According to Irigaray, within our tradition of thought, men's bodies (or 'morphology') are assumed to be neat and solid, whereas women's morphology is perceived as 'messy' and fluid. These evaluations, she suggests, pervade the most abstract thought of the Western tradition: *chora*, or 'place', in the writings of Plato (Irigaray, 1985a, pp. 243–64) and Aristotle (Irigaray, 1993, pp. 34–55), for instance. Through her critical engagements with philosophers from Plato to Derrida, as well as her more programmatic texts, Irigaray sets out to 'deconstruct' Western discourses through which 'the feminine' is denigrated. Her work on Nietzsche is part of that project.

Irigaray's texts are challenging to read. Indeed, it is often remarked that the book with which this chapter is concerned, *Marine Lover* (*Amante Marine de Friedrich Nietzsche*), is difficult, even opaque. For this reason it is an under-read, and underestimated, commentary on Nietzsche. As with Nietzsche's own style, Irigaray's writing is poetic, and sometimes obscure compared to most philosophical writing. Irigaray does not proceed by means of careful exegesis or explanation of either Nietzsche's or her own position. She expects her reader to have done their homework, not only on Nietzsche, but also the other philosophers to whom her discussion refers. And she does not provide footnotes or other textual bearings to orient the reader's understanding. One could say that reading *Marine Lover* is like being thrown into the sea: ambiguously pleasurable once prospects of reaching firm ground are abandoned.

Far from operating according to a mandate of transparency and clarity, then, Irigaray writes elliptically, communicating at an emotional and sensual level by sharing the 'tonality' of her relation to Nietzsche. Irigaray immerses herself within the writing of the philosopher she interprets, appropriating his or her 'voice'. To an English-language reader, raised on a diet of plainly articulated arguments, Irigaray appears to lack objectivity. Her manner of engaging with the philosophers is intimate, and this challenges readers used to a detached style of philosophical prose. For Irigaray, however, such 'intimacy' is strategic. Indeed, far from lacking critical distance, this approach provides her critical methodology.

For these reasons, Irigaray requires her reader's indulgence: that we read carefully, slowly, between the lines – much as Nietzsche had advised his own readers in *Daybreak* (Preface 5). To appreciate why she is so demanding, it helps to understand the stakes of her reading of Nietzsche: to make room within his philosophy for a feminist interpretation. As such, she attempts to engage with Nietzsche not only as she finds him, but also as he might become for an *amante marine*: an active woman-marine-lover, rather than the passive, feminine 'beloved' (*aimée*).[1] This strategy of writing herself into the philosopher's work is consistent throughout her oeuvre.

To render Irigaray's interpretation of Nietzsche more accessible, this chapter will first examine Irigaray's 'position' – her strategy of inserting herself 'within' philosophers' texts as the repudiated, forgotten 'feminine' – with reference to examples from *Marine Lover*. Next, 'Irigaray's methodologies' turns to a fuller examination of her style of interpretation, and will introduce some philosophical tools she draws upon to form her interpretation of Nietzsche. The section entitled 'The Deployment of Affect' considers the meaning of 'lover' in the title of Irigaray's Nietzsche book, so apparently obscure and yet critical to understanding her interpretation. Finally, 'Nietzsche's Irigaray' explores the extent to which, despite her criticisms, Irigaray is indebted to Nietzsche for her own philosophical values, style of writing, and methodology. Indeed, it is these affinities with Nietzsche that motivates Irigaray's close reading of him, ultimately enabling her to occupy the position of Nietzsche's female lover (*Amante*) convincingly.

Irigaray's 'Position'

Irigaray situates herself always as a woman, and as a *feminist* reader and correspondent of the philosophers. She is acutely aware, however, that to occupy such a position is not without problems. What she calls 'the feminine' (*le féminin*) is barely legible within Western philosophy. It is the obscured or 'othered' position the denial of which, for Irigaray, founds the philosophical position per se. The texts of the philosophers rehearse and formalize a cultural prejudice against the feminine, according to Irigaray. While 'man' is counted as 'one' – the subject of experience – 'woman' is considered nothing in herself, a mere accomplice to the affirmation of masculine subjectivity. Expressing this in terms of binary opposition, 'man' is 'A' to 'woman's' 'not-A': so that insofar as 'man' is defined as the positive value in opposition to 'woman', 'he' depends upon 'woman' to shore up 'his' identity.[2] 'Woman' is represented by this discourse only in (a negative) relation to 'man', and so insofar as women are neither simply 'masculine' nor 'feminine' (understood only as what masculinity rejects), conventional philosophical writing fails to represent sexual difference. Irigaray demonstrates this view at the outset of *Marine Lover*:

> And you had all to lose sight of me so I could come back, toward you, with an other gaze.
>
> And certainly, the most arduous thing has been to seal my lips, out of love. To close off this mouth that always sought to flow free.
>
> But, had I never held back, never would you have remembered that something exists which has a language other than your own. That, from her prison, someone was calling out to return to the air. That your words reasoned all the better because within them a voice was captive. Amplifying your speech with an endless resonance. (p. 3)

Irigaray's strategy involves staging a withdrawal of 'woman's' labour of supporting negation to masculine identity. She then interrogates how women might find an identity *beyond* binary opposition: a relation to 'man' of 'B' (pure difference) instead of 'not-A' (where 'A' is the primary term). She writes:

> Nothing? This whole that always and at every moment was thus becoming new? Nothing? This endless coming into life at each moment? Nothing? This whole that had laid by the mantle of long sleep and was reviving all my senses? Nothing, this unfathomable well? (p. 5)

Once the philosopher's silent substratum, the 'feminine' now speaks – reanimated by Irigaray's interpretation. Irigaray introduces an interesting rhetorical device to the scene of Nietzsche scholarship: by addressing her text to Nietzsche directly in the form of a 'love letter' that is also a 'Dear John' letter, she occupies the roles of various figures of women that populate his texts as metaphors for 'Life', 'Truth', and 'Destiny', as well as more obviously negative clichés such as the barren feminist or crone. In this guise, She admonishes Nietzsche for neglecting to listen to a forgotten, self-affirming feminine concealed beneath his philosophy.

Irigaray accuses Nietzsche of using 'woman' to amplify for his own opinions: 'That your words reasoned all the better because within them a voice was captive', (p. 3); and as a mirror for his own likeness: 'he refused to break the mirror of the (male) same, and over and over again demanded that the other be his double' (p. 187). Despite Nietzsche's acknowledgement that women's social position reflects Western ontology[3] – and his critique of philosophers' ineptitude regarding 'Truth', figured as a woman (see BGE Preface) – Irigaray treats Nietzsche, in his relation to women, precisely as one of the dogmatic philosophers he ridicules. Nietzsche may be aware of philosophers' shortcomings: their blindness to different viewpoints, and reifications of social dynamics as the essential types, 'man' and 'woman'. Yet for Irigaray, Nietzsche, too, relates his philosophy through a usage of 'the feminine' that denies women their own voice because it speaks only *his* truth. In short, she argues, Nietzsche reduces 'woman' to a maternal metaphor tied to the creation of his philosophical ideas. By interpolating herself as a character within Nietzsche's philosophy, Irigaray attempts to open his work to new possibilities and new understandings of femininity: 'This is not a book *on* Nietzsche but *with* Nietzsche who is for me a partner in love' (Irigaray, 1981, p. 44).

The interim aim, then, of Irigaray's conversation with Nietzsche – and her interludes with the philosophers more generally – is to render the function of 'the feminine' visible and the philosopher accountable for ignorance of feminine subjectivity. Integral to this approach is a destabilization of the 'masculinity' that philosophical discourse presumes. This, in turn, prepares a further aim, to produce a position from which a 'woman-philosopher' might speak. Irigaray's deconstructive reading is in this way also a creative act: she renegotiates *with* the philosopher a discursive practice that refuses to subordinate one voice to the other.

Reading and understanding Irigaray's work, then, involves challenging accepted modes of philosophical writing, even subverting the manner in which philosophy is 'staged': a staging that must remain un-interrogated – even invisible – for the business of philosophy proceed as usual. This is because, as Nietzsche knew well, the way philosophy is staged organizes the kinds of relation possible between the text and its reader. Philosophical criticism supposes that each pole of dialogue – occupied by philosopher or commentator – is 'equal' to the other. Reason – understood as simple, objective, and expunged of emotion – is supposed to mediate the textual relation in philosophy. Neutrality is the expected 'stance' for both philosopher and commentator, and affective involvement is viewed as compromising objectivity.

These 'rules of engagement' assume a uniform perspective, and uniform material and social circumstances that influence one's viewpoint. To this extent, Irigaray suggests, they effectively exclude a feminist reading. First, the notion that the philosopher is 'neuter' – that philosophy can represent a neutral perspective – is mistaken and deceptive. For Irigaray, philosophy is always political, especially where it claims not to be. 'Neutrality' is a cloak worn by politics that fails to recognize itself as such. And by universalizing its perspective by means of the misnomer of neutrality, philosophy does violence to alternative perspectives it excludes. As we will see in the final section of this chapter, Irigaray draws in part from Nietzsche's insights for this 'diagnosis' of philosophy.

Second, philosophy's antagonism towards emotion and partial interest doubly excludes women, frequently equated with the particular and the emotional. Because women often have different, sometimes competing interests to male philosophers, there is a suspicion that their interpretations might import social concerns into the 'purified' arena of reason. The feminist may be too 'involved', too focussed on women's issues to take account of the 'real' stakes of philosophy: a universal 'Truth', determined from 'no-man's' perspective.

Importantly for Irigaray, philosophy's supposed 'neutrality' refers to a set of (actually very partial) qualities and attitudes taken for granted within philosophical discourse. These attributes understood to be 'neutral' designate, Irigaray suggests, a *masculine* point of view, serving masculine interests (see 1985a, p. 133). While objectivity and distance is routinely equated with masculinity, the 'feminine' has come to stand for the material that masculine philosophers reject, rework, and value-add: 'matter' to his 'form'; 'emotion' to his 'reason'; 'body' to his 'mind'; and 'object' to his 'subject'.[4] 'Femininity', then, designates precisely the proximity to emotion and the body over which the philosopher must prevail in order to philosophize. For Irigaray, it will be impossible to philosophize *as a woman* before first correcting philosophy's othering of the 'feminine'.

Significantly, in spite of Derrida's claim that Nietzsche 'writes with the hand of woman' (1973, p. 299) – and Nietzsche's own claim to be a 'psychologist of the eternal feminine' (EH 'Books' 5) – Nietzsche's 'position' is also typically masculine. Irigaray argues that Nietzsche's is a philosophy of overcoming par excellence, and that his rhetoric reflects a desire to skirt over rather than absorb or be absorbed by the materiality of life. This signals a sexual division of labour within Nietzsche's work consistent with more traditional works of philosophy: In *Thus Spoke Zarathustra*, for instance, 'Life' is represented by a woman with whom Nietzsche's protagonist flirts and lightly converses. And, as Irigaray points out in *Marine Lover*, for Nietzsche, women and the material elements are always kept 'at a distance':

> It is always hot, dry, and hard in your world. And to excel for you always requires a bridge. Are you truly afraid of falling back into man? Or into the sea? (p. 13)

We will discuss Nietzsche's relation to materiality and embodiment in the sections on methodology and 'Nietzsche's Irigaray'.

As a feminist reader, Irigaray seeks to establish through an engagement with Nietzsche a position from which to speak, without which the 'critical distance' demanded by philosophy is unattainable. In so doing, she complicates the very notion of 'critical distance' by emphasizing the importance of (the sexual) 'relation' to the establishment of identity. That humans 'exist' in the context of relationships that support them is a critical element of the enunciation of 'who one is' for Irigaray. 'Masculine' identity is unstable, she suggests, because it disavows its relations of dependence, valuing instead self-actualization through separation from others. Irigaray, conversely, situates her reading in the context of her relationships – to those whose philosophy she interrogates, and a feminine 'genealogy' (actual and symbolic mothers, such as Simone de Beauvoir, and prospective 'daughters' or readers). These relations are elaborated affectively in terms of love, disappointment, fear, and anger, thereby emphasizing the 'situation' of subjectivity, which is embodied and emotional as well as rational.

Irigaray's manner of establishing her position from which to speak, then, is to insinuate herself within the philosopher's writing. By appropriating his language, his metaphors and figures, his mode of address, she enacts a resonance within his 'voice', which produces a disturbing effect. Irigaray's 'position' is this uneasy *proximity*, which touches but does not coincide with the place of the philosopher. Irigaray establishes her voice by mimicking the words of the philosopher, but with minor, telling, differences. These differences produced through repetition disturb the philosopher's seeming authority and neutrality, and reveal 'the feminine' – the elision of which had given him voice.

Irigaray's Methodologies

The philosophical tools with which Irigaray constructs her argument are eclectic, varying according to whom she critiques. This is due to the importance of relation to the articulation of a position, discussed above. But her eclecticism is also connected to what she sees as a more empowering position for women readers: 'infidelity' to any particular philosopher. First, each particular approach taken to 'truth' excludes another, thus concealing the multiplicity of viewpoints that could comprise a philosophical conversation. By shifting from approach to approach, Irigaray optimizes textual openness, producing a poly-vocal writing that resists reduction to one particular stance.

Second, Irigaray finds strategic 'infidelity' empowering as it permits a distance between the woman-reader and the philosopher all too easily closed where fidelity is upheld. In their intellectual relationships with men, women are often seen as complementary rather than owning a place of their own: the woman-partner as advocate, affirming *his* truths, *his* desire. 'Infidelity' enables the assertion of difference within the relation between the philosopher and his woman-interlocutor, reminding us of her difference. With this strategic 'infidelity' in mind, the following approaches feature in Irigaray's critical toolbox:

Psychoanalysis

Despite her troubled relation to psychoanalysis,[5] its influence pervades Irigaray's interrogations of the philosophers. Yet her 'use' of psychoanalysis is provisional, pragmatic, and self-reflexive. Her method of reading philosophy against itself is like psychoanalytic therapy, where the analyst interprets the analysand's (patient's) words to reveal hidden meanings. Irigaray's frequent tactic of repeating (by quotation or paraphrase) and then interrogating the philosopher's text can be understood as a manner of analysing the 'unconscious' of the philosophical work.

What she finds in this unconscious is a repressed femininity: a mode of expression, and variety of experience, that must remain concealed for the philosophy to cohere. In the course of articulating the philosophy, 'femininity' – as matter, emotion, or softness for instance – is repudiated. This repudiated material reappears in another guise, however, like a 'slip of the tongue' or symptom in the clinic. By catching the philosopher in the midst of repudiation, Irigaray disturbs the consistency the disavowal fabricates.

Her voice 'identifies' with the repudiated femininity that returns to haunt the philosopher. Thus her writing is, like the psychoanalytic treatment, *dialogical*: actualizing an encounter between the (conscious) philosopher and the (unconscious) female interlocutor his writing excludes. As we will see in the later section, 'The Deployment of Affect', Irigaray exploits this tactic to great effect in *Marine Lover*.

Destruction/Deconstruction

Two other significant influences for Irigaray are Martin Heidegger and Jacques Derrida. From Heidegger, Irigaray makes use of the motifs of 'forgetting' and 'ontological difference'. Irigaray frames *An Ethics of Sexual Difference* in terms of Heidegger's claim that philosophy neglects its most fundamental question: what is Being? For Heidegger philosophers tend to quibble over questions concerning the nature of this or that being and call it 'ontology', while forgetting to interrogate the conditions of Being itself, and its integral relation to thought and humanity (*Dasein*). Irigaray responds by suggesting that the oblivion that organizes Western thought is *sexual* rather than ontological difference. Sexual difference is obscured by the presumption that what distinguishes types of human being is the presence or absence of a penis. For Irigaray, conversely, this binary arrangement of sexual difference recognizes only one model of being human. 'Difference' is understood as sameness, or a relation of privation to masculinity.[6]

Irigaray's use of Derridian 'deconstruction' also concerns the conception of difference. Derrida famously targets binary oppositions and slippages of meaning through which philosophy is crafted and conventional values maintained. Deconstruction reveals that when philosophers employ binary oppositions – where a higher priority is given to one term over another apparently derivative term – difference is understood in terms of an underlying sameness. For Derrida the paradigmatic opposition of Western philosophy that reinforces the value of sameness is the privilege given to speech over writing, or 'phonocentrism'. In 'Plato's Pharmacy' Derrida reads Plato's *Phaedrus*, where writing is characterized as a 'pharmakon' – both poison and medicine – that ' . . . will introduce forgetfulness into the soul of those who learn it' (Plato, 1995, p. 79 (275A)). For Plato speech is essential, immediate, and alive, while writing imperils oral discourse and memory. Derrida notes the ambivalence of the key term, 'pharmakon': it is both good and bad; an aid to and corrosive of memory; and this 'undecidability' generates binary difference. The ambiguity of the 'lesser' term of the pair *supports* the privileged term. 'Speech' is understood by virtue of writing: when pressed to explain what speech is, Plato characterizes it as a living, interior *writing*, engraved upon the soul (see Derrida, 1981, p. 154).

Irigaray argues in a similar vein against what she sees as the prevalence of 'phallocentrism' in Western philosophy: whereby sexual difference is mis-construed as sameness according to the privilege awarded to the 'phallus' (a symbolic value organized according to a masculine morphology). One of Irigaray's approaches is to demonstrate the instability of masculinity as a measure of cultural value, as it repudiates femininity while also drawing upon 'feminine' metaphors to elucidate its value. In *Marine Lover*, for instance, she challenges Nietzsche's representation of his doctrine of eter-nal recurrence (in Z 'The Seven Seals') as an attempt to ground his creativ-ity in 'woman' figured as Eternity:

> And you ask a woman to help you in this operation. To redouble your affirmation. To give yourself back as a unit—subjects and objects of all your ecstasy. To fold all your becoming back into your being. To give you back, in the here and now, everything you have believed, loved, produced, planned, been. (pp. 34–5)

Nietzsche conceives of his own creativity in terms of maternal metaphors, but denies women's creative potential by characterizing it as merely repro-ductive. The reduction of 'womanhood' to 'motherhood' in this way serves, Irigaray suggests, a phallocentric sexual economy that values masculinity by obscuring feminine difference.

Elemental Philosophy

Finally, Irigaray's methodology references Gaston Bachelard: a thinker whose influence on French philosophy is barely registered in anglophone coun-tries. In *Marine Lover*, Irigaray draws out elemental metaphors in Nietzsche's writing, diagnostically analysing the values, commitments, and fears expressed therein. Her elemental lexicon is derived in part from Bachelard's reading of Nietzsche in *L'Air et les songes* (Bachelard, 1988).[7] It would be unfair to reduce her reading to a variety of Bachlardian interpretation (as does Farrell Krell, 1994), however: Irigaray's elemental analysis expresses her own feminist con-cerns, developed through a relation of affect to Nietzsche (see below).

For Bachelard, we only comprehend a philosopher's work after consider-ing the imaginative aspect of their writing. This is reflected in the variety of metaphors they employ – considered not as simple *vehicles* for meaning, but as intrinsic to it. Bachelard interprets how Nietzsche feels about each element according to the adjectives and values he ascribes to it, and whether such images make good use of that element's potential. According to this analysis, Nietzsche – the self-described 'prophet of the meaning of the earth' (Z Prologue 3) – does not in fact love the earth:

> *Soft earth* disgusts him. How he scorns things that are 'spongy, cavernous, compressed' . . . It is one of the most reliable touchstones; only an impassioned lover of the earth, only a terrestrial who is also somewhat under the influence of water, can avoid the *automatically pejorative* nature of metaphorical *sponginess*. (128)

Nietzsche does not celebrate the earth within the terms of the element itself. He favours, rather, aerial metaphors: affirming only eroded earth, impoverished of its own uniqueness – an earth that has become subject to the air (desert earth, and the rocks of the mountain peaks). Nietzsche's preference for 'pure air', for Bachelard, expresses a *dynamic* rather than material imagination: a preference for action (movement, dance), overcoming, and freedom over matter.

Irigaray's 'elemental' approach to reading Nietzsche – through an exploration of his relation to the properties of water – is clearly influenced by Bachelard's diagnosis of Nietzsche's elemental affinities, and what they reveal about his philosophical values. Irigaray does not analyse his work in terms of the element in which he is most comfortable, however. Irigaray focuses instead on the element Nietzsche most fears. In an interview Irigaray states:

> I chose to interrogate Nietzsche from the perspective of water because it's the strongest point from which to interpret, it is the element of which he is most afraid. In *Zarathustra*, you detect his fear of the Deluge. Water is also what obscures frozen forms: ice/glass, mirrors. It is a pole, I wouldn't say opposed to, but a pole in a relation of otherness to the sun. (1981, p. 43)

This fear of water, she suggests, is symptomatic of a general disposition of his philosophy: first, a preference for lightness and Apollonian facade that (Dionysian) fluidity obscures; second, an envy of women's procreative power, represented by amniotic fluid; and, third, a fear of the sexual relation and an ambiguous, engulfing proximity suggested by fluidity.

For Irigaray, then, Nietzsche's fear of water rejects both the maternal and sexual relation. Distance, masks, and surfaces mediate Nietzsche's relationships with others in his writing. More surprisingly, she suggests that Nietzsche's fear of water indicates a fear of 'becoming': thereby revealing an inconsistency between Nietzsche's avowed values and the metaphorical register of his writing. Irigaray sets her relation to him in *Marine Lover* to water in order to remove Nietzsche from a complacency that stifles his becoming. The 'marine lover' returns by virtue of a great thaw, the end of an age of ice: ' . . . no sails, no skiff, no bridge remain in the breaking up and thawing of ice' (p. 36). Irigaray, as the 'marine lover', figuratively casts Nietzsche into the sea, returning him to a materiality that resembles that intra-uterine place of first movement, the place of his first becoming.

> Henceforth you would be separated from her only by a single membrane. And even so . . . Through that membrane, might you not, with some horror, discover the back that corresponds to your front? Your silence is brushing the bottom of something it had thought never to touch again. You are now immersed and reenveloped in something that erases all boundaries. Carried away by the waves. Drowning in the flood. Tragic castaway in unrestrained turmoil. (ibid.)

By subjecting Nietzsche's philosophy to fluidity, then, Irigaray attempts to test his commitment to becoming. And his avowed preference for becoming over being – of movement, internal difference, and change over static ideals – suggests he should be amenable to Irigaray's treatment. She suggests that Nietzsche's becoming, explicated in terms of eternal return, is a 'simulacrum of becoming' (p. 32), safely mediated by the stylized image of woman as Eternity. Her own engagement with Nietzsche in *Marine Lover*, conversely, is posed as an invitation to a becoming that can only take place once he embraces fluidity and a relation to sexual difference.

The Deployment of Affect

Male commentators have engaged with Nietzsche without first having to establish the authority to do so. The 'relation' between them is easily imagined in terms of fraternity or friendship, and is supported by caricatures of women (as 'nymph', 'dominatrix', 'mother', and 'barren feminist'), which serve as objects of exchange between Nietzsche and the men he envisions will read his philosophy. Nietzsche's readers are invited to converse with him about women, even if they're *actually* talking about philosophy. This relation to woman secures philosophers' social privilege, while apparently destabilizing 'Truth' and subjectivity. Indeed, for Derrida, 'woman' provides the very materiality for his relation with Nietzsche, as the script through which 'man' writes himself: 'if style were a man . . . then writing would be a woman' (1979, p. 57).

For women readers, conversely, 'friendship' with Nietzsche is complicated by this material use of 'woman'. In 'Of the Friend' (Z) Nietzsche even explicitly excludes women from that relation, stating that woman 'knows only love'. Prohibited friendship with Nietzsche, Irigaray consents to a relation he invited, but perhaps did not anticipate: love. Irigaray issues the relation as a challenge to adapt to a woman who is not a mere prop for his philosophy. Instead of using woman as an object of exchange between his text and its reader, Irigaray offers *Marine Lover* to Nietzsche as a bridge between them. This also challenges Nietzsche's impoverished conception of love as a degraded form of friendship rather than as having its own radical potentialities. For Irigaray, Nietzsche's conception of love, limited to selfless care or destruction, reflects fantasies about his own mother. 'Woman' for Nietzsche always has maternal contours:

And because you don't distinguish yourself from the other, you are now sinking down as in a current, so you can barely come up for air. And as soon as that brief moment of alertness is over, you [*tu*] dive back into her who bears you, and never do you break completely free of her. For that is not your fortune. (p. 30)

Marine Lover demonstrates to Nietzsche what a woman 'lover' rather than a 'mother' might be to him – and more crucially, how *Nietzsche* would need to develop to accommodate such a woman. Irigarayan love is then a transformative rather than palliative relation. Love that recognizes the other's difference enables a becoming impeded by a reification of that other: as Eternity, for instance. Love is, Irigaray suggests, a relation that enables a shared existence, and need not sacrifice one of the pair to the other: 'Why are we not, the one for the other, a resource of life and air?' (p. 31). Love can be a 'resource', however, only insofar as one is mindful of the other's need to be who they are. Irigarayan love, then, breaks down the binary (master/slave) arrangement of forces between Nietzsche and his 'woman', who only reflects what he hopes to be/come. Through this intermediate entity – love, figured as the book itself (written *with*, not *on* Nietzsche) – Irigaray hopes that she and Nietzsche will be able to 'unlimit their spaces'

(p. 5): to open a becoming Nietzsche had desired, but hadn't the resources to achieve alone.

Nietzsche's Irigaray

Irigaray is critical of Nietzsche, and takes him to represent a philosophical tradition that excludes women as readers. Her philosophy is sympathetic to his, however, and even acknowledges a debt to him. From her encounters with Nietzsche Irigaray takes not only the rhetorical landscape and mode of address assumed in order to stage their conversation. They also share important critical insights, values, and commitments, consideration of which will aid an understanding of her critique.

First is Nietzsche's value for feminism generally. Although he penned many ambiguous statements about 'woman' and feminism, feminist philosophers have been attracted to Nietzsche's writings in recent decades for good reason. In *Beyond Good and Evil*, *On the Genealogy of Morals*, and *Thus Spoke Zarathustra*, for instance, Nietzsche vigorously condemns philosophers who believe their philosophies to represent one universal point of view. With his concept of 'perspectivism', Nietzsche diagnozes personal undercurrents within philosophical writing passed off as universal truth. He calls Spinoza's love of an apparently neutral system in the *Ethics*, for instance, 'the masquerade of a sick hermit' that betrays his 'personal timidity and vulnerability' (BGE 'Prejudices' 5). Nietzsche's critique of the philosophical myth of objectivity allies him to a feminist critical program that seeks to reveal the personal stakes of philosophers pretending to speak in the name of all rational subjects, and thus marginalizing those with a different viewpoint.

Irigaray, then, shares with Nietzsche a critique of philosophy's conceit to speak a 'big-T-Truth', unmediated by social and material situation. She also shares with him a positive evaluation of *the body* philosophers attempt to overcome and undervalue, again in the name of objectivity. In relation to 'will to power' – a conception of life as a self-organizing diversity of drives – Nietzsche argues that philosophy is contingent upon the particularities of the philosopher's body. This resonates with Irigaray's notion of sexual difference, and her attempts to sketch a language consonant with feminine morphology, namely, those bodily qualities that philosophical writing repudiates, rather than the 'phallic', masculine body it takes for granted.

Nietzsche's own claim to understand feminine psychology, while no doubt overstated, can be taken to mean that he frequently spoke on behalf of those dimensions of human experience most associated by the philosophical tradition with femininity. Nietzsche affirms that there are as many truths as there are concrete circumstances, or bodies that live and think. This emphasis upon the plurality of perspectives works in concert with a feminist epistemology that stresses the *standpoint* of the one who makes knowledge claims. Nietzsche also affirms the primacy of the body as an interpreting, intelligent organism, over consciousness – the body's abbreviated, abstracted tool (see Z 'Of the Despisers of the Body'). As the body is often associated with femininity, the effect of a *male* philosopher speaking for embodiment disturbs this assumption.

Irigaray also shares with Nietzsche a poetic style of writing that, again, is conventionally aligned to femininity. Nietzsche emphasized the materiality of language – contrasting, the rhythm, timbre, and tempo of German against French and Italian – and its relation to 'metabolism' (BGE 28, 247). Accordingly, Nietzsche associates poetic style with a corporeal sensitivity to milieu, or life's material, sense-giving context. Nietzsche saw this relation between materiality and language as reciprocal, holding that the attempt to write in a different tempo/metabolism may open a different perspective. Likewise, Irigaray presses for an experimental writing she calls *l'écriture feminine*: a mode of writing that produces new perspectives, with reference to 'sexual difference'. Charged with producing new expressions of feminine embodiment and desire, *l'écriture feminine* privileges modes of communication conventionally denigrated by philosophy. Non-linear, proximate, expansive, plural, open-ended, cyclical – and, indeed, more poetic – language is opposed to linear, rigid, closed, and contained 'phallic' writing. Nietzsche, similarly, favoured an 'aphoristic', fragmentary, non-linear writing practice, and encouraged his readers to interpret his books in novel and unexpected ways. (Irigaray obliged Nietzsche at least in this respect.)

Finally, in *Thus Spoke Zarathustra*, Nietzsche held that philosophy's pretension to 'disembodied' discourse is symptomatic of a pathological hatred of life and the body. In a related vein, Irigaray argues that the bloodlessness of philosophy indicates a disavowal specifically of the 'feminine' body, which has come in Western thought to represent the body insofar as it is beyond the subject's control. Irigaray can thereby be seen to work with Nietzsche as well as against him, extending and sharpening his critique of dogmatic philosophers' troubled relation to their bodies.

With *Marine Lover*, then, Irigaray attempts to harness Nietzsche's critical insights to her feminist revaluation of philosophy, while also challenging the vestiges of phallocentrism within his writing. Irigaray resists simply falling into line with Nietzsche, instead using his best insights to open a critical perspective on his work. Her strongly motivated interpretation is compelling for the same reason that it sometimes repels readers: because, as with Nietzsche, her writing is dense with affect, unabashedly partial, poetic, and sometimes hyperbolic. *Marine Lover* documents a turbulent love affair, grounded in Irigaray's ambivalence for Nietzsche. It is a productive ambivalence, however, that establishes a new mode of engagement with Nietzsche's philosophy, and serves to caution other of his feminist readers against complacency about their authority as such.

Notes

[1] The French '*amant*', for lover, is gendered masculine. Irigaray thereby draws a connection between women's possibilities in love and grammatical gender: by adding the 'e' to feminize '*amant*', she allows us to imagine that women might be active 'lovers' rather than passive 'beloveds'.

[2] Penelope Deutscher explains this relation with reference to Irigaray in *Yielding Gender* (1997), p. 79.

[3] Nietzsche at times demonstrated a delicate sensitivity to the cultural parameters of femininity, and their connection to the construction of masculinity. See TI 'Maxims' 13; BGE 237a.

[4] For an account of the meaning of woman throughout the history of philosophy, see also Lloyd (1993).

[5] Irigaray wrote her PhD dissertation (later published as *Speculum of the Other Woman*) in response to the teachings of Jacques Lacan at the *École Freudienne de Paris*, which led to her expulsion. Her chief criticism of psychoanalysis is that it is a 'phallocentric' discourse blind to specifically feminine possibilities and interpretations.

[6] For in-depth accounts of Irigaray's relation to Heidegger, see Mortensen (1994); Chanter (1995); and Faulkner (2001).

[7] Margaret Whitford (1991, pp. 55–6) acknowledges Gaston Bachelard's influence upon Irigaray's critical methodology.

Bibliography and Guide to Further Study

Irigaray's Nietzsche Interpretation

Irigaray, Luce (1991), *Marine Lover of Friedrich Nietzsche*, trans. Gillian C. Gill. New York: Columbia University Press. Irigaray's major text on Nietzsche.

— (1994), 'Ecce Mulier? Fragments', in Peter J. Burgard (ed.), *Nietzsche and the Feminine*. Charlottesville and London: University Press of Virginia. A parody of Nietzsche's (already quite parodic) 'autobiography', *Ecce Homo*, arguably less successful than *Marine Lover*.

Irigaray on Methodology

Irigaray, L. (1981), *Le Corps-à-corps avec la mère*. Montrèal: Plein Lune. This (French language) interview with Irigaray addresses her writing style, and how she envisages her relationship with philosophers (including Nietzsche).

— (1985a), *Speculum of the Other Woman*, trans. G. C. Gill. Ithaca: Cornell University Press. Originally Irigaray's doctoral thesis, this work contains sustained engagements with Plato and Freud, with briefer interludes on Descartes, Kant, Hegel, Aristotle, and science more generally.

— (1985b), *This Sex Which Is Not One*, trans. Catherine Porter. Ithaca: Cornell University Press. A compilation of essays dealing with psychoanalytic theory, women as objects of exchange, discourse, pornography, sexuality, women's morphology, and *l'écriture feminine*.

— (1992), *Elemental Passions*, trans. Joanne Collie and Judith Still. London: Athlone. Explores relations between the sexes in terms of the elements, and is instructive regarding the elemental dimension of her reading of Nietzsche.

— (1993), *An Ethics of Sexual Difference*, trans. Carolyn Burke and G. C. Gill. Ithaca: Cornell University Press. Irigaray's account of the forgetting of the feminine that founds philosophy.

Works on Irigaray's Nietzsche

Burke, Carolyn (1989), 'Romancing the Philosophers: Luce Irigaray', in Dianne Hunter (ed.), *Seduction and Theory: Readings of Gender, Representation, and Rhetoric*. Urbana: University of Illinois Press. An important essay on Irigaray's strategy of 'flirting' with the philosophers.

Butler, Judith (1993), *Bodies That Matter: On the Discursive Limits of 'Sex'*. New York and London: Routledge. Contains a clear account of Irigaray's notion of the repressed feminine.

Chanter, Tina (1995), *Ethics of Eros: Irigaray's Rewriting of the Philosophers*. New York and London: Routledge. A comprehensive study of Irigaray's philosophical criticism and ethics of reading.

Deutscher, Penelope (2002), *A Politics of Impossible Difference: The Later Work of Luce Irigaray*. Ithaca: Cornell University Press.

Farrell Krell, David (1994), 'To the Orange Grove at the Edge of the Sea: Remarks on Luce Irigaray's *Amante Marine*', in Peter J. Burgard (ed.), *Nietzsche and the Feminine*. Charlottesville and London: University Press of Virginia. Addresses *Marine Lover* specifically, but is quite an unsympathetic reading.

Faulkner, Joanne (2003), 'Voices from the Depths: Reading 'Love' in Luce Irigaray's *Marine Lover*'. *Diacritics* 33, (1), 81–94.

Mortensen, Ellen (1994), 'Woman's Untruth and *le féminin*: Reading Luce Irigaray with Nietzsche and Heidegger', in C. Burke, Naomi Schor and Margaret Whitford (eds), *Engaging with Irigaray*. New York: Columbia University Press.

Oliver, Kelly (2006), 'Vision, Recognition, and a Passion for the Elements', in Maria C. Cimitile, and Elaine P. Miller (eds), *Returning to Irigaray: Feminist Philosophy, Politics, and the Question of Unity*. Albany: SUNY Press. A useful account of Irigaray's attention to materiality and her elemental philosophy.

Oppel, Frances (1993), '"Speaking of Immemorial Waters": Irigaray with Nietzsche', in Paul Patton (ed.), *Nietzsche, Feminism, and Political Theory*. London: Routledge. Addresses Irigaray's interpretation of Nietzsche specifically.

Whitford, Margaret (1991), *Luce Irigaray: Philosophy in the Feminine*. London and New York: Routledge. The first book-length consideration in English of Irigaray as a philosopher, and very influential upon the anglophone reception of Irigaray.

Other Works Cited

Bachelard, Gaston (1988), *Air and Dreams: An Essay on the Imagination of Movement*, trans. Edith Farrell and Frederick Farrell. Dallas: The Dallas Institute of Humanities and Culture.

Derrida, Jacques (1973), 'Discussion', in Maurice de Gandillac and Bernard Pautrat (eds) *Nietzsche Aujourd'hui?: 1. Intensités*. Paris: Union Générale d'Éditions.

— (1979), *Spurs: Nietzsche's Styles*, trans. Barbara Harlow. Chicago and London: The University of Chicago Press.

— (1981), *Dissemination*, trans. Barbara Johnson. London: Athlone.

Deutscher, Penelope (1997), *Yielding Gender: Feminism, Deconstruction, and the History of Philosophy*. London and New York: Routledge.

Faulkner, Joanne (2001), 'Amnesia at the Beginning of Time: Irigaray's reading of Heidegger in *The Forgetting of Air*'. *Contretemps*, 2, 124–41.

Lloyd, Genevieve (1993), *Man of Reason: 'Male' and 'Female' in Western Philosophy*. London: Routledge.

Plato (1995), *Phaedrus*, trans. Alexander Nehamas and Paul Woodruff. Indianapolis and Cambridge: Hackett Publishing Company, Inc.

Chapter 13

Nehamas's Nietzsche

Mark Tomlinson

In Anglo-American Nietzsche studies, few works over the last 30 years have proved as popular or influential as Alexander Nehamas's *Nietzsche: Life as Literature* (1985). One sure reason for this is the book's accessibility: those looking for a clear and reliable introduction to Nietzsche's major themes can do no better. Historically, however, what really ensured the success of Nehamas's work was the way it effected a synthesis of key aspects of both European and Anglo-American interpretations at a time when such a synthesis seemed necessary. For many years, the tendency among anglophone scholars had been to criticize, if not ignore, the aesthetic, specifically literary, aspects of Nietzsche's work. By the early 1980s, however, under the increasing influence of contemporary European currents of thought, anglophone scholars began to pay attention not only to *what* Nietzsche wrote, but to *how* he wrote it. They began, that is, to see the latter as somehow essential to the former. Nehamas's genius was to integrate both approaches: to be sensitive to the literary dimension of Nietzsche's work without abandoning the careful conceptual analysis that had characterized previous Anglo-American interpretations. The result was a unique, highly inventive, and as we shall see, often brilliant interpretation of Nietzsche, one that in a certain sense played to both sides of the divide.

Formally, this chapter seeks to introduce readers to the specificities of Nehamas's Nietzsche, and in particular to the novel interpretive rubric through which it approaches Nietzsche's work: aestheticism. It aims to demonstrate the precise way in which Nehamas deploys this rubric across three key, notoriously difficult, Nietzschean themes: perspectivism, the will to power, and the eternal recurrence.[1] As we will see, according to Nehamas, Nietzsche views the world as if it were an artwork, and most often, as if it were a literary text. It is this peculiar way of looking at the world, he argues, that motivates the majority of Nietzsche's philosophical doctrines. It also helps explain Nietzsche's own idiosyncratic philosophical practice, including his writing style: Nietzsche not only sees the world as a text, but life as literature.

Perspectivism

In order to introduce Nehamas's Nietzsche more fully, let us turn at once to his treatment of perspectivism. At its most basic, perspectivism is the view that there are no views independent of interpretation, 'perspectivism' itself included. Or as Nietzsche puts it, 'facts are just what there aren't, there are only interpretations . . . Perspectivism' (Nietzsche, 2003, p. 139). Over the years, many of Nietzsche's readers have taken this as little more than a recapitulation of Kant's famous idea that we can only know, and represent, things as they appear to us, not as they really are. But, as Nehamas rightly points out, such a reading fails to capture the true essence of the doctrine: '[t]he idea that we are necessarily incapable of representing the world accurately presupposes the view that the world's appearance is radically different from its reality' (1985, p. 45).[2] It presupposes a split between a so-called true world (the one we cannot access) and a false one (the one we can access). But, *contra* Kant, the upshot of Nietzsche's perspectivism is not simply that we cannot access the true world, it is that such a world does not exist. Nietzsche's perspectivism, Nehamas explains, entails that in itself, the world has no features, and that therefore '[these features can be] neither correctly nor wrongly represented' (ibid.). Perspectivism is not the view that we can only ever see things from a particular perspective – our own – and never as they truly are. Rather, perspectivism denies that there is, or ever could be, such a thing as 'the way things truly are'. That we see things from a particular perspective is not an obstacle to knowing, or a defect in our interaction with the world (and thus something we must strive to overcome), it is rather the *ground* of such knowing.

In order to understand the way in which perspectivism might be said to ground knowledge, we must first understand more about perspectivism itself. What does it mean to say that we see things from a particular perspective? For Nehamas, it means that when we engage in any activity or inquiry 'we must inevitably be selective' (p. 49). We must 'occupy ourselves with a selection of material and exclude much from our consideration' (p. 50). When Nietzsche claims that there is only a perspectival seeing, a perspectival knowing, he does not mean that we see or know an appearance of the world instead of the actual world itself; he means that knowing and seeing involves 'an inherently conditional relation to its object, a relation that pre-supposes or manifests specific values, interests, and goals' (ibid.). If we were not selective – if we did not see things from a particular perspective, with particular values, interests, and goals – we would not see anything at all.

At this point, Nehamas makes his first appeal to Nietzsche's so-called aes-theticism – the reliance upon artistic models to understand the world – in order to clarify the argument. For Nietzsche, Nehamas argues, knowing is like painting. Just as the latter involves seeing things from a particular per-spective, so too does the former:

> [t]here is no sense in which painters, even if we limit our examples to realistic depictions of one's visual field, can ever paint 'everything' that they see. What they 'leave out' is in itself quite indeterminate, and can be specified, if at all, only through other paintings, each one of which will be similarly 'partial.' Analogously, Nietzsche believes, there can be no total or final theory or understanding of the world. On his artistic model, the understanding of everything would be like a painting that incorporates all styles or that is painted in no style at all—a true chimera, both impos-sible and monstrous. (p. 51)

In order to see anything at all we must see things from a particular perspec-tive, just as in order to paint anything at all we must paint them from a particular perspective or in a particular style. A perspectival relation to the object of one's knowledge is a *necessary* condition of knowledge, not some-thing to be overcome (an impossibility in any case).

In linking perspectivism to aestheticism, Nehamas is able to present a sophisticated account of an otherwise difficult doctrine. But this is not its only strength. As in much of *Nietzsche: Life as Literature*, Nehamas's chapter on perspectivism skilfully negotiates some of the more difficult problems that might be raised against it. Nehamas recognizes that Nietzsche's com-mitment to perspectivism presents him with a serious problem: how can one argue for a position, as it seems Nietzsche wants to do with perspectiv-ism, without holding that position to be true? The problem is, if perspectiv-ism is true, then it seems there are some facts, or rather *a fact*, independent of interpretation after all, namely perspectivism itself. It seems, then, that Nietzsche's theory of knowledge is self-refuting. For many, this has been reason enough to dismiss the doctrine outright. However, as Nehamas clev-erly shows, this particular charge, while serious, is not fatal. In fact, the charge rests on a false assumption, namely, that interpretation and truth are mutually exclusive; that if something is an interpretation it is necessarily false. But as Nehamas reminds us, Nietzsche's point is that truth and inter-pretation are *not* mutually exclusive. The latter (as the means by which we see and come to understand anything at all), *grounds* knowledge, it does not negate it. If Nietzsche is right about the relationship between perspectivism and knowledge as outlined earlier in this section, then he can hold his view without contradiction. The only way to refute perspectivism is to disprove that relationship; or (which amounts to the same thing), to actually pro-duce a fact that is independent of interpretation, a non-perspectival perspective.[3]

Will to Power

The '*world is the will to power—and nothing besides!*' (Nietzsche, 2003, p. 39). This statement – along with the doctrine to which it gives voice – has puz-zled even Nietzsche's best readers. Does it not seem utterly incompatible with everything that has just been said about perspectivism? Perspectivism claims that in itself the world has no features and therefore no ultimate character. It is always in the process of being created. How then are we to reconcile it with the doctrine of the will to power, a doctrine which, if the above statement is anything to go by, very much appears to be attributing to the world a definite character? As with his response to the problem of per-spectivism, Nehamas's approach is highly inventive. The will to power, he argues, is not so much a description of the world as it really is, but an account of why such a description could never be given. The will to power is not at odds with perspectivism, but its perfect complement.

Nehamas's suggestion is that the will to power has more to do with hermen-eutics than metaphysics: 'what there is is always determined from a specific point of view that embodies its particular interests, needs, and values, its own will to power' (p. 81). The will to power is the name Nietzsche gives to a set of purposes and values embodied in a perspective which comes to condition the kind of world we create and experience. 'Each way of dealing with the world manifests the will to power of those who engage in it as at the same time it arranges this indeterminate world into a definite object' (p. 97). A religion such as Christianity, for example, is a manifestation of the will to power in that it involves and seeks to propagate a particular way of interpreting the world and our existence within it. It takes '[t]he lives of the ascetic, the poor, and the downtrodden' and appropriates, or reinter-prets, them 'from calamities to be avoided into ideals to be pursued' (ibid.). And this is why the will to power is not a description of the world as it really is but an account of why such a description could never be given. If the will to power is Nietzsche's name for a set of purposes and values – be they Christian, Zarathustran, or otherwise – which come to condition the world and the objects within it, then different manifestations of the will to power produce different worlds and different objects. Therefore, when Nietzsche writes that the world is will to power and nothing besides, he is not claiming that the world has a determinate character called the will to power, he is claiming that in itself the world has no character. Nehamas puts the matter this way: 'the world of the will to power is "in itself" radically indeterminate: it can be described in a large number of ways, none of which need, or indeed can, make a claim to constituting its ultimate correct representation' (ibid.).

The account Nehamas gives of the will to power may fit nicely with his account of perspectivism, but it is not without difficulty. The version of the will to power Nehamas puts forth implies a radical ontology. In the world of the will to power, things, including human beings, would appear to lack all substance. Nothing has being beyond its subjection to a particular manifestation of the will to power.

> Nietzsche . . . allows for a serious fluidity in our interpretations of the world and so also for a serious fluidity in what there is. His view implies that ontological categories are subject to change, and this in turn suggests that there are no such things as ontological categories. (p. 83)

But how can there be interpretations of the world without there being, in some substantial sense, a world in the first place? How can there be an interpretation of a thing without there being some *thing* to which that interpretation refers?

Nehamas thinks we can go some way to answering this objection if we consider Nietzsche's critique of the self. We typically think of ourselves as having some underlying essence or substance that makes us who we are. It is this self that performs actions (attends class, eats dinner, takes the train, and so forth). It is the 'I' in 'I'm thirsty' or 'I'm hungry'. For Nietzsche, however, there is no such thing as the self, at least not in this sense. In a revealing passage from the *Late Notebooks* he writes '[i]f I think away all the relationships, all the "qualities", all the "activities" of a thing, then the thing does *not* remain behind: because thingness was only a *fiction added* by us . . . ' (Nietzsche, 2003, p. 206). In other words, there is nothing – no self – that is distinct from, more than, or behind my actions. There is not my self on one side, and my actions on another. As Nietzsche famously puts it, there is no doer behind the deed (GM I, 13; Nietzsche, 1989, p. 45). I am the totality of my actions, nothing more, nothing less. And if I were to set any of my actions aside, if they were erased from my history, I would not now be the same person. It is not only, then, that I am no more than my actions, it is that I cannot do without even a single one of them. This means that who I am is not fixed, but at every moment subject to change. As I do more things, I continue to create myself, I continue to become who I am.

What this account of the self reveals is that in order to be an object of interpretation, a thing need not have a fixed character or underlying essence. A thing is the sum of its effects. Its being lies not in some atemporal, essential identity, but in its relation at any given moment to other objects in an interpretive whole (what we might also call a 'will to power'). These relations or interconnections – and hence the things themselves – are in flux; they are always in the process of being reinterpreted in the light of subsequent events, and by a particular person or group of people for particular reasons. If at any point a single relation or interconnection is dropped, the object changes, since it is nothing over and above those relations. To refer to our earlier example, the lives of the poor and the downtrodden existed before Christianity gave them their specific *Christian* significance. But these lives did not exist in themselves as bare facts (p. 97). They did not possess some underlying essence. They simply had a prior significance; a significance determined, Nietzsche might say, by a prior will to power – for example, a noble mode of valuation rather than a Christian, slavish, one. The point is, at no time do these lives exist apart from a particular interpretive whole.

At this point in the argument, Nehamas once more appeals to Nietzsche's aestheticism. The radical ontology entailed by the will to power makes a great deal more sense, Nehamas thinks, if we bear in mind that Nietzsche views the world as a literary text. Consider literary characters. They do not exist as bare facts. By this Nehamas means two things: first, that a character is nothing beyond or aside from his or her actions and statements – 'absolutely everything characters do makes them what they are'; if we remove or alter any aspect of them, we automatically alter the whole (p. 89). Secondly, that the natures of those actions and statements are themselves not fixed, but subject to interpretation. Let us consider the first aspect of Nehamas's claim. 'Literary characters', he writes,

> are exhausted by the statements that concern them in the narrative in which they occur: they are in fact nothing more than what is said of them, just as they are also nothing less. Every detail concerning a character has, at least in principle, a point; it is to that extent essential to that character . . . [To]

change even one action on the part of a character is to cause both that character and the story to which it belongs to fall apart . . . [Could] Anna Karenina, for example, not have fallen in love with Vronsky? Could she not have left her husband? Could she have loved her son less than she did? (p. 165)

Nehamas certainly appears to have a point. It is difficult to imagine Anna without Vronsky, just as it is difficult to imagine Odysseus without his cunning. If we were to subtract the one from the other, we would not have the same story, nor the same characters. But there remains a question, I think, over this part of Nehamas's claim. The literary character Nehamas appeals to is a particular kind of character, one that is perhaps not common to all forms of literature, or even all forms of the novel. Dickens, for example, seems full of characters that are almost the opposite of Nehamas's description. If you took a significant portion of events and description away from Uriah Heep, he'd still be 'umble'; if you took the same away from Joe Gargery, he'd still be sitting beside his stove. Of course, critics of Dickens might say that he doesn't have characters, just caricatures. But that particular criticism presupposes a certain type of character – one in which growth, development, and change are privileged.[4]

The second aspect of Nehamas's claim seems much safer. The meaning of a character's actions and statements – and hence the nature of that character – is itself not given. Take Captain Ahab from Melville's *Moby-Dick*. His character does not exist as a bare fact, as something prior to or beyond his actions and statements. But neither are those actions and statements bare facts. They require interpretation. In fact, we might say that Ahab is nothing prior to or beyond his place in an interpretive whole – a whole that itself changes as we continue to read. Nehamas puts the point this way:

We cannot possibly suppose that in reading *Moby-Dick* we can understand what Ahab means when he yells, 'I would strike the sun if it insulted me,' without having already made at least a tentative commitment as to who Ahab is . . . A moody, solitary cripple can be transformed into the novel's 'crazy Ahab' through such a statement, and his other actions now appear in a new light; they turn out to be literally different actions. But is Ahab crazy because he seeks revenge for an action performed by a senseless, irresponsible beast? Or is he crazier still, and so perhaps more human, because he refuses to submit to a power greater than he can master? Is he suffering from the loss of his leg, the loss of his pride, or from the limits to his strength? Each one of these elementary questions conditions our interpretation of the original statement and is in turn conditioned by it;

an answer to any one of them commits us to answers to the other questions as well. Ahab emerges through such answers. (p. 89)

The parallel with the will to power is clear: '[a]s in the literary case, so in the world', to interpret or reinterpret events 'is to rearrange effects and therefore to generate new things. Our "text" is being composed as we read it, and our readings are new parts of it that will give rise to further ones in the future' (p. 91). As with perspectivism, then, by reading the will to power 'aesthetically', Nehamas is able to wring from an otherwise perplexing, and to some preposterous, doctrine, a comprehensible, even attractive, one.

The Eternal Recurrence

Book 4 of *The Gay Science* contains one of Nietzsche's most intriguing passages:

> *The greatest weight.* – What, if some day or night a demon were to steal after you into your loneliest loneliness and say to you: 'This life as you now live it and have lived it, you will have to live once more and innumerable times more; and there will be nothing new in it, but every pain and every joy and every thought and every sigh and everything unutterably small or great in your life will have to return to you, all in the same succession and sequence—even this spider and this moonlight between the trees, and even this moment and I myself. The eternal hourglass of existence is turned upside down again and again, and you with it, speck of dust!'
> Would you not throw yourself down and gnash your teeth and curse the demon who spoke thus? Or have you once experienced a tremendous moment when you would have answered him: 'You are a god and never have I heard anything more divine.' If this thought gained possession of you, it would change you as you are or perhaps crush you. The question in each and every thing, 'Do you desire this once more and innumerable times more?' would lie upon your actions as the greatest weight. Or how well disposed would you have to become toward yourself and to life to crave nothing more fervently than this ultimate confirmation and seal? (GS 341; Nietzsche, 1974, pp. 273–4)

Those familiar with Nietzsche's work will recognize this passage at once: it is the famous formulation of one of his most mysterious ideas, the eternal recurrence.

Like the will to power, the eternal recurrence has often been read as a cosmology, as a highly speculative account of how the universe works. On that reading, the world of the eternal recurrence is said to be a world in which

> everything that has already happened, and everything that is happening at this very moment, and everything that will happen in the future, has already happened and will happen again, preceded and followed by exactly the same events in exactly the same order, an infinite number of times. (p. 142)

In as much as the eternal recurrence has been read that way, it has won Nietzsche few admirers, and it is not difficult to see why. As an account of the universe, the eternal recurrence looks like nothing more than a naïve metaphysics. It also seems to violate any number of Nietzsche's own antimetaphysical premises. Given the difficulties a doctrine like the eternal recurrence presents, many of Nietzsche's interpreters have simply left it to one side. It is part of the remarkable strength of Nehamas's work that he refuses to ignore the difficult nature of Nietzsche's core ideas. Where others have struggled to see a way through, Nehamas beats a path of his own.

Nehamas begins by agreeing with Nietzsche's critics: *qua* cosmology, the eternal recurrence is highly dubious, maybe even logically impossible (see pp. 141–9). However, whether the eternal recurrence stands up as a theory about the physical nature of the universe is in the end, according to Nehamas, of no great concern: '[p]hilosophically . . . the use Nietzsche makes of the eternal recurrence does not require that this highly doubtful cosmology be true or even coherent' (p. 150). For Nehamas, the most significant aspect of the doctrine is not its metaphysical validity but its psychological consequences. Its application is not to physics or metaphysics but to life: '[t]he eternal recurrence is not a theory of the world but a view of the self' (ibid.).

As a cosmology, the eternal recurrence is often taken to claim that one's life will recur in exactly identical fashion. But that misses the point. The lesson of Nietzsche's teaching, according to Nehamas, is not that one's life *will* recur, but that *if* one's life *were* to recur then it could only recur in identical fashion. That is, Nehamas takes the eternal recurrence as an assertion of a conditional, not as a statement of fact. This seemingly insignificant detail shifts the focus of the eternal recurrence from the nature of the universe to the nature of the self, and ultimately to an account of the ideal life.

It is common to wish from time to time that we had not acted as we did – to dream about going back in time to change things. We often in our lives entertain counterfactual statements in the form: 'if only I had done x instead of y'. But rarely do we stop and think about the validity of such statements (other than to say, of course, that what's done is done). According to Nehamas, however, the validity (or otherwise) of such counterfactuals is precisely what the eternal recurrence is about. For Nietzsche, wishing things had been different is pointless. And not just because what is done is done, but because it involves a radical misunderstanding of the nature of the self. Think of the will to power and in particular Nietzsche's critique of the self. Nietzsche argues that the self is not something beyond, or separate from, its actions and experiences. It is rather the totality of those things. Nehamas's idea is to connect this aspect of the will to power to the eternal recurrence. To say that the self is inseparable from its actions and experiences is to say that everything I do depends on everything I have been. And to say that is to say that were something about my past different, I too would be different. 'Any change in [my] features would . . . altogether eliminate the person [I have] been as well as the world [I have] lived in' (p. 164). There can be no true counterfactuals in the form expressed above, for 'a person's life cannot be in any way different and still be the life of the same person' (ibid.). Everything I do is crucial to who I am. The eternal recurrence does not posit the repetition of the universe, but the inseparability of the past from the present, and the present from the future. What Nehamas's interpretation reveals especially well is the way that the eternal recurrence presents us with a choice between two extremes: either one accepts one's life in its entirety, or else one rejects it in its entirety. There is no middle ground. We cannot be selective in what we wish to accept of ourselves, for everything about us is equally essential to who we are. '[I]f anything is different, everything is different' (p. 163).

But why might Nietzsche consider this particular insight so telling? For Nehamas, Nietzsche's theory is a theory with practical intent. It is supposed to help transform the self, not merely provide new information about it. Indeed, as Nehamas argues, it is the eternal recurrence that provides the framework for Nietzsche's view of the ideal life. It will not, I hope, surprise readers to learn that for Nehamas the best way to illustrate this point is to once more call on Nietzsche's so-called aestheticism. Nehamas suggests that a perfect example of Nietzsche's ideal life can be found in Marcel Proust's *Remembrance of Things Past*. In Proust's book – a fictional autobiography – the narrator famously relates 'all the silly, insignificant . . . accidental, sometimes horrible' details of his life – the life of a budding author (p. 167). At first, those details can seem gratuitous, pointless even. But as the novel progresses they become essential. Gradually we come to realize that it is precisely these details and events that enable Proust's narrator to become the person he is, and the author he hopes to be. They become the details of a book he – Proust's narrator – has not yet begun to write, but which we have just finished reading.

Like Proust's narrator, Nietzsche's ideal is the person who is able to create or fashion a self out of everything that has happened to him. In so doing, that person redeems and in a sense alters the past by making of it a necessity. The perfect self is like the perfect narrative or the perfect literary character. Nothing is inconsequential. Every detail has a purpose. Every part is integrated into the whole. Even though our every experience is always already essential to who we are, it is only very rarely – in the strongest, most admirable people – that we are able to integrate those experiences into our characters, that we are able not only to affirm everything that has happened, but to fashion out of it a work of art.

The Eternal Recurrence . . . Again

Nehamas's pyscho-aesthetic reading of the eternal recurrence faces at least three difficulties. First, Nietzsche's ideal self, as portrayed by Nehamas, would seem to excuse and even actively perpetuate injustice and suffering in our own lives as well as the lives of others. Nietzsche's formula for greatness is '*amor fati*: that one wants nothing to be different, not forward, not backward, not in all eternity' (EH 'Clever' 10; Nietzsche, 1979, p. 37). The eternal recurrence demands that we not only accept but affirm the world as it is and as it has been. But what of those for whom this world is a nightmare? What of inequality, starvation, mass murder . . . ? Are we supposed to affirm those too? At times, *amor fati* seems less a formula for greatness than an apology for barbarism. Secondly, it seems it would be entirely possible to achieve Nietzsche's ideal and yet be 'deeply repulsive from a moral point of view' (Nehamas, 1985, p. 7). What is most important for Nietzsche is to give style to one's character; to create – like an artwork – an organized, coherent whole out of the material of one's life. Whether one is good rather than evil is another matter. 'Organization is the most crucial feature of literary characters' – the quality of their actions is secondary (p. 193). Thirdly, as with perspectivism, Nietzsche's notion of the ideal self (at least as understood by Nehamas) seems self-refuting. Surely Nietzsche is the last person who should be prescribing a way of life. Does not the very notion of an ideal life, or an ideal self, contradict Nietzsche's anti-dogmatic, perspectival philosophy by issuing a set of principles and practices for all to adopt? Although Nehamas finds all three problems troubling, he does not abandon Nietzsche's philosophy – nor his own interpretation of that philosophy – on account of them. The third problem in particular, he thinks, can be readily overcome.

Indeed, the manner in which Nehamas extracts Nietzsche from this difficulty is masterful. Were Nietzsche to issue a set of principles and practices for all to adopt it would certainly go against the spirit of his own philosophical project. But that is not what the eternal recurrence is about. Nietzsche's ideal individual is just that – an individual. To shape one's life into a work of art means to create something unique. It does not mean to follow a set of instructions. Just as there is 'no general set of considerations that can determine in advance what can and cannot, what must and must not be part of a great artwork', nor is there such a set of considerations that can determine what must and must not be part of a life of value and importance (p. 229).

> A true individual is precisely one who is different from the rest of the world, and there is no formula, no set of rules, no code of conduct that can possibly capture in informative terms what it is to be like that. (p. 225)

Great artworks are often the ones that break the rules, not follow them: '[n] ew art movements are often successful precisely because they show that what the tradition, explicitly or implicitly, had excluded from art can become the source and matter of a new genre' (p. 229).

If we read Nietzsche looking for a set of instructions on how to become a great individual we are bound to be disappointed. He does not provide any because there are none. And yet, although he does not describe his ideal character, he does 'produce a perfect instance' of one (p. 230). In this regard, 'it is not only Nietzsche's model that is literary. In a serious sense his product is literary as well' (p. 233). Through his highly idiosyncratic style and individual ideas, Nietzsche fashions out of his own life a true work of art. He creates one of the greatest characters in the history of Western philosophy: himself.

The Perfect Reader?

As I hope is clear by now, *Nietzsche: Life as Literature* achieves something rare in the field of Nietzsche studies. It manages to distil from Nietzsche's corpus a single, unified interpretation of the latter's major philosophical doctrines, and in a clear manner. It also pays close attention to the literary and aesthetic dimension of that work. But Nehamas's Nietzsche is far from perfect. Though at times the notion of a Nietzschean aestheticism works to spectacular effect, at others it can feel forced, as if it were being used to squeeze from Nietzsche's work a unity that is not always there. Several of Nehamas's critics, such as Brian Leiter and Richard Schacht, have noted this very point (see Schacht, 1995; Leiter, 1992). Both have been sceptical of how much Nietzsche's aestheticism is actually Nietzsche's and how much of it is Nehamas's.

It is certainly true that nowhere (to the best of my knowledge at least), does Nietzsche explicitly mention that he views the world as a literary text, nor that the point of his work is to produce a literary product. In that sense, Schacht and Leiter would seem to have a point. Nevertheless, with a thinker such as Nietzsche, it is not at all apparent that such strict fidelity to the text guarantees a more fruitful – and for that matter, truthful – interpretation. Nietzsche demands a great deal of his readers. As he writes in *Ecce Homo*, '[w]hen I picture a perfect reader I always picture a monster of courage and curiosity . . . something supple, cunning, cautious, a born adventurer and discoverer' (EH 'Books' 3; Nietzsche, 1979, p. 43). Nehamas may not be Nietzsche's perfect reader, but he is nothing if not courageous – a born adventurer and discoverer.

Notes

1 In *Nietzsche: Life as Literature*, Nehamas also devotes chapters to Nietzsche's writing style, to genealogy, and to the moral (or otherwise) dimension of Nietzsche's ideal self. For reasons of space I have not been able to discuss them in detail here. What can be said, however, is that Nehamas's remarks on all three extend naturally from his aestheticist interpretation.

2 Unless otherwise indicated, page numbers throughout this chapter reference Nehamas's *Nietzsche: Life as Literature* (1985).

3 As Nehamas puts it: 'Perhaps not all views are interpretations. But we shall know this to be true only when one is actually produced. Perspectivism cannot be shown to refute itself as easily as we have often assumed' (p. 67).

4 I am indebted to Martin Lee for this particular insight. I would also like to thank him for his invaluable comments on an earlier draft of this chapter.

Bibliography and Guide to Further Study

Nehamas's Nietzsche Interpretation

Nehamas, Alexander (1980), 'The Eternal Recurrence'. *The Philosophical Review*, 89, (3), 331–56. An early statement of the position elaborated in *Nietzsche: Life as Literature*.

— (1981), 'Getting Used to Not Getting Used to It: Nietzsche in the Magic Mountain'. *Philosophy and Literature*, 5, 73–88.

— (1983), 'Immanent and Transcendent Perspectivism in Nietzsche'. *Nietzsche-Studien*, 12, 473–91.

— (1985), *Nietzsche: Life as Literature*. Cambridge, MA: Harvard University Press. Nehamas's major work on Nietzsche.

— (1986), 'Will to Knowledge, Will to Ignorance and Will to Power in *Beyond Good and Evil*', in Yirmiahu Yovel (ed.), *Nietzsche as Affirmative Thinker*. Dordrecht: Martin Nijhoff Publishers. A discussion of Nietzsche's view that truth and error, knowledge and ignorance, are not essentially opposed to one another, but rather points along a single continuum.

— (1988), 'Who Are "The Philosophers of the Future"?: A Reading of *Beyond Good and Evil*', in Robert C. Solomon and Kathleen M. Higgins (eds), *Reading Nietzsche*. New York: Oxford University Press.

— (1989), 'Different Readings: a Reply to Conway, Magnus, and Solomon'. *International Studies in Philosophy*, 21, (2), 73–80.

— (1994), 'The Genealogy of Genealogy: Interpretation in Nietzsche's *Second Untimely Meditation* and in *On the Genealogy of Morals*', in Richard Schacht (ed.), *Nietzsche, Genealogy, Morality*. Berkeley: University of California Press. Traces the development of Nietzsche's theory of interpretation with particular emphasis on the nature of our relationship to our past.

— (1996), 'Nietzsche, Modernity, Aestheticism', in Bernd Magnus and Kathleen M. Higgins (eds), *The Cambridge Companion to Nietzsche*. Cambridge: Cambridge University Press. Places Nietzsche's aestheticism in its broader social-historical context. An excellent companion piece to *Nietzsche: Life as Literature*.

— (1996a), 'What Should We Expect from Reading? (There Are Only Aesthetic Values)'. *Salmagundi*, Summer, 27–58.

— (1996b), 'Nietzsche as Self-Made Man: On Graham's Parkes' *Composing The Soul*'. *Philosophy & Literature*, 20, (2), 487–91.

— (1998), 'Truth and Value Diverge: On Arthur Danto's *Nietzsche as Philosopher*'. *International Studies in Philosophy*, 30, (3), 5–12.

— (2002), 'Nietzsche and "Hitler"', in Jacob Golomb and Robert S. Wistrich (eds), *Nietzsche: Godfather of Fascism?* Princeton: Princeton University Press. A fascinating and searching discussion of Nietzsche's immoralism.

— (2010) 'Friedrich Nietzsche', in Jonathan Dancy, Ernest Sosa, and Matthias Steup (eds), *A Companion to Epistemology*, 2nd edn. London: Blackwell.

Works on Nehamas's Nietzsche

Conway, Daniel (1989), 'Literature as life: Nietzsche's Positive Morality'. *International Studies in Philosophy*, 21, (2), 41–53. An enthusiastic response to Nehamas's interpretation.

Corngold, Stanley (1995), 'The Subject of Nietzsche: Danto, Nehamas, Staten', in Manfred Pütz (ed.), *Nietzsche in American Literature and Thought*. Columbia: Camden House. Useful contextualisation of *Nietzsche: Life as Literature*.

Fowler, Mark (1990), 'Nietzschean Perspectivism: 'How Could Such a Philosophy – Dominate?' *Social Theory and Practice*, 16, 119–44. Includes a critical discussion of Nehamas's account of perspectivism and the will to power.

Higgins, Kathleen (1986), 'Nietzsche: Life as Literature'. *The Journal of Aesthetics and Art Criticism*, 45, 199–200.

Leiter, Brian (1992), 'Nietzsche and Aestheticism'. *Journal of the History of Philosophy*, 30, (2), 275–90. A critical discussion of Nehamas's Nietzsche, in particular, the concept of aestheticism.

Magnus, Bernd (1993), *Nietzsche's Case: Philosophy as/and Literature*. New York: Routledge. Contains several critical remarks pertaining to Nehamas's discussion of Nietzsche's style.

Pippin, Robert B. (1999), *Modernism as a Philosophical Problem: On the Dissatisfactions of European High Culture*, 2nd edn. Oxford: Blackwell. Includes a brief, but important, discussion of Nehamas's interpretation. Pippin suggests the aestheticist reading of Nietzsche is not so much incorrect as incomplete.

Schacht, Richard (1995), *Making Sense of Nietzsche: Reflections Timely and Untimely*. Urbana: University of Illinois Press. Contains a chapter on Nehamas's Nietzsche. Schacht, like Leiter, is highly critical of Nehamas's aestheticist model.

Shusterman, Richard (1988), 'Nietzsche and Nehamas on Organic Unity'. *Southern Journal of Philosophy*, 26, 379–92.

Solomon, Robert C. (1989), 'Nietzsche and Nehamas's Nietzsche'. *International Studies in Philosophy*, 21, (2), 55–61.

Staten, Henry (1990), *Nietzsche's Voice*. Ithaca: Cornell University Press. Contains a critical discussion of Nehamas's remarks on the importance of style in Nietzsche's work.

Nietzsche Translations Cited

Nietzsche, Friedrich (1974), *The Gay Science*, trans. Walter Kaufmann. New York: Vintage Books.

— (1979), *Ecce Homo: How One Becomes What One Is*, trans. R. J. Hollingdale. London: Penguin Books.

— (1989), *On the Genealogy of Morals*, trans. W. Kaufmann. New York: Vintage Books.

— (2003), *Writings from the Late Notebooks*, ed. Rüdiger Bittner; trans. Kate Sturge. Cambridge: Cambridge University Press.

Index